18. Jan-92
Los Angeles

C-SIX

Konichiwa!

Mick & Joanne Yoshii

I'm sorry you've had to read the English version of the book .... back to Japanese language school!

Great to have met you both. I hope that this won't be your last cruise with us on QE2 & that you enjoy my version of 'Dr. of Sea'

Very best wishes

Nigel Roberts

Sayonara!

C-SIX

Ten years as the Doctor of the QE2

Nigel Roberts

SIDGWICK & JACKSON
LONDON

Dedicated to the memories of my parents, George and Lucy Roberts,
and of my brother, Douglas Roberts.

First published in Great Britain in 1988 by Sidgwick & Jackson Limited

ISBN 0-283-99672-2

Typeset by Hewer Text Composition Services, Edinburgh
Printed by Adlard & Son Limited,
Letchworth, Hertfordshire
for Sidgwick & Jackson Limited
1 Tavistock Chambers, Bloomsbury Way
London WC1A 2SG

C-Six

Queen Elizabeth 2 is the most acclaimed ship in the world today, and befitting the Liner's great reputation, the Ship's Medical Department is acknowledged as the finest in the passenger shipping industry.

QE2 has thirteen decks which have either a name or number, and from forward to aft these are divided vertically by eight stairways and lifts, lettered A–H. The locations of various areas of the ship are identified in relation to the various stairways and decks.

In order to afford maximum stability and comfort, most ships' hospitals are specifically positioned directly on the waterline at the centre of the ship, and by total coincidence, this particular region aboard *QE2* is at C stairway on 6 Deck. Hence, ironically but appropriately, the 'address' of the world's most prestigious *sea*-going *sick*-bay is C-SIX.

Contents

Acknowledgements

My thanks to my agents, Jennifer Watts and Roger Schlesinger, for their support; to Susan Hill of Sidgwick & Jackson who understood the potential, and to Juliet Van Oss, my editor, for her sensitivity. Thanks also to Les, Fran and Stewart Rolinson for their help, and to my family and the many friends who followed the saga, and sought for a title. My sincere thanks especially to all the past and present members of the numerous ships' medical teams with whom I have served: their company and special character have been the principal attraction of the very unique branch of our profession which has given me so much satisfaction and pleasure. Their achievements and emotions are reflected in the pages of this book.

Prologue

Both geographically and socially, there are few places in Britain further from the ocean than Birmingham, the industrial centre of the nation. However, it was into this land-locked region of the country that I emerged, in April 1941. I was born of an Irish mother with an amazing combination of a fiery temperament and an enormous ability to love, and a father with identical traits who hailed from Shropshire, near the borders of Wales, where presumably the name Roberts originated. Being the youngest-but-one of an extremely close family of six children, I grew up under the sheltering and educational influence of my three elder brothers, John, Gerald and Stefan and elder sister, Pat, enjoying the close companionship of my younger brother Douglas during my early years.

The very first of all my childhood memories has probably been the greatest influencing factor of my life. At the tender and impressionable age of three, I developed scarlet fever, no minor ailment in those pre-penicillin days of the mid-forties. While Hitler blitzed the country around us, I began an extended sojourn in the local fever hospital. Although my internment was for a significant percentage of my three-year-old life, the illness was not severe and the memories of doctors, nurses and frequently visiting sympathetic relatives were indelibly imprinted as happy experiences, and following my recovery I resumed my childhood with the obsession that one day I would return to the soothing, fascinating world of medicine, but this time at the other end of the stethoscope. Whilst my contemporaries were still enjoying the thought of careers as engine drivers, firemen and soldiers, I had decided to become a doctor.

I have loosely referred to my home territory as the Birmingham region, but I was in fact born in Walsall, Staffordshire, and having completed my primary education at the charmingly named 'Sunshine' primary school, I received my secondary education at one of the oldest-established grammar schools in the Midlands, Queen

Mary's Grammar School, Walsall. With my childhood ambition of joining the medical profession firmly in mind, I manoeuvred my way through the various streams in the school eventually to qualify to become a medical student at London University, at one of the top medical schools in the country, King's College Hospital. I was a medical student! In London! In the sixties! Apart from the terrific formal education, the introduction to 'life' was invaluable, and the whole experience dynamite!

In 1966, having completed my five and a half years of training at medical school, I left behind the bright lights of London, returned to my home county of Staffordshire, and commenced a very happy engagement as a houseman at the North Staffordshire Royal Infirmary at Stoke-on-Trent. I emerged a year later as a fully qualified Doctor of Medicine.

The initial decision to enter the medical profession is, for most, not easy. Equally, having completed your houseman year, the choice of what to do with your medical degree can be difficult and sometimes bewildering. In the first year of medical school, a general census amongst the students would reveal that ninety to ninety-five per cent have decided to pursue a career in one of the hospital specialities, such as neurosurgery or cardiovascular surgery, the 'glamour' jobs, when they graduate. The fact is that less than ten per cent actually take up these positions. The remaining ninety per cent enter general practice, industrial medicine, research or the armed forces. Throughout Britain there are less than a couple of dozen doctors in permanent positions as Medical Officers at sea. This means that maritime medicine comprises one of the smallest sub-groups of doctors in the profession.

I am sure that my seafaring associates in medicine could produce an extremely varied and interesting set of replies to the question, 'Why did you become a ship's doctor?' Generally speaking, other seafarers in the deck, engine and hotel departments are asked, 'Did you always want to go to sea?', but the doctors are asked, 'What made you?' This presumably is linked to the correct assumption that most doctors have a much broader choice of application in the profession on land, and to choose the romantic but footloose and unsettled branch of an otherwise relatively staid profession appears to be a contradictory decision. The other major consideration which prompts this question is that in days gone by a ship's doctor was considered to be very low on the ladder of the medical profession. Times have changed, and I am sure that this book will illustrate just that.

One of the major influences that led me to become a ship's doctor was my attraction to the ocean from an early age. Considering the distance between my birth-place and the nearest sea-shore, I must have been born with some chromosomal memory which gave me the determination, similar to that of a freshly hatched turtle high on the beach, to make the long journey to return to my primeval roots, the sea. The ocean has always been a driving force in my life, surpassed only by my primary ambition, to be involved in the world of medicine. I can recall, vividly, standing at the rail of the Irish ferry as a child, totally mesmerized by the vast, heaving cauldron stretching to the horizon and who knew where beyond. In later years, the excitement and the romanticism of ships and the ocean caught my attention more, but at this stage it was still only part of a background impression.

I first became aware of the opportunity to combine my attraction to the sea with medicine when the armed forces developed a cadet-ship scheme whereby the three services approached individual medical students with an offer to join Her Majesty's forces and become a fully paid officer whilst still under medical training. In return for this, the student entered into a contract whereby, after qualification and completion of his house-jobs, he spent a five-year short-service commission with whichever of the services he had chosen to enter.

It is impossible, in retrospect, to condense the multitude of whys and wherefores, the pros and cons, but joining the Royal Navy gradually seemed a good idea. The prospect of travel, the excitement associated with the armed forces, the opportunity to broaden horizons, the challenge of a new sector of the community, the variety of experience, and perhaps the uniform, were some of the many influencing factors. In addition, I was single, unattached and uninvolved. Marriage and a settled career was for the future.

Many people will naturally be unaware that a doctor in the Royal Navy does not necessarily mean you are a doctor at sea. It is in fact possible to spend a short-service medical commission with the Royal Navy and not serve on a ship. My own five years offered an interesting and stimulating variety.

One of my early commissions was to the submarine base of HMS *Neptune* in Scotland, where I came into contact with nuclear and underwater medicine, both new and fascinating fields for me to have touched. After spending a year involved in, amongst many other activities, the dubious delights of crash diving hundreds of fathoms in the frail cigars of conventional submarines, and standing on the decks of target ships hoping that the torpedoes would pass beneath the hull, it was quite a physical and mental step to move on into the world of flying.

My next appointment was to the Fleet Air Arm at HMS *Heron* in Yeovilton, Somerset. Here I was a medical officer involved with the general health and care of the station personnel, but was also involved in aviation medicine. I don't suppose too many doctors have the opportunity – or the inclination for that matter – to flit around at supersonic speeds in a Phantom military aircraft between lunch and evening office hours or, at the other extreme, to suffer the heartache of digging the remains of a friend and breakfast companion from the side of a hill when a young life has been suddenly snuffed out at the speed of sound, as I had to on more than one occasion, following the tragedies of mechanical failure or pilot error in these temperamental thoroughbred war machines. Despite other traumatic incidents, these were fabulous days: I added flying and gliding to my experience, and the people were electric, alert, daring, full of *joie de vivre* . . . and crazy! A number of my contemporaries during this period were eventually to demonstrate their prowess in the Falklands war, and I am more than proud to have known them and worked with them.

After the world of foamed runways and helicopter rescues, my next location was more peaceful. In 1969 I joined the families' clinic in Malta in the role of General Practitioner, taking care of the wives, children and relatives of the Naval personnel and auxiliary workers on the island. Eventually, my principal involvement was with the families of the Royal Marines and the Marines themselves: another totally different group of characters and another great experience. These highly tuned, highly trained groups of men were one large, very close family, of which it was a privilege to be considered a member.

These additional Royal Naval experiences were a terrific bonus to my original ambition to become a ship's doctor, but during the early days of my introductory course, a sea-going commission was my primary concern, and naturally I was hoping for the best available. Consequently, on being issued with a form asking me to state my preference for my first commission, I completed the questionnaire as follows:

1st preference – Flag-waving tour of the West Indies.
2nd preference – Flag-waving tour of the West Indies.
3rd preference – Flag-waving tour of the West Indies.

Believe it or not, contrary to every corny skit regarding appointment systems, the Appointments Officer arrived, and much to the chagrin of my introductory course companions I was offered the commission of the Medical Officer to HMS *Leopard*. She was to undergo sea trials from Portsmouth and then proceed . . . on a flag-waving tour of the West Indies! Shortly afterwards, I joined my ship and was introduced to the Royal Naval version of *Doctor at Sea*.

My time spent as Surgeon Lt. on a Royal Naval frigate was memorable not particularly from the medical point of view, but for the totally new and enjoyable general experience, and the introduction to a previously unknown corner of life which it offered me.

HMS *Leopard* had been commissioned to sail on detached duty on its tour of the West Indies, as a consequence of which I was to spend the next eight months being responsible for the health of a mere handful of 214 very fit men – not an overly demanding medical task! However, from a professional point of view it is easy for time to soften the memory of apprehension and the wavering of confidence I experienced when I initially entered the very alien environment of a floating community.

Having cast off from the shore, I had great difficulty relating to my previous land-based knowledge and experience, and for the first time ever I was totally 'on the spot' medically. There were just myself and a shelf full of books, no consultant, no registrar, no senior house-officer, not even another doctor to refer to or bounce comments off. As small as the community was, and as few patients as there may have been, every crew member who entered the sick bay was a potential drama, and every problem appeared proportionately larger in the isolation of the ship at sea.

Almost by definition, the crew members of a war vessel are medically fit, since they are all comparatively young and athletic, and serious troubles have mainly been dealt with or weeded out during recruitment. The majority of sick bay attendances, then, are for minor ailments such as head colds, athletes foot, dhobi itch, and the like. The more serious cases are often associated with trauma, from the engine room, the galley, the decks and frequently the sports fields.

The treatment of trauma is no new aspect of ship-board medicine and, indeed, in days gone by, when doctors were first carried aboard the wooden men-of-war, the vast majority of medical work was involved with the trauma of battle – amputations, removal of shrapnel, and suturing of lacerations, for instance – and consequently the ships did not carry medical doctors, but surgeons. Thus the ship's doctor was in fact the ship's surgeon and was naturally always titled as such. This title became a seagoing tradition, and even to this day the Medical Officer on British ships is referred to as the ship's surgeon.

The ensuing eight months on HMS *Leopard* settled quickly into an easy medical routine, very different from my recent experiences on the floating towns of the Merchant Navy. However, my early days on *Leopard* certainly afforded me a very abrupt introduction not only to the fun and enjoyment of the Royal Navy, but also to the more dramatic aspects of life on the ocean waves, particularly the difficulties and complications of medicine and surgery on the high seas.

In 1971 I completed my short-service commission, and leaving my experiences with the Royal Navy behind me, I spent the next few years on land, based first in Toronto, Canada, before moving on to take up residence in the Arctic circle, in the North-west territories of Canada. Here, I lived amongst the Eskimos for several months as the Medical Officer for a flying doctor service based in Cambridge Bay, and covering an incredibly huge, barren expanse of territory, almost the size of Europe. My experiences were amazing and often thrilling; however, in 1974 I returned to sea, this time with the Merchant Navy.

My Royal Naval experiences were, of course, great training for life at sea, but there was no way that I could have guessed how different the role of doctor of a passenger ship might be! I have spent the past fourteen years of my medical career with the Merchant Navy, and I have thoroughly enjoyed the contrasts between different ships and shipping companies, from Union Castle to P&O and Princess Cruises, and finally Cunard Shipping. The majority of my time at sea, however, has been associated with one ship in particular, the *Queen Elizabeth 2*.

There is no question that whatever faults, politics or controversies may be associated with her, the *QE2* is at present the greatest ship in the world. Her name and reputation as possibly the last of all the great ocean liners will live in maritime history. Why should this be? What is so special about the *QE2*.

On 20th September 1967 a tremendous cheer was heard along the banks of the River Clyde, the proud centre of Scotland's ship-building industry. Down a slipway eased the *QE2*, over 67,000 tons of metal, rivets, glass, wood, plastic and rubber in a multitude of sections, all beautifully designed and put together in the graceful modern lines of a long-awaited, greatly publicized ship, the successor to the magnificent transatlantic liners, the *Queen Elizabeth* and the *Queen Mary*. The ship had been christened and launched by none other than our monarch, Queen Elizabeth herself, who remarked in awe, 'Oh, look at her, she's beautiful.'

But why had the people cheered so loudly on that day in 1967? What was so special about this structure which, after all, was basically only a load of inert material put together by a group of craftsmen?

Considering this vessel in totally practical and analytical light, it could easily be regarded as just another ship, a structure which sits relatively comfortably on water and which if, heaven forbid, it should ever sink, would not leave any devastating hole in world affairs and would soon become just a collection of rusting debris on the ocean floor. The structure, admittedly, had been created with tremendous care and attention, but even so, as an unmanned shell it had the cold stark character of an empty building. But add the other ingredients: make this structure large, *huge*, with beautiful lines and magnificent proportions, to outshine all competitors, or even its renowned predecessors; fill it with the ultimate in comfort and luxury, and add the most up-to-date, state-of-the-art equipment and facilities; give it *haute cuisine* and a tremendous wine cellar; provide the best of service, the closest of attention, an unrivalled concern for safety; add the finest hospital and medical facilities aboard any passenger ship in the world; make it the most outstanding in its class, disregarding costs; place it almost out of reach, known by all, but accessible to only a few; make it the last of its kind, never to be repeated.

The magnificent end product of all this dedicated effort was authoritatively considered to be 'the most carefully planned ship ever built'. On 30th May 1969, the co-ordinator of the ship's interior design, Mr Dennis Lennon, received a telegram from Lord Snowdon, which stated, 'What you have personally achieved with *QE2* makes one proud to be British. The overall creative design, the meticulous detailing and simple, honest sophistication combined with the change of pace and mood is breathtaking. Many congratulations.' In keeping with the ship's status, the advance publicity was overwhelming; in the three years prior to *QE2*'s sailing, the COI, Britain's official information office, put out 36,500 pictures of the ship to over 80 countries, creating a news personality termed in the US 'the most exciting thing to be launched since *Apollo I*'.

Greater even than three football pitches in length, the ship is 963 feet long by 105 feet wide, being specifically laid down to allow her to pass through the Panama Canal, with astonishingly few spare feet at either end and a few spare inches on each side when she sits in the locks. Towering 13 decks high, her structure contains more than 900 state rooms, carries 1850 passengers with more space per passenger than any other ship, and her crew of 1050 gives a remarkable passenger/crew ratio of less than 2:1! 25 miles of carpeting cover her decks and over 60,000 sq ft of leather help cover her walls.

There are four superb passenger restaurants, every one of which presently boasts an international 5-star rating. The public areas include two huge, dazzling ballroom/entertainment rooms, the 'Queen's room' and the largest public room afloat, the two-tiered 'Double Room', recently converted to the 'Grand Lounge'. Passengers can choose to relax in any of the nine individually styled bars, visit a 530-seat, 2-floored cinema/theatre, gamble in a sumptuous casino, luxuriate in a world renowned health spa, pamper themselves in extensive beauty and hairdressing salons, swim in a choice of four different pools, be educated in one of the most up-to-date computer centres, or indulge themselves on a designer shopping spree through glittering arcades.

Having created this 'entity' now cast off the lines, and let her float free, to become a totally independent, unprecedented structure of beauty, grace, prestige and status. *This* was why the crowd had cheered so loudly. But this was only the beginning.

The prestige, status and reputation exerted their magnetism. From every walk of life were drawn the cream of characters – the rich, naturally, but also the celebrities, the leaders, the politicians; people from the top of every field, in arts, sport, science, medicine, travel, research, religion; heads of state, presidents, astronauts, military leaders, explorers; the famous . . . and the infamous. Many giants in character, achievement, reputation and position have visited, travelled with, or contributed to the functioning of the ship, and have inevitably enhanced the ship's status and character. Gradually the ship became more mature and developed an aura which fed upon itself and grew with its maturity, until from this chrysalis stage emerged what we know and admire today, the greatest passenger ship in the world. Despite the fact that she is still the same basic collection of pipes and boilers, decks and steel plates, the aura is indisputable, it is exciting and stimulating and unfortunately will probably never be repeated: RMS *Queen Elizabeth 2*.

Way back in 1967, during my service with the Royal Navy, attached to the nuclear submarine base in Gareloch, Scotland, I had lived and worked within only a few miles of this ultra-modern wonder as she was being created. Later in that same year, I had stood alone on the far banks of the Clyde, and watched in silent admiration as this superb structure, this pinnacle of world shipping, passed slowly by on its maiden voyage to its new home in Southampton, England, to be fitted out prior to commencing its glittering career. Little did I realize, as I watched quietly and pensively that day, that ten years later I would fly from England to Hong Kong to take charge of the medical department of this great ship sailing majestically past.

In March 1978, I took up appointment as Principal Medical Officer of the *QE2*.

Starlight

Starlight . . . starlight . . . casino. Starlight . . . starlight . . . casino.

The piercing, adrenalin-injecting words rang out from the public address system throughout the *QE2* – in every cabin, every bar, every corridor, and every corner of the ship.

Starlight . . . starlight . . . casino.

I caught my breath, and with a strange, prickling sensation, stiffened in mid-sentence. The code world for a medical emergency – starlight – which we had selected for its clarity, crispness and commanding sound, exerted its Pavlovian effect, and with an almost explosive reflex I was transformed from a relaxed, chatty host to a clear-thinking ship's doctor.

Forty-five minutes earlier I had been met at the door of the First Class dining room, the Columbia restaurant, by the maitre d', who was immaculately turned out in black tails, and escorted to my table to join my guests and dinner companions for this voyage. 'All well this trip, doctor?' the maitre d' asked on the way.

'So far, so good,' I replied. 'No dramas yet, Ron!'

Whilst the maitre d' patiently held my chair, I moved quickly around the table as was my custom on the first night of our dining together, shaking hands and introducing myself to the sophisticated and beautifully dressed group of people with whom I would share my meal times for the next few evenings, during our voyage to England from New York. Although this was the second evening of the voyage, it was the first official dress night. We had all attended the Captain's pre-dinner, welcome-aboard cocktail party. Everyone was relaxed and jovial, pleased and eager to acquaint themselves with their new companions, and the meal progressed smoothly. The seas were calm, the company excellent, the food and wine equally so. The service was attentive, and I was being offered a mouthwatering portion of Beef Wellington. What better way to spend an evening?

Starlight . . . starlight . . . casino.

Almost catching the waiter in midair as he served me, I rose immediately from my chair.

'Please excuse me,' I said briefly to my guests, 'but I'm afraid I have to leave you.'

Without further delay I hurried towards the exit, leaving the maitre d' to explain the details to my startled companions.

Four seconds . . . five seconds. . . . The briefest time had passed since the call had rung out through the restaurant. The casino was almost as near as it possibly could be on the ship, on the next deck, only twenty steps up the stairway outside the restaurant door. A head waiter, seeing me approach, pulled open the entrance door and I slipped quickly out.

Seven seconds . . . eight seconds. . . . Three long strides and a right turn onto the stairway. Up the steps, three at a time. . . . *Eleven seconds . . . twelve seconds . . .* a right turn and a controlled burst through the doors into the casino . . . *thirteen seconds . . . fourteen seconds. . . .*

I halted, gazing rapidly around the area for a fraction of a moment. The scene appeared frozen. My adrenalin was surging, every object, every movement in the room was strikingly apparent . . . *fifteen seconds . . . sixteen seconds . . .* the hubbub of voices, the bleep-bleep of electronic gambling machines, the tack, tack, tackle of a ball bouncing in a roulette wheel, the tinkle of glasses, laughter from the bar, the rasping waterfall shuffle of a deck of cards, the calls of the dealers. The majority of the room appeared entirely as on every other night of the year, but somewhere in here a patient was desperately ill, probably dying, possibly dead. I dashed forward into the crowd.

Towards the far end of the room the Casino Manager, a tall, slim figure, was waving at me frantically. He stood in the midst of a small group of motionless, curious passengers who were gazing down below the edge of a blackjack table. At the adjacent table the dealer had paused and was looking on, unsure whether or not to abandon this round of cards. Two players had turned from the table, one leaning casually on the back of his chair, puffing billows of smoke from a Churchillian cigar whilst he watched the scene as though it was a TV drama. One table further on, the world of the casino ticked along unruffled, unaware, buried in its own importance.

Pushing politely but firmly through the small crowd, I dropped onto my knees beside the spread-eagled figure and looked him over: late forties, stocky build, salt and pepper hair receding slightly from a flushed forehead, where small glistening beads of perspiration had collected over his brow . . . *seventeen seconds . . . eighteen seconds. . . .*

'What's happened and how long?' I demanded quietly of the Casino Manager, who had dropped down beside me.

'He's only a casual gambler, and he was getting excited over winning a few dollars,' he replied. 'He was OK one moment, playing cards. Got up laughing about his good luck, and then collapsed on the spot. About twenty seconds before I phoned the bridge,' he added.

Twenty seconds, I thought, and added another fifteen seconds for the 'starlight' call and around another twenty seconds for me to get to this point. I had reached him in less than one minute . . . excellent!

The man lay sprawled face down amongst the fallen chairs and scattered cards. His head rested against the leg of the blackjack table, his hair had fallen across his closed eyes. High on his cheek there was a small, deep gash caused by his impact with the floor. One arm lay entwined with the legs of a broken chair, and balanced loosely between the fingers of his other hand was a solitary round, black disc, which only moments earlier must have seemed important enough to him to cause him great stress, but was now a meaningless piece of plastic.

As I began to talk, my mind was racing, absorbing the picture, assessing the situation, commencing a rapid examination.

'Did he move after he hit the floor?' I demanded of the crowd.

'Yes, he sat up and held his chest before he slumped down,' someone called back.

Good, I thought to myself, cervical injury is unlikely. I grasped his shoulder and turned him onto his back. He rolled over gently, still, lifeless. His facial muscles were slack, his mouth half open, cheeks sunken. A pale, dusky blue was already colouring his features . . . *twenty-four seconds . . . twenty-five seconds. . . .* I placed my ear to his mouth – no sound. I felt for his carotid pulse – nothing. I ripped open his shirt, placed my ear on his chest, still warm and perspiration soaked – no pulses, no respiration, no heart beat.

At 9.35 p.m., in the middle of the vast expanse of the North Atlantic Ocean, a relatively young man lay on the deck of the *QE2* casino, dead . . . *thirty-two seconds . . . thirty-three seconds . . .* but not brain dead.

I had arrived well within the four-minute limit, after which time the brain cells would have been irreversibly damaged due to cessation of blood flow and lack of oxygen. If we could recommence circulation and oxygenation of his brain while we attempted to restart his heart, he could possibly be saved.

'Clear this area please,' I commanded the onlookers as I raised my hand in the air, clenched it tightly, and brought the ball of my fist down fast and hard against the centre of the patient's breast bone with a loud thud, startling the bystanders, who quickly moved back from the scene.

If the man was in ventricular fibrillation – his heart muscles contracting minimally and ineffectually at many times the normal rate – the heavy blow to the chest directly over the heart might convert the rhythm back to normal. If his heart was in asystole, when the muscle is completely motionless, it would be a different problem.

I examined him again – no response. I bent down over the patient, checked inside his mouth, then tilting his head backwards I took a deep breath, placed my mouth to his, and blew all the oxygen-carrying, life-giving air from my lungs to his. As I blew, I watched his chest expand from the corner of my eye. I drew back, breathed in, and repeated the process twice more; some oxygen, at least, would now be in his system.

I quickly switched positions and, leaning over his chest, I pressed down firmly on his sternum, compressing the heart inside his chest and forcing blood out of the chambers into his lungs to collect oxygen, and then out of the lungs around the body to carry the oxygen to all of his tissues. 1 ... 2 ... 3 ... 4 ... 5. ... The chest wall was depressed repeatedly, each time squeezing more blood into the circulation.

Back at the top end again, I took a deep breath and blew ... *fifty-one seconds* ... *fifty-two seconds*. ... As I raised my head to return to the chest massage, a voice interrupted me, 'OK Nigel, I've got this end.'

Alan Kirwin, the other man in our two-doctor medical team on board *QE2*, had quietly arrived on the scene, breathless after galloping up the stairs and along from the other end of the ship. Dropping to his knees opposite me, he took over the cardiac massage, 1 ... 2 ... 3 ... 4 ... 5, whilst I sucked in another deep breath and blew. The sequence was established. As we worked, I quickly filled Alan in on what few details we had.

Suddenly, there was a small commotion from beyond the edge of the spectators as the remainder of the emergency medical team arrived. From the various corners of the ship all the medical staff had been torn from their activities by the emergency call.

In the hospital, the night sister had been tidying up a dressing on a laceration. *Starlight ... starlight ... casino.* She rushed for the emergency bag which contained essential medications and equipment and then made a heart-racing dash up flight after flight of stairs to the casino, seven decks above. Close behind her, with more equipment, followed a medical attendant who had been sitting quietly reading in his cabin across the corridor from the hospital. The second medical attendant dashed down the stairs in the opposite direction on his way from the crew mess, where, seconds before, he had surrendered a winning hand of cribbage. Into the hospital, he snatched up the remaining gear, and off to the casino.

Up in the petty officers' club, the medical PO stood chatting with his pals, just about to enjoy a pint of beer, after a hard day's work. *Starlight . . . starlight . . . casino*. The beer spilled onto the counter, and before the swirling froth had settled, the door had closed behind the bolting figure.

In her cabin up towards the bow of the ship, the second nursing sister stood in her night coat, catching up on some ironing, and mentally working out what she would do on her leave. *Starlight . . . starlight . . . casino*. She whipped out the ironing plug and threw off her night coat. Frantically she grabbed a uniform dress from the wardrobe, pulled it on quickly together with a pair of shoes, and burst from her cabin with her hair flying – no hat, no stockings, no belt, no make-up – a streak of efficiency responding automatically to the call.

The third nursing sister was sitting watching the early cabaret in the Queen's Room, unknowingly only yards away from the victim's wife, who continued to watch the show undisturbed by the unknown significance of the signal which interrupted the comedian's punch line. From every corner of the ship, the team arrived with all the necessary equipment.

Resuscitation was now well under way, the team was assembled – and all within two minutes.

The patient was looking better: his cheeks were pink, his pupils small and equal, initial resuscitation was adequate; but there was still no response at all from his ailing heart. There was no spontaneous output or breathing.

'OK, let's get some room,' I called quietly. 'We want him in that area over there, towards the corner.'

Automatically, several pairs of hands grasped his trunk and limbs, and with his head supported, he was extricated from his entanglement with the chairs and blackjack table into a more open space. As he was lifted, his tie was plucked off and his jacket and shirt, shoes and socks disappeared in the blink of an eye. The onlookers were cleared, and the desperate struggle continued, whilst in the distance, the rattle of a roulette ball rang out, cards were ruffled, dice thrown, and dollars passed backwards and forwards as the crowds insisted on returning to the 'important' events of the moment.

'Pauline,' I called to one of the sisters, 'see if his cabin key is in his coat.' 1 . . . 2 . . . 3 . . . 4 . . . 5 . . . blow.

'Yes,' she replied quickly.

'OK, go down to the cabin and see if his wife or anyone else is there. Bring her up here quietly, don't panic or upset her. Find out whatever history you can from her about the patient. Anything at all that's relevant.' 1 . . . 2 . . . 3 . . . 4 . . . 5 . . . blow. 'If she's not there, check the bathroom cabinet, the drawers and usual places, see if you can find any medicines he may be taking. Take Derrick with you. If his wife's not there, get hold of their bedroom steward, he'll be able to recognize her, get him to dash round the public rooms and find her.' 1 . . . 2 . . . 3 . . . 4 . . . 5 . . . blow.

Pauline and Derrick were gone before I'd finished. They knew the routine.

There was still no response. As we talked, emergency equipment appeared hurriedly from containers and was assembled around the patient. The wires of the cardiograph machine snaked out like tentacles and were attached to the limbs of the prostrate form at the centre of all this sudden activity. Now we had a picture of what was going on inside his chest.

'Ventricular fibrillation,' I stated flatly. 'Defibrillator, 200 Joules,' I called unnecessarily to the senior nursing sister, Michelle, as she handed me the paddles already in her hands. A green tube appeared and, with a squelch, electrode gel was squirted onto the surface of the paddles. I placed them firmly on his chest, warned everyone to stand clear, and pressed both buttons. The patient's muscles contracted as the tremendous electric shock passed through his body. Arching and stiffening, he leapt briefly into the air. All eyes turned to the cardiograph. There was no change, he was still in fibrillation.

'Again,' I said quietly. Like a tortured soul in nightmare sleep, his body leapt again. There was a pause. 'Still fibrillating!' Disappointment showed on everyone's faces, but there was no time to lose. 'Continue resuscitation!' 1 . . . 2 . . . 3 . . . 4 . . . 5 . . . blow.

Alan had taken over at the head. Without my having to ask, an intravenous catheter was placed firmly in my hand by Angela, the second nursing sister, who moved quickly to take over the massage whilst I looked anxiously for a vein to receive the catheter. A thin blue vessel ran down the centre of his forearm, the needle was slipped in, a line was attached, and fluid ran slowly into the man's circulatory system.

'Five per cent dextrose,' stated Michelle, as she reached out and grabbed one of the onlooking casino staff to act as a human hanger for the plastic bag of fluid.

At the head, Alan had stopped blowing. 'Sucker,' he called out, and from behind his shoulder an arm appeared like a third limb and a slurping, gurgling suction pipe immediately emptied the patient's mouth. Using the laryngoscope, an endotracheal tube was introduced quickly into the patient's throat, down past his vocal cords and into the trachea. The cuff was inflated, the bag connected, and a hissing plastic pipe coiling down from the oxygen bottle was attached. Now, with the aid of the tube and bag, pure oxygen flowed into his lungs.

'Adrenalin 0.5 milligrams,' I called to my unseen helpers over my shoulder, and was immediately offered the syringe. The adrenalin shot into the intravenous line. 'Flush,' I instructed, and the dextrose solution hurried the chemicals into his vein where it was pumped around the body by Angela's continuing massage.

'I want eighty mils sodium bicarbonate,' I advised Michelle. The solution was passed by Brian, the medical PO, from the emergency bag to Michelle to myself in quick succession, and then into the patient's circulation through the catheter. 'Flush.'

Pauline reappeared opposite me and told me quietly and calmly, 'The patient's name is Andrew Lyons; he's forty-eight. No significant past medical history at all. Not taking any medications. Apparently he's been perfectly well recently, with no complaints. His wife is in the manager's office, a member of the cruise staff is with her. He has three children on board, all teenagers. They haven't been told anything yet.'

Bloody hell, I thought. When the patient takes on an identity, the struggle always becomes more personal, so much more draining.

'OK Angie, stop massaging for a moment. Let's see what's happening on the graph,' I instructed. The team paused briefly, all eyes glued to the graph.

It must have appeared a strange scene: two formally dressed doctors in crumpled mess-jackets, dress shirts with buttons popped, bow-ties pulled aside, perspiration running down our cheeks; a nurse on her knees, her long black formal dress pulled up, her high-heeled shoes discarded, coiffured hair over her face, necklace thrown over her shoulder; the second nurse half dressed, panting, catching her breath; the rest of the team in various states of undress, coats discarded, shirt collars undone, and towering above us all, like the Statue of Liberty, the casino staff member, holding aloft the intravenous fluid bag. Everyone's eyes were wide with anticipation, willing the graph to change. The cardiograph spilled out more paper . . . there was no change, he was still fibrillating.

'Defibrillator again please. Set for 360 Joules.' The squelch of gel. Paddles in position. 'Stand clear!'

Andrew Lyons's body leapt again, and slumped back to a motionless, lifeless posture. Still fibrillating! Damn! . . . Damn! . . . DAMN!

'Lignocaine please, seventy-five milligrams,' I called, 'and set up a lignocaine infusion, two milligrams per minute.' The massage was restarted automatically. The oxygenated blood pumped around his still body, and the lignocaine flowed through his veins. 'Defibrillator again. 360 Joules. Stand clear!' Another contorted leap. No change! We weren't winning at all.

'Let me have some more adrenalin, one milligram, and forty mils sodium bicarbonate solution please.' The speed and urgency were still very apparent, but an air of frustrated, hopeless failure was gradually spreading through the team. Andrew Lyons was slipping into another world.

'Flush, please'. The drugs again coursed around his body. 'Defibrillator. 360 Joules,' I announced with waning optimism. 'Stand clear!'

Now, as though in slow motion, Andrew Lyons's body leapt again in an almost grotesque, depressing dance of death. We paused sadly and watched. The despair of fruitless effort showed in anxious eyes.

'THE GRAPH!' somebody gasped. Suddenly there was a burst of human electricity throughout the group; all of us were immediately fully alert. As a body, we caught our breath. The graph had changed! An indescribable and fabulous charge passed through the circle. Andrew Lyons's heart was responding! The graph faltered, became irregular, and then ticked quietly on. We'd done it! Sinus rhythm! However, we weren't out of the woods yet; there was still no spontaneous respiration.

With renewed enthusiasm, we adjusted his intravenous flow, and blew more oxygen into his lungs. The graph remained steady, and now he had a palpable pulse and a measurable blood pressure, but still no respiration. 'I'm stopping the pumping for a while,' Alan advised, 'let's see what happens.'

We stared down at Andrew Lyons, willing him on, whilst his wife sat in the Manager's office, tearful, frightened, praying. Unconsciously we all held our breath with Andrew.

Ten seconds . . . 'Come on!' . . . *Twenty seconds* . . . 'Come on . . . COME ON!' *Thirty seconds.* It seemed an eternity, and then . . . he breathed! A long, slow, deep breath. There was a pause, and then another breath, and then – what seemed almost miraculous – steady breathing!

I looked up and took in the faces. There were huge smiles, and here and there, amongst the streams of perspiration, tears of relief and satisfaction.

This is what medicine at sea and being Doctor of the *QE2* is *really* all about.

Andrew Lyons, husband and father, had been brought back from the dead.

I
MEDICINE AT SEA

General Hospital

All shipping companies vary somewhat in their attitudes towards medicine at sea, and the standards which they are prepared to maintain for their crew and passengers. The first consideration faced by the ship owners and ship builders is whether the medical department is a necessity or a luxury. The basic requirement regarding doctors on British ships is simple – all vessels with a hundred or more total crew and passengers must carry a designated, fully qualified doctor of medicine, and the ship is not allowed to leave port without one. Interestingly, since the eighteenth century and before, there have always been three positions which must be filled before a ship can sail: the captain – or master – of the ship, the ship's cook, and the ship's surgeon. Nowadays, the same requirements still stand, but circumstances have changed.

On all larger ships of more than a few hundred tonnes, there are several deck officers, who, although they may not have been the masters of their own ship, may have passed their examinations to acquire their Master's qualifications, or 'Master's ticket', therefore at any one time on a larger vessel, there will be more than one officer who could, if necessary, take over the role of captain. Whereas it would be extremely unlikely that a ship would sail without its designated captain, under the regulations the ship can in fact leave harbour as long as an officer with a Master's ticket is on board. The obligation to carry a ship's cook dates from the days of disease and debility which resulted from poor standards of food and malnutrition, and the regulation requiring a ship to carry a specifically nominated crew cook still stands. In the event of an emergency, however, one of the many passenger chefs could be nominated as crew cook.

In contrast to this, the majority of ships which are required by law to carry a doctor carry only one of the species, and only the very large vessels holding upwards of around 1500 passengers and crew will carry

3

two. Therefore, if for instance the doctor has been injured or detained ashore for some reason, the ship is unable to sail until he arrives or a replacement is appointed. During my time at sea this has occurred on only one occasion.

The ship at that time was in Vancouver, Canada, and was due to sail in the early evening. I had been ashore in the city enjoying lunch with some local friends, and was returning in good time by taxi. As the taxi made its way along the main street, an elderly couple suddenly stepped onto a pedestrian crossing in front of the car ahead of us and the old lady was knocked down. My taxi of course halted and I jumped out to help. The old lady had received several minor injuries which I was fortunately able to treat until an ambulance arrived, and she was taken off to hospital. The time was getting on, and I turned back to my taxi, but it had disappeared! Presumably the driver didn't want to be dragged into court as a witness!

A small group of agitated people were centred around the pedestrian crossing, their voices raised, arms waving and gesticulating. From the centre of the group, a wide-eyed anxious man suddenly sprang forward and grabbed me by the arm – he turned out to be the driver of the car involved in the accident.

'I want a statement from you! I want you to tell the police what happened!' He was pulling and pushing at my arm, shoving me along the pavement towards a police officer.

'Look,' I said, 'I'm sorry I can't help, but I'm in a hell of a rush.'

'Everyone always is after an accident!' he shouted.

'But you don't understand, I work on a ship and it can't sail until I arrive!' I said, suddenly thinking to myself, I hope!

'Look, you've got other witnesses, I'm sure they'll help,' I added.

'No, they all say the same!'

'But I won't even be here!'

'Officer!' he shouted, 'this man will give you a statement.'

'Wait a minute,' said the officer.

'A minute! I haven't got a minute!' I exclaimed. Jostling back and forth with a near hysterical driver swinging from my arm, I was scrutinizing my watch with increasing trepidation. From my point of view, it was one problem for the ship to be held up because I wasn't on board, but what if they didn't realize or check that I wasn't back, and sailed without me!

The policeman eventually came over. 'Now then, these two people first,' he said, bringing forward a couple of pedestrians who had witnessed the accident.

'But I'm in a rush, officer!'

4

'One at a time, sir, one at a time,' he replied ponderously.

I turned to the driver and said emphatically, 'Now then, my main concern was the old lady, and by the looks of it you've got your witnesses, so I'm off!'

'Ah, but you're the main witness,' he said, refusing to let me go. I paused and considered . . . there had to be some way out of this.

'Oh, all right,' I said. 'Just excuse me a minute while I get my bags.' He released my arm and I strolled around the corner to collect my non-existent belongings, and kept going! However, despite the street having been seemingly full of nothing but taxis only a short while earlier, suddenly there was no such thing as an empty cab. I couldn't believe it. The ship's probably well on its way to Alaska by now, I thought. Eventually I spotted a cab for hire. I could have hugged the driver.

By this time the ship had now theoretically sailed. The cab driver, it would appear, had been waiting all his life for someone to give him a $20 bill and instruct him to 'Make it as fast as you can!'

With my stomach in my chest, and my head rebounding off the cab roof, we creamed through Vancouver, and eventually through the dock gate. The ship was still there, complete with an agitated captain and hundreds of increasingly raucous passengers, itching to start their vacation. As we drove up the dock, the captain spotted me, and several shrill blasts came out of the ship's whistle. Arms and fists were waved, blasphemies and expletives rained down together with advice on how to move my rear end quicker. Cheers and hoots went up from the passengers on deck, who through the uncannily rapid ship's bush telegraph, had soon learned that the absent doctor was the reason for the hold up, and a cascade of streamers bounced off me as I stepped onto, and rapidly off, an already uncoupled gangway.

What I was not aware of was that, as usual, the bush telegraph had also added its own trimmings to the story: I had supposedly been ashore to visit a girlfriend. Try as I did, I couldn't for the life of me convince anyone that their vacation hadn't been held up because the doctor was ashore enjoying some 'light refreshment' – and the story followed me throughout that cruise.

So, the regulations state that certain ships will carry a medical officer. However, other than this basic requirement, there are few specific regulations regarding the department itself.

For fairly extensive periods of time, the ship is home for the crew members, and in effect the regulations require that the medical facilities are provided specifically for the ship's staff. Although available to both crew and passengers, the clauses controlling the total number of beds in the ship's hospital is based on the number of crew carried.

There are entire books full of stringent international requirements concerning the actual building of the ship which regulate every aspect of the structure and the ship's usage of materials. Depending upon where the ship is built, and in which country it will be registered, there may be further specifications involving principally the health and safety of the crew and passengers. On the *QE2*, for example, the water tight door integrity, fire fighting facilities, life boats, navigational aids and medical facilities are second to none. Directed by their consciences, their bank balances and their regard for their own reputations as shipping companies, and always aware of the threat of litigation, the owners may well add a further list of their own requirements to the ship builders' specifications, such as non-slip decking, adequate lighting of cinema steps, warning notices, increased hygiene awareness and the like.

A major consideration which the ship owner must face is the amount of space which must be allotted to the medical, and every other department, on board. The design and construction of a ship is extremely complex. If you can imagine creating an entire town and then placing it in a container, you may get some inkling of the problem. This is vastly compounded by the fact that the town must fit the container, and not vice versa. Most people consider a town as being a collection of shops around the village square, surrounded by a housing complex. Whereas a community such as this may obtain its water from a reservoir perhaps a hundred miles away, its electricity from a power station ten miles away, and its food supplies from depots scattered in the surrounding countryside, on a ship, all these facilities must be built in alongside the community. Thus, a ship must contain *all* the means to supply its everyday needs, and consequently every inch of space has a very high premium.

With this in mind, let's consider the earlier question: What, in relation to the medical department, is considered essential, and what a luxury?

The larger the hospital, the more potential passenger area and revenue lost. The larger the staff, the more wages to find; and, more important and costly, the more accommodation has to be provided. These considerations apply throughout each and every department.

Within the medical department, the essentials, generally speaking, include the capacity to handle whatever medical or surgical emergency that may arise out on the ocean. In addition, we must provide attention for minor, day-to-day medical problems, and maintenance of basic health for both crew and passengers.

The facilities or services which are not essential include the capability to continue adequate medical attention beyond the time when a serious case would, on lesser ships, be put ashore into a land-based hospital. The off-loading of the unfortunate patient would occur at the first port of call, whatever or wherever that port might be.

A seriously ill patient will require round-the-clock monitoring and also basic laboratory investigation, but most ships don't have the staff to continue this intensive care for prolonged periods of time. For a small medical department of two or three personnel to maintain intensive care and supervision of a cardiac patient for twenty-four hours a day and meanwhile continue to run the department, may be possible for twenty-four to forty-eight hours, but certainly, if this continued for several days, the staff also would end up needing intensive care, especially if further medical or surgical emergencies should arise at the same time. Therefore, under normal circumstances, the average ship will land its seriously ill passengers ashore at the next port.

As bad as this may be, it may at least be acceptable if it is a home port or a port in one of the major civilized cities of the world. This unfortunately isn't always the case. The next port may well be a small South Pacific island, it may be in the extremes of Alaska, or a nowhere port in the Far East. The local populace may not speak English. The facilities could be primitive, some very primitive. Usually the disembarking patient will be accompanied by a spouse or relative and the escort will have to stay in an hotel, or whatever accommodation is available. It is possible that there may not be an air service from that location, for evacuation after recovery. So what alternative can a ship offer?

If the medical practice on board is of a good enough standard, if the ship has sufficient staff, and if there are modern facilities to carry out basic investigations, then, under necessary circumstances, the patient *could* stay on board. Is this a luxury? Unquestionably, from my point of view as the ship's doctor, it isn't. If I, as a passenger, were aware of the possibilities, I would most definitely prefer the ship that offered this additional attention, whatever the extra cost.

As you would expect, the medical department on the QE2 has more to offer in the way of facilities and staff than all other passenger

7

ships presently in commission. At full complement, the medical department is made up of eleven people. The Principal Medical Officer is in charge of the department. He is supported by, and shares medical responsibility with, a second doctor. Although it is necessary for both doctors to be *au fait* with all aspects of medicine, it is certainly preferable, when faced with a major surgical procedure, for one doctor to have a leaning towards surgery and the other towards anaesthetics. However, this isn't a priority, as every other specialist field must also be considered.

Next, we have four nursing sisters, who are all British or Commonwealth-trained and registered. We are fortunate in being able to choose from a great number of applicants, and are often able to select nursing sisters with experience in casualty care, coronary and intensive care, and operating theatre work. They are therefore well able to handle any of the emergency situations which may occur, and we can boast a standard of nursing care equal to any in the world.

Next we come to the Dispenser – or Medical Petty Officer. He, as his title suggests, is in charge of the ship's pharmacy, the ordering and maintainance of stocks, and the dispensing. In addition, under the medical officer's supervision, he is the ship's radiographer, and also carries out the laboratory work performed on board.

Working under the senior sister's supervision we have two medical attendants, who are the work horses of the department. They are mainly responsible for the condition of the hospital, for its upkeep and cleanliness. They are also in charge of the general needs of the hospitalized patients, their non-technical nursing requirements, their meals and maintenance. They also assist in whatever area may require an extra pair of hands.

It isn't always considered necessary to carry a dentist on board ships, but on the *QE2* World Cruise, although he may be considered a luxury by some, he's invaluable. When you remember that the full complement of the *QE2* is around 2900, made up of approximately 1050 crew and 1850 passengers, you can see that this constitutes quite a large practice. For many of the crew, the ship's dentist is their only dentist. He is able to carry out routine maintenance of their dental condition and dental health. This can be important and very time-saving for crew members who may only get home infrequently, and for short periods. For the passengers, of course, the dentist is a godsend for their emergency problems. Broken teeth, dental abscesses, lost fillings, detached crowns and fractured dentures constitute a continuous stream of work.

Last, but by no means least, we have our physiotherapist. In Britain, the physiotherapist plays a major role in the treatment of certain categories of illness, and similarly, on board ship, her contribution can make a tremendous difference. Many accidents occur amongst the deck personnel, in the engine rooms, and in the kitchens; elderly passengers experience a high incidence of serious respiratory infections; pneumonia, back pains, arthritis and stiff necks are all conditions which occur irrespective of being on holiday, and in all of these illnesses the physiotherapist's armoury of heat treatments, ultra sonics, exercises and massage can make life so much more comfortable.

That's the team. Now, what are the hospital facilities?

Most ships' hospitals are positioned low down, near the waterline, around the mid-section of the ship. This is the most stable and consequently the most comfortable area of the ship, and theoretically the easiest area to work in when wielding a scalpel or carrying out delicate procedures. The hospital is similarly located on *QE2*.

The hospital area, although very compact, offers quite extensive facilities. To begin with, there are five separate wards: the intensive care unit, the male and female passenger wards, the crew ward and the isolation ward, for use in case of contagious illness.

All our hospital beds have a piped oxygen supply. The intensive care unit has all the usual emergency equipment available, including cardiac monitors, defibrillator, cardiograph, suction, oxygen, intravenous equipment and medications, and in addition we carry a respirator.

The operating theatre is as fully equipped as any standard shore-side theatre, with all the necessary instruments for whatever surgical emergency may arise; sterilizing units, scrub sinks, diathermy, X-ray viewers and of course a complete anaesthetic facility. Along the corridor we have the X-ray department, a facility much in demand, mainly for chest problems and fractures or 'trauma'. Further along still is the dental department, with one of the most up-to-date units available. Opposite this is the physiotherapy department, with a small gymnasium/exercise area, pullies, weight-lifting and mobilization appliances. We have the most up-to-date electronic equipment and, of course, massage and treatment tables. Around the corner there is a small laboratory, for basic investigations. Near the entrance is the reception area and treatment room, and adjacent is the dispensary with an extensive collection of drugs, covering every category of medicine including the various serums and vaccinations for polio, cholera, typhoid, yellow fever, tetanus and rabies which are required for our extensive world travel. Here also in the hospital is the crew clinic, with consulting and examination rooms. Of course, there are linen lockers and rooms full of stores, with sufficient supplies to last several months away from home, and rooms jammed with cylinders of anaesthetic gases and oxygen reservoirs which are piped to all the areas of the hospital. Finally, we come to the area which hopefully always remains closed, the ship's morgue – a large refrigerated unit with space for three bodies, which during my time, I am more than pleased to say, has never been full.

Four decks up from the hospital, in an area more conveniently located and accessible for our on-board guests, is the doctor's surgery, for passenger consultations and examination.

I'm certain that together with many hundreds of people with whom I have discussed the subject in the past, you're thinking, 'Why on earth would they want such extensive facilities on board?' Allow me to answer this for you by considering the medical workload which we would normally expect to encounter on QE2.

Prior to becoming a ship's Medical Officer in both the Royal and Merchant Navy, my own impressions of doctors and medicine at sea were in many aspects far from the true picture. It is easy now for me to be amused at questions put by passengers who have considered the job only as superficially as I once did in those pre-maritime days: Do you get bored just treating seasickness? Do you enjoy being at sea with nothing to do? Do you ever get any illness that's serious? What do you do on shore when you've finished here and go back to real medicine? Don't you miss practising proper medicine? Don't you feel that you're wasted at sea? Surely no-one is ill when they go on holiday! It is a totally incorrect but perhaps understandable assumption that there is very little serious medicine practised at sea, but this is presumably based on the idea that the crew members are all young and fit, and that the passengers must be fit to embark on a vacation in the first instance.

The assumption that people on holiday are necessarily healthy would be a splendid idea; however, it would be most remarkable if we could choose our time of ill health. Unfortunately, there may well be the odd occasion when a passenger has died between booking his cruise and the date of joining the ship. There are, however, many varieties of physical condition between fit and dead! Of course, anyone who is seriously ill at the time that they should be setting out for their holiday will most likely change their plans. Consequently, on each voyage there will obviously be one or two last minute cancellations due to ill health. Frequently, however, a passenger who has booked up their cruise six months ahead, and has spent the interval preparing and looking forward to the holiday, is often going to disregard a minor illness and sometimes a more serious condition, unless their doctor has specifically instructed that they shouldn't travel, particularly if they're accompanying relatives or friends, or if they're not insured for cancellation. In addition, there are people who are in the later years of their lives, or who have a chronic illness, whereby the opportunity to take another cruise may never arise. On the other side of the coin there are passengers taking cruises because their doctors have suggested that it would be good for them. Other people may be in transit from one country to another: moving home or completing an overseas appointment; others may be returning home after an illness contracted abroad whilst on holiday or business. For whatever reason, therefore, the ship may well be carrying passengers who have boarded in an already unhealthy condition.

Amongst the passengers who are well initially, there is no way to predict the onset of a serious acute medical problem. In fact, sometimes the incidence of illness will be increased by being on holiday. The excitement of travel, the additional running around prior to commencing a holiday, the rigours of air travel, the rigmarole of getting to, and onto, the ship, all build up stress – as, of course, with any other holiday. In addition to this, whilst on their holidays many people will dance for the first time in years, they'll eat often and to great excess, they'll drink more alcohol than usual, be more active on tours, on the beaches and around the decks. Instead of using lifts as they normally do, they will climb stairs to help lose some of the extra pounds they've gained - and help ease their consciences! Cardio-vascular crises thrive on these new conditions.

Other illnesses are also affected by travel. When people from many different areas are brought together on any holiday, on either land or sea, they will inevitably share their various home-town bugs amongst each other. Being exposed for the first time to a new virus or agent to which they have no herd immunity, the happy throng of travellers will unknowingly exchange infections with their neighbours – an unwelcome present with which to start off their holiday.

Another factor influencing travellers occurs when they are exposed to foreign cuisine and hygiene standards. There are many expressions which have developed over the years whereby the unfortunate traveller has jokingly tried to make light of his affliction; 'Tourista', 'Montezuma's Revenge', 'Delhi Belly', 'Gyppy Tummy',

'Montezuma's quick-step'. Unfortunately, as one of our comedians always jokes, 'You can call it what you like, but there's only one way out!'

The inexperienced sailor has more problems to face yet. Despite the unerring determination of ship designers and marketing departments to create floating hotels, believe it or not, despite their stabilizers, ships still have a tendency to move about far more than their land-based cousins (except perhaps in California!). Weatherwise, there are low pressure areas which, in full fury in mid-Atlantic, can stir your drink just as well as any electrical mixer and, for an encore, dump you unceremoniously from your stool to the floor.

Of course, there is one major factor which influences the incidence of illness amongst cruise passengers, and that is the average age. For several reasons – including cost, image and promotion – travelling by ship does attract a higher age group than alternative holidays, particularly on a world cruise, when the younger people who have sufficient money are usually too busy earning it to be able to take a three month break!

Having referred to the expense of a world cruise, you may be interested to learn of the approximate costs. The two most sumptuous cabins on the ship are the 'Queen Elizabeth' and 'Queen Mary' suites. These suites are identical and both have a split-level lounge/bedroom, a dressing room and a fully equipped bathroom. There is an adjoining room which can be used as either a day-room or an extra bedroom, and this cabin also has a bathroom. The suites have large private balconies, and these are larger, in fact, than some of the small cabins on the ship. When you consider the premium placed on any space on board, you will realize that a balcony is a very valuable piece of ship's real estate! The present cost for one of these cabins is around £2,500 per day. Yes, *per day*! Amazingly, these cabins are rarely empty, and the demand for them on a world cruise is such that they never need advertising, despite a total cost of around £250,000 upwards for the full cruise.

However, don't give up the idea of a world cruise yet, because at the more acceptable end of the scale, we have the cabins on five deck. On a ship of *QE2*'s status, of course all cabins are first class, but the least expensive accommodations on the ship are the inside cabins on five deck, which is the lowest of the passenger accommodation decks. That is, a cabin on the inner side of the corridor, which doesn't have the ship's side as a boundary, and consequently doesn't have a porthole. These cabins have all the basic requirements: adequate wardrobe space, bathroom with shower, telephone, TV, radio, and are fully carpeted. The cost per person per day for these cabins is approximately £150. During slow cruises, and at certain times of the year, special deals may be offered, and these may also include sections of the world cruise. Fifty per cent of our world cruise passengers are made up of those who are only taking a short section of the cruise. So you see, taking a world cruise doesn't necessarily mean going into bankruptcy, and in fact there is always a cross-section of younger passengers who manage to join us.

At this point, it has to be said that there are certain ships and itineraries which attract a much older clientele than others, not necessarily only because of the cost, but also by reputation. On some of these more geriatric cruises the enormous number of walking sticks on board could possibly be considered a fire hazard! and I must confess that there have been times, on surveying the newly embarked passengers on the occasional, very elderly cruise, when I have thought that the ship looked more like a maritime division of God's waiting room! However, as we are all aware, happiness and enjoyment is not dependent on age, and I personally derive great pleasure and satisfaction from caring for, socializing with, and sharing the memories of some of these fabulous old characters.

I'm sure that there must be many younger people now reading these lines who are deciding that cruising isn't for them. I can assure you that you're wrong. I personally feel that younger people can get one heck of a good holiday out of a cruise. Some ships have developed a reputation for the younger crowd, and if you choose or are advised on a suitable cruise on *QE2* or an appropriate alternative ship, I promise you you'll have a ball!

Returning to our subject, many of the older passengers will already be under long-term treatment for chronic problems and may have several long-standing illnesses running concurrently which are kept in fine balance by the supervision of their own doctors. I always feel that these unfortunate folks with multiple problems can be compared with a house of cards, or a juggler – take one card away, or drop one ball, and the whole lot may come tumbling down. Similarly, it may take only a minor acute illness to upset the fine balance of all the chronic problems being controlled by a multitude of drugs. So, far from passengers being exempt from illness on holiday, there is no shortage whatsoever of problems to tackle.

In addition to the run-of-the-mill passenger illnesses, there is also, of course, the constant turnover of the crew's day-to-day problems. All the usual host of common ailments encountered on land can be seen in the crew clinic, but there is a greater likelihood of seeing certain

13

categories of illness. Psychological problems are understandably more frequent when you consider the added stress of life at sea, with its 24-hour-day, seven-day-week captivity within limited surroundings, and the separation for long periods from wives and families, and from one's roots. As a further consequence of these stresses, together with the lack of outdoor or diverse recreational facilities, the amount of alcoholic intake on ships must surely be amongst the highest levels in any section of society. Another influence on crew health is that, in exactly the same way as members of the Royal Navy, merchant seamen get what might be considered more than their fair share of social encounters. In addition to the rapid turnover of female company on board ship, there are generally a number of nights out in home and foreign ports . . . and what more can anyone say about Bangkok!

Understandably then, crew surgery will entail routine problems, peppered with a good cross-section of seafarers' complaints! However, just as on land, common things are common. The everyday illnesses encountered include colds and flu, respiratory infections, intestinal upsets, skin rashes, athletes foot, minor accidents, back problems, eye and ear infections, haemorrhoids, and the like. Amongst the serious problems more frequently encountered on board are cardiac disease – particularly coronary thrombosis – serious respiratory infections such as pneumonia, and fractured bones.

On board QE2 during a world cruise, when the number of people on board may be anything up to 2800, we could see up to eighty patients a day between the two doctors during busy periods. The majority of these will be crew members. These consultations will not all be merely brief visits, but will include major problems which may require hospitalization and investigation; some cases will also require cardiographs, X-rays, laboratory work or minor surgery. On average during these long cruises, there will probably be a major cardiac emergency every second or third day. There will usually be a fracture of some description every day, and a steady stream of strokes, pneumonias and other serious problems throughout. In addition to the usual Western illnesses, all the tropical illnesses which may be encountered around the world can occur. Not only does the ship sail around the globe, but also foreign travellers from all areas, and crew members from a host of different countries, fly in to join the ship.

A quiet morning could soon be shattered by a fractured skull, a serious chest injury, a third degree burn, an acute abdomen, a heart attack, a kidney stone, intestinal haemorrhage or a perforated ulcer.

14

Alternatively, it may be a long day full of brain teasers such as blood diseases, liver or renal problems, or psychiatric cases. In short, no illness is exempt; anything and everything in the book – from A to Z – can walk into the hospital. There is one exception: obstetrics. Although babies are occasionally born on the high seas, I personally have never had to deliver a baby on board.

It is interesting to speculate, in the event of a child being born on the high seas, on what nationality it would adopt. The country of origin of the parents? The country of nationality of the parents? – one could be French, the other Chinese. The country of the next port of call, where the birth would be initially registered? Or even the country of registration of the ship? The answer to this teaser, in fact, is that the child would be allowed to take on the nationality of either one of its parents, provided that that parent's nationality was by descent. In addition, depending upon the specific laws of the individual countries, the baby could be allowed to take the nationality of the country in which the ship is registered. In the case of British ships, however, this alternative would be subject to the Nationality Act of 1981.

Having mentioned almost every category of illness in the book which can be encountered at sea, there remains one which preoccupies almost everybody – seasickness. There are more myths, jokes, folk cures and old wives' tales relating to this subject than to any other aspect of the sea. However, as flippant as some may be about the subject, I've no doubt at all that everyone who steps on board any form of ship or boat must have considered it seriously, to a greater or lesser extent. Whether or not they've actually ever been sea sick, it must have crossed everyone's minds. Many hundreds and thousands – and perhaps hundreds of thousands – of potential passengers are lost to the cruise industry because of their fear of seasickness. There is an old saying concerning seasickness: 'Initially, you're afraid you're going to die, and eventually you're afraid that you're *not* going to die!' Seasickness isn't just a matter of vomiting. It's accompanied by the most demoralizing malaise, whereby the entire system, both physical and mental, feels totally dreadful. If, in the midst of suffering seasickness, the patient were to be told that the ship was going to sink, I guarantee that most would reply, 'Great! That'll solve the problem!' There are those who argue that it's all in the head. Let me tell them, it doesn't matter two hoots if it starts in your head or your boots: once you've got it, you're in trouble! But I would like to stress, so that everyone is totally convinced, that there is no need at all for *any* of the above. Unless there are extremely

15

unusual circumstances, seasickness is *totally* treatable: it can be quickly brought under control, however severe the case!

Believe it or not, seasickness is not very common. Almost by definition, a cruise ship itinerary will be chosen to provide the most pleasant and relaxed weather and sailing conditions to keep the passengers happy, the principal aim of any leisure industry. Therefore, you're unlikely to be placed in a situation where you may be affected by rough weather in the first instance. Secondly, nearly all, if not all, modern ships will be stabilized. Stabilizers, or 'fins' as they're often termed, can be compared to two short aeroplane wings, which are positioned on each side of the ship below the water line. They move on pivots to alter the flow of water across their surfaces, giving lift or drop to the fin, and consequently to that side of the ship. If, however, you should be unlucky enough to hit rough seas, or you're one of the unfortunate folks who is sensitive to motion, then there are many forms of cure, including the less effective old-fashioned remedies of a glass of port wine and brandy, dry biscuits, or watching the horizon. There are nearly as many folk cures as days of the year, and possibly one will suit you. For those who prefer more reliable treatment, there are various forms of medication, including the many traditional seasickness pills available on every pharmacist's shelves, which now have very effective modern counterparts such as Stugeron. For those who need something stronger than tablets but don't like the idea of an injection, there are rectal suppositories, but remember to take the wrapping off! You think that's a joke? You'd be amazed how many people pop them up, complete with aluminium foil!

Recently, in America, a further method of treatment has become available: the patch, a small Band-aid impregnated with anti-nauseant medication which is usually stuck behind the ear, and the chemical is slowly absorbed through the skin. On the *QE2*, however, we don't recommend or dispense these patches. When the world seems near to its end, when you feel that the only thing left to come up from your stomach are your boots, you're cursing the travel agent for recommending the cruise, you've sworn to yourself never to come within a hundred yards of a boat in future, you're depressed and just want to cry, and you can't believe that the captain could be so incredibly callous not to run the ship into the nearest port to end your misery, don't despair! Help is just a 21-gauge hypodermic needle away! I promise you that, unless there are unusual circumstances, the worst of all seasickness can be controlled within half an hour, or one hour at the most, if a sufficient dosage of anti-nauseant is given intramuscularly. In fact, you start to feel better within fifteen minutes of the injection. Forget about the myths and apprehensions, seasickness really isn't a reason to miss a great time!

There are some aspects of medicine at sea which are actually made easier by the circumstances. Few people want to be ill on holiday, but when they are unwell, they're much more likely to attend the doctor early than when at home. Whereas they may be prepared to put up with a throat infection in the office, they're certainly not going to let it spoil their holiday! So people attend for treatment of problems which they would normally tolerate, for a while at least. On the surface, this would appear to create a potentially very full waiting room. In practice, these minor problems are easily and quickly dealt with.

This attitude does have a major benefit. Take, for example, the busy husband at home. He may awaken one morning with pain in his chest, which isn't severe enough to stop him in his tracks. His wife urges him to go and see the doctor. He replies, 'There's no time this morning; I've got a meeting at 9 a.m., another at 11 a.m. . . . if it doesn't ease off by this evening, I'll see the doctor tonight.' At 4 p.m., having unwittingly ignored the danger signals throughout the day, he sustains a full-blown coronary thrombosis, followed by cardiac arrest, and dies! How many times has this sequence occurred? On the other hand, however, whilst on holiday, as I've mentioned, the patient is damned if he wants his early morning chest pain to spoil his day. The doctor is virtually next door, so he sensibly checks it out. By this process alone, the survival rate and avoidance of complications is dramatically improved! In exactly the same way, many other potentially serious problems are diagnosed and treated early on board ship; even surgical problems can be corrected by early presentation, diagnosis, and medical treatment, rather than surgery.

If the ship's doctor can be presented with the same range of medical problems as his shore side counterpart, is there any difference in medicine at sea? Apart from the obvious observation that the incidence of seasickness in Piccadilly Circus is likely to be lower, the principal difference in medicine at sea is not in the type of cases, but the means of dealing with them. Basically, a problem arising at sea must be dealt with by the single doctor on board and the limited facilities available. As the ship's doctor, whenever you reach for the phone to request a second, or specialist opinion, you're on both ends of the line, so to speak.

Many people may consider this area of medicine to be general practice; however, it is what I consider to be frontier medicine. At sea, your clinical knowledge and techniques take on a role of heightened importance. When confronted with a serious case, which may be from any field – orthopaedics, cardiovascular, neurological, intestinal, urological, gynaecological, geriatric, paediatric, or whatever – a comprehensive clinical history and thorough physical examination are the bedrock on which to build your case. Next, you must take on the supportive roles which, on land, others provide. There may be electrocardiographs to take, minor laboratory investigations to carry out, an X-ray may be necessary. You'll be responsible for, and may need to carry out alone, all of these investigations in order to obtain enough data to diagnose, assess, and treat the problems with neither the comforting support of your colleagues or the full range of medical diagnostic techniques available on land today. The information must be sifted, and, sometimes in the isolation and loneliness of the deep hours of the night, your decision made.

Having decided upon your direction, you may now have to switch roles again. If it should become necessary to carry out an operation, then suddenly you're very busy! The operating theatre must first be cleaned and prepared. Instruments, which will have been pre-packed and sterilized, must be made ready and all the paraphernalia of the operating theatre checked, and rechecked. Whereas this can be achieved in a shore-side hospital by merely lifting the telephone to the theatre sister, on board ship – you have to do it! On a small ship, you and your faithful nurse, and perhaps a medical attendant, must get everything ready. Meanwhile, the patient must also be cared for. An intravenous drip may be required, possibly a catheter to drain the stomach, another to drain the bladder. Blood must be obtained for possible transfusion.

'Hold on!' you may say, 'where's the blood bank?' The answer is simple, it's on the hoof, walking around in very convenient and effective two legged containers! Volunteers from amongst the crew usually register with the hospital and are categorized according to their blood groups. Hence, they can be called upon as necessary. Having organized the volunteers and collected sufficient blood, it must then be cross-matched for compatibility with the patient.

Next the patient has to be prepared and pre-anaesthetic medications given, and all this time he must be clinically monitored and assessed. Who is doing all of this work? Yours truly again, with his trusty nurse. All these functions which appear to occur so automatically in a shore-side hospital, must be painstakingly carried out, until finally all is ready.

Now the patient must be anaesthetized. Who is the anaesthetist? Me. Having put the patient to sleep, who is the surgeon? Me. When the operation is finished, who will be in charge of post operative care? Me.

These are of course extreme circumstances. Nonetheless, it can and does happen that on a small ship your very limited staff may have to cope without any other medical support. I am always surprised how efficiently and easily the routine flows, once the decision to 'go in' has been made. In fact, the hardest aspect of the problem is making that very lonely decision: to weigh up the pros and cons, possibly go in too early and then lose the patient, following what may have been an unnecessary operation; alternatively, go in too late, and not succeed. Major surgery at sea should only be carried out in life-threatening circumstances. Consequently, under these conditions, if the decision is well made, you can only win – without the operation, the patient has lost anyway.

Having considered the demands of surgical problems, what of medical emergencies? A medical emergency may be just as demanding of time, if not more so, than a surgical emergency. For instance, having admitted an acute coronary thrombosis to the ship's hospital, the patient will be placed under intensive care. Initial medications will be administered, and oxygen and intravenous therapy will probably have been commenced. Simultaneously, the patient will have been placed on a cardiac monitor. Who makes up the cardiac team? Who else but the lonely doctor, and once again, his trusty nurse.

Meanwhile, while you're busy watching the monitor night and day, and, in addition, catering to the routine daily demands of the job, someone decides to pick this moment to break a leg. Somehow, you must find time to carry out the X-rays, reduce the fracture – perhaps under intravenous anaesthetic – and then immobilize with a cast. You can guarantee that if you're busy, chances are you'll be *very* busy! It's what we all know as Sod's Law!

Having now provided you with a picture of the potential work-load which we might encounter on board *QE2*, you will presumably be wondering how we are, in fact, able to cope with all these problems. What do we do with serious cases? If a serious illness occurs whilst the ship is in port, of course we'll call upon the local facilities if they're considered adequate. Once the ship is at sea, however, we're usually very much on our own. What about helicopters? When the *QE2* is on a North Atlantic crossing from Southampton to New York, it will usually travel at around 29 knots – approximately 33 m.p.h. so that within just seven hours she has travelled over 200 miles, and is effectively out of return-range of the

19

nearest land-based helicopter. A further consideration is that, even if the ship is close enough for helicopter support, would it be in the interests of the patient to put them through what is, at best, a very traumatic procedure for an unwell patient, when there are good facilities on board for maintenance of the acute stage of an illness until the patient could be transferred comfortably and safely when the ship reached port? In actual fact, during fourteen years at sea, I personally have never been involved in a helicopter evacuation. What we do, then, is just get on with the problem!

Indeed, rather than off-loading patients, the *QE2* is the most immediate and efficient referral centre for whatever area of open seas she may be sailing. There are occasions when we're called upon, in the middle of the ocean, to render emergency medical help to ships not carrying a doctor, and there will be more details and examples of this in a later chapter.

In essence, the on-board medical team must be prepared to function in an isolated situation, with no back-up facilities from ashore. This means having the capability to deal with any and all of the variety of potential problems referred to throughout the earlier part of this chapter.

I am, of course, pleased to say that our record of success with emergency problems, including our survival rate for acute myocardial infarctions for example, can compare very favourably with any comparable medical centre in the world. Considering the high number of serious problems with which we're faced, the mortality rate on board the *QE2* is surprisingly, and gratifyingly, low. This, in many instances, is due to circumstances which I've already outlined, the principal one being that, in an emergency situation, the patient is probably closer to medical help on a ship than in any community ashore, and more importantly, we probably have more 'front-line' experience than any other cross-section of doctors.

Finally, let's consider what might be regarded as a routine day's work at sea. Is there such a thing? Not usually, and of course this variability is one of the attractions of the job. However, if all runs according to plan, what might a routine day include?

At 8.30 a.m. each morning the department meets together, and the day kicks off. Apart from the opportunities for social pleasantries, this meeting officially takes place to enable the night sister to hand over to the day staff. Any questions or problems for the day are usually sorted out and organized at this meeting.

One of the two doctors will then take the morning's crew clinic. The ship is home for the crew, and they go to their GP with the day-to-day problems which I related earlier. Having completed the crew surgery, doctor number one will next visit and examine any in-patients who have been admitted to the hospital wards. If all's well he then sets out on his house calls – or cabin visits – to see any new patients not well enough to attend the doctor's office; also any patients who aren't sufficiently unwell to be in the ship's hospital, and are being treated in their own cabins.

Following the cabin visits there are often a number of practical tasks to carry out around the hospital: perhaps a couple of minor operations such as excision of cysts, ingrown toenails or the like; maybe microscope slides to examine, or some other laboratory investigation, X-rays to be read, or electrocardiographs that have been taken that morning to check.

The morning's routine for doctor number one, will be interrupted each day at sea by 'rounds'. Each morning a cross-section of the ship's officers meet together and then set off in various directions around the ship to carry out inspections, or rounds, which include general rounds and crew accommodation rounds, whereby these areas are inspected for cleanliness, tidiness, breakages, wear and tear and other defects. On other days there will be hygiene rounds, when all of the food storing, handling, preparation, cooking, serving and eating areas and practices are checked in minute detail.

The second doctor, meanwhile, will have started his day by visiting his hospital patients and making any necessary follow-up cabin visits. These will be carried out in the first part of the morning, as he is due to start passenger surgery a little later, at a more convenient time for the patients. Accompanied by one of the sisters, he'll then work most of the morning in the passenger consultation office, where he'll usually have a busy time sorting out the host of various problems already discussed.

The period after lunch is relatively quiet medically and throughout the ship, but the hospital is still ticking. There are a number of on-going programmes which must be kept up to date, including routine crew medicals. Also, *QE2* is a registered vaccination centre and, as such, we're responsible for maintenance of immunization programmes for all the staff and, during world cruising, for the passengers also. Stock-taking, documentation, paperwork, cleaning, and in-patient care continues, and the team is prepared at all times for the usual flow of urgent cases or emergencies.

In the late afternoon, routine office hours recommence, and this time the two doctors change places, doctor number one taking the passenger clinic, and number two taking care of the crew. Again, after clinic hours, ward patients, cabin visits and tail-end jobs in the laboratory and around the hospital are tied up.

Included at some stage during the day are the various committee meetings with which the MO is associated. The principal one concerns the administration of health and hygiene, but there are also a safety committee, personnel executive committee, and the general manager's meetings, which all heads of department attend, and where all current problems on the ship are aired and discussed.

Outside the daily routine, one of the two doctors will be on call at all times from 9 a.m. to 9 a.m. on alternate days. He is responsible for whatever emergencies arise and any problems which can't be resolved by the duty nurse, and he'll also carry out follow-up visits to in-patients and the more serious of the cabin patients.

As you can see, the day's routine for both doctors can be demanding, enjoyable, well paced and rewarding, sometimes tranquil, but often full of drama. Medicine at sea is certainly not boring!

So, in a large nutshell, these are the basic facts and statistics of medicine at sea. However, perhaps I should repeat that there are more than a few variations from the routine day. The smooth flow may well be interrupted by emergencies, but fortunately there are many lighter diversions also, as for example with the frustrating but amusing difficulties of 'interpreter medicine'.

On board *QE2* a great many of the crew members are British, but in addition there is a mixture of almost any and every nationality who make up the full complement. This pot-pourri of nationalities and characters can add a great deal of interest, variety and spice to the morning's work. On the other hand, it can create a considerable medical headache from all the complexities created by language barriers. Although medical school covers all the obvious aspects of the profession, I occasionally think how useful it would have been to have undertaken a course in mime. You'd be amazed how far you can get with only one key word, such as *dolor* – the Spanish for pain – and pointing to your head, ear, throat or stomach. However, when it comes to Scandinavians, Africans, Indians, the Middle and Far Eastern languages, then you haven't even got the benefit of key words to rely on, and though some of them bring interpreters, how the heck do you tell them to go and fetch one if they haven't!

If the ailment is simple, then pointing at bruised toes, cut fingers or a pimple is quick and easy; if it's complex, you're in for a very long session. Even with an interpreter, how do you set about a psychological or psychiatric problem? Most foreigners usually have the foresight to bring along an English-speaking friend; that is, all except

Americans! You think that's a joke? You should try some of the southern drawls, or a really good Brooklyn twang! What if they should also stutter? Or how about some little old Southern belle with a partial stroke? I think it was George Bernard Shaw who once said: 'Britain and America are two great nations, separated by a common language.'

With British terminology you can even start off on the wrong foot. Try for example, as I did in my early days, asking Mr Cohen what his Christian name is. 'Christian name? Christian name?' he replied, 'with a name like Cohen, you want my Christian name?!'

Most countries have their characteristics. Indians tend to move their heads from side to side when they talk, so you're often left guessing whether an answer was yes or no. Italians, of course, speak with their hands, even the interpreters! On one occasion, I asked an interpreter why, even when he was interpreting someone else's words, he still waved his arms around?

'Oh, I'm sorry!' he replied, and then continued, 'Well, he's 'a got 'a headache, and he's 'a got 'a cough.' Uncharacteristically he remained perfectly still. 'And he's 'a got 'a chest pain,' . . . still no movement . . . 'and he's 'a got the phlegm,' his hands were twitching. 'And it's 'a give him 'a stomach-ache,' his control started to disintegrate, he clutched his stomach and grimaced. 'And he's 'a vomit, and he's 'a diarrhoea,' his arms leapt up, as though of their own accord, 'and he's 'a feel like 'a death!' He was in full swing now, arms waving and flailing, his restrictions abandoned! He finished with a flourish, relaxed, content, smiling – like someone just released from bad constipation!

The Chinese always confound me. 'What's his problem?' I ask. The interpreter speaks in Chinese for what seems like three sentences to the patient, and the patient replies with another three . . .

'A cough,' the interpreter informs me.

'Is there anything else?'

There is a wait while he asks the patient, and a longer wait while the patient replies.

'Well?'

'No,' says the interpreter.

'No? Just no?'

'No, nothing else!'

'Any other symptoms?' I persist.

The question is posed, and then comes the long, long reply. I wait patiently for the answer, and eventually I'm forced to ask, 'What did he say?'

'No.'

'What else?'

'Nothing.'

'What do you mean, nothing? What else were you talking about?' I ask in exasperation.

'His problem, of course,' he explains to me slowly, as though I am simple minded.

'So, what else does he want you to tell me?' I say, almost pleading.

'Nothing.'

And so on! Minutes of discussion, and one word answers. I've never yet got to the bottom of all the chatting! 'Just the Chinese way,' explains the interpreter, as though that answers all!

I suppose that the prize for most amazing interpreter must go to a South African lady who travelled with us. As we all know, it's the tendency when talking to someone who doesn't understand our language to not only speak more clearly and slowly, but for some unexplainable reason we all also tend to raise the level of our voices, and the more difficulty we have in getting through, the louder we get. It doesn't make any sense but we do it all the same.

I'd never really met an Afrikaaner until now. This particular Afrikaans lady accompanied a female friend into my office one morning and announced, 'My friend is German, so I thought that I would come along to interpret for her.'

'That's very thoughtful of you,' I replied. 'Thank you. What's her problem?'

'She has some pain in the chest,' said the interpreter.

'Oh yes? Well chest pains can originate from various problems,' I explained. 'It's important to know where the pain is located precisely and what sort of pain it is. I wonder if you could ask her to describe it for me, please?'

The interpreter edged her chair closer to her friend, and sat quite near, face to face. Very slowly and precisely, with exaggerated lip movements, she gave her Afrikaans interpretation of my question: 'WHERE IS YOUR CHEST PAIN?' she yelled, almost at the top of her voice, then continued shouting in perfect English, 'WHAT SORT OF PAIN IS IT?'

Her friend replied quietly, in broken English.

I was speechless! To my total amazement, the interpreter carried on through the entire interview at the same pitch. I was so dumbfounded that I didn't intervene. I thought it was some sort of Afrikaans joke! Perhaps it was!

All Passengers, Great and Small

By now you will be aware that there is more to the role of doctor at sea than is initially apparent, and certainly more than seasickness injections and cocktail parties! There are two more unconventional roles of the doctor at sea to consider, particularly on the *QE2*. One of these is that of ship's dentist.

As I've mentioned, a dentist is sometimes carried on board the *QE2*, and our present dentist, Keith Mason, usually travels for around one third of the year, which includes the annual world cruise. However, during the remainder of the time on *QE2*, and at all times on smaller ships, when a dentist is needed, you're it! This doesn't necessarily mean that the passengers and crew have to rely on the dental guesswork of some uninformed, unpractised doctor to fill the gap, so to speak, as basic dental training is included in the medical school curriculum. In my own case, I have also managed to glean a fair background knowledge and some know-how of emergency dental techniques by attending classes, looking over the shoulder of dental colleagues and assisting in some of their work. However, I do stress that the dental treatment carried out by the medical officers is of an emergency or temporary nature.

The more frequently occurring dental problems which are seen and treated on a cruise include dental infections, fractured teeth, lost fillings and detached dental caps or bridges. You can imagine the upset and panic which arises on the occasion when some lady has gone to the trouble of getting all dressed up in her new gown, had her hair specially styled in the beauty salon and spent an age perfecting her make-up for the captain's private cocktail party followed by dinner and a full social evening . . . and then loses a dental cap just as she's all ready to go. I've seen many ladies who would quite seriously consider the options if offered the choice of a lost dental cap or a broken bone, and I suppose there will be many female readers who would be totally in sympathy with this dilemma.

You'd be quite amazed at the disproportionate degree of gratitude which results from having rescued unfortunate patients – some of them men – from this apparently relatively minor predicament. Of course, it goes without saying that no-one goes to the expense and trouble of taking a cruise, and then happily accepts the need to attend the captain's party with a gap-toothed smile! I've salvaged many a disastrous situation, whereby the unlucky passenger was intending to stay in their cabin for the remainder of the cruise! As ridiculous an over-reaction as this appears to be, take my word, it happens! Perhaps you have to be on the sticky end of the situation to understand it.

Generally speaking, the MO's amateur dental attention is more than adequate, and achieves satisfactory results. However, there were understandably odd occasions, in the very early years, when a little more experience would have helped, as with my first extraction at sea, carried out on one of the ship's crew in the Royal Navy, miles and miles away from supervision and advice.

I'm sure that every young dentist must go through the same ordeal when faced with their very first case out on their own, but I was determined that, if nothing else, the patient wouldn't have any complaints about pain. Consequently, I gave him a good full dose of local anaesthetic, and a measure more to be sure, and a drop more for good luck, and one more for the pot. It worked like a charm: he felt no pain at all. The only problem was, I could also have taken out most of the other teeth in his head, and maybe removed his mandible, or perhaps even a vertebra or two, and he still wouldn't have felt any pain! And drool! I would never have believed anyone in the world could drool so much, and for so long. The patient was like a snail: everywhere he went, he left a trail of saliva behind him. At times he looked like the centre of a spider's web, with long streaks of saliva stuck to everything around him.

'Great, doc, great!' he said, genuinely and thankfully, as he replaced a soggy cigarette back in the corner of his drooping mouth for the umpteenth time, only for it to drop from his numb lips and frozen face yet again. On balance, it was a success.

An alternative to using local anaesthetic is to give a short-lasting, general anaesthetic with inhaled gas, or to give an intravenous anaesthetic. Back in 1978, during my first months on board *QE2*, I received a visit from a gentleman who is one of the great names of the film world. He was almost equally well known for his reputation as a boozer, bon viveur and tearaway. He complained of a recurring dental problem which was ruining his holiday, and he was adamant that the damned tooth should be removed. The tooth in question was a molar and extraction would not alter his appearance, not that this was of any consequence as his face, to say the least, was well lived in. I advised him that we should attempt a temporary remedy, and wait a few days until we reached New York, but he would hear nothing of it. In addition, he insisted that he must be 'put to sleep'. We debated the subject, and I decided to administer intravenous valium anaesthesia.

Now, one of the more well known phenomena in medicine is that heavy alcoholic drinkers usually have a resistance to the effects of certain medications. Large doses of certain chemicals may be necessary to achieve the desired effect, and this includes the sedative effects of valium given intravenously – the procedure which I was about to carry out. Despite his infamous alcoholic reputation, our patient was very guarded regarding the full extent of his intake, and wouldn't admit to the amounts. I calculated the dosage of valium to be given, taking his size and alcohol history into account. Having prepared all the dental equipment for the extraction, with the medical assistant in attendance and the emergency gear at the ready, I slowly administered the valium into a forearm vein.

The patient sat, bright-eyed and bushy tailed, chatting away.

'Feel OK?'

'Yep, no problem thanks, doc,' he replied.

More valium.

'Feeling drowsy?'

'No, I'm feeling pretty good.'

More valium.

'Sleepy?'

'No, wide awake!'

More valium.

'Count slowly for me from 1.'

'1, 2, 3, 4, 5, 6, 7,' and on, and on . . . '41, 42, 43, 44, 45,' . . . . More valium . . . '61, 62, 63, 64, 65 . . .'

I was now well over my calculated dosage and approaching the maximum which I felt could safely be allowed.

'71 . . 72 . . . 73 . . . . 74 . . . . 75.' Eventually he became groggy. His eyelids, becoming heavier, finally closed. He was in a light state of anaesthesia.

'Right, that will have to do,' I decided. 'Let's get this thing out!'

Another phenomenon associated with intravenous valium, and some other forms of sedation which aren't intended to take the patient into deep anaesthesia, is that the light level of anaesthesia which is required allows the patient to feel some discomfort. Consequently, they may react to the pain. However, following recovery from the anaesthetic, the patient doesn't have any recollection of the incident whatsoever – of the pain or the response.

Our patient's eyes had remained closed and his breathing was heavy, deep and even. His features and body were now relatively relaxed. I grasped the tooth firmly with the extractor forceps.

'Uuh,' groaned the patient.

I took a firm grip on the tooth.

'Uuuuuuuh,' he said.

The medical assistant held the patient's head firmly, while I pushed the tooth back into the socket to break the cement grip. Suddenly the assistant's hands slipped, and he jumped in alarm as, with acute embarrassment, he found himself holding the patient's toupee, which had slipped down over his ear. The startled assistant was bug-eyed as he gazed in total disbelief at the bald pate of one of his screen heroes! Fortunately I still had a firm hold on the tooth.

'UuuuuuhhhH . . . ooohH,' he moaned.

I twisted the tooth to dislodge it in the socket.

'OooooohhHH . . . aaaaaahHH.'

The medical assistant, to say the least, was looking very shaken and apprehensive at all the shouting and reaction from his hero. Another twist.

'Oh . . oooh . . oooooh. . . . . . OH!' He finally yelped as I yanked, and out came the tooth in one piece.

More than pleased with the result, and smiling at the achievement, I turned to the M.A. 'Don't worry,' I said, full of confidence and pleased to have demonstrated my dental prowess, apparently so efficiently. 'When the valium wears off, I guarantee you that he won't remember a thing about the entire procedure.'

Whereupon the patient's eyes snapped open. He sat bolt upright in the chair. Taking us both in with his gaze, he loudly declared, 'OH YES I ....ING WELL WILL!'

And so he did, much to my continued embarrassment, for a long, long time. And having remained friends over the years, he still continues to remind me! Oh well, you can't win them all!

Fortunately, even with our two cases mentioned above, I can't remember anyone ever complaining about our dental services – and that's not because of the after-effect of valium on the memory!

Over the years there are occasions, of course, when perhaps either the dental machinery is defunct or the appropriate instruments are missing. If this should occur, then a degree of compromise or adaptability is required. An example of this could be the use of a small, very fine file, such as an electrician's rat-tail file, to take the sharp edge off a broken tooth that may be cutting a patient's tongue or cheek.

In this very situation, on one occasion, my reputation as a dentist was shattered amongst the Italian section of the crew. One of their particularly nervous members attended with a broken tooth. We would be in port within two days where correct dental care would be available, but meanwhile I decided to file off a nasty jagged point which was cutting the patient's tongue. I explained at length, through an interpreter, what I was going to do and both men silently regarded me as though they were not sure whether I was joking or serious. As there was no appropriate dental equipment on board, I phoned the chief electrician for the loan of his fine files which he'd kindly supplied on previous occasions. The chief electrician said that one of his men would deliver the tools.

Our apprehensive Italian sat, perspiring, with his eyes glued to the door, exchanging occasional worried glances with the interpreter. Abruptly, the door opened and a young electrician's assistant stepped forward and stated, 'The chief asked me to let you have these files.' Apparently not realizing the circumstances, or which files the chief had been referring to, he had duly gathered up a selection of tools and now thrust out a bunch of full sized, eighteen-inch-long, one-inch-wide rasps and course files!

With no more comment than a strangled, 'AaaaaaahhhH!' our patient leapt from the chair, and disappeared through the door faster than a startled jack rabbit. The interpreter, without any comment at all, backed slowly out of the room, looking sideways at me as though I was some sort of weirdo!

As I recall, there were very few dental problems amongst the Italian crew following that incident!

The second of the less conventional medical roles – one which the average passenger and even many of the crew members aren't aware of – is the doctor's role as ship's veterinary surgeon.

Many ships have the capacity to carry animals, but the QE2 is particularly well equipped in this respect. Way up at the top of the ship, just forward of the funnel, is a surprisingly large area which is fitted with built-in kennels and cages with separate accommodation for up to two dozen animals. Here can be found a whole host and variety of dogs of all sizes and shapes, and cats of all colours and breeds. At any one time the ship may carry up to three fully trained kennel maids.

I imagine that you'll be fairly surprised to learn that so many animals may be on board ship, or even that there are any animals at all. Bear in mind, however, that for a considerable proportion of the year the ship voyages between Europe and America, and that there will be many people who are either emigrating, returning home, or crossing to the other side of the Atlantic for a long period, and aren't merely cruising. Obviously there will be a number of these passengers who don't wish to leave their pets behind. There are others who don't like to be, or even refuse to be, separated from their pets even for the short period of a cruise. For these, the kennel facilities offer their only opportunity to travel. They can rest or play below, content that their four-legged darlings are being pampered and cared for up above in a canine or feline equivalent of *QE2* luxury. The *QE2* kennels have an outdoor exercise area and walkway, which, believe it or not, is even equipped with a genuine London lamp-post for the use of the dogs! This must be the most sophisticated, well-used, and well-travelled canine lavatory in the world.

Cats and dogs are naturally the most common animals to be carried, but theoretically there is no limit to the type of animal which can be transported by ship. Fortunately for the amateur ship's doctor/vet, the *QE2* sticks to the less exotic varieties of animals, and usually carries only house pets. During my first days at sea, however, the line for which I was working ran round-trips to South Africa with ships which carried a combination of cargo and passengers. On my first voyage with them to South Africa we carried a couple of race horses in boxes on the forward deck. Life must have been strange and difficult for these poor animals, so far from a green pasture and so restricted in their movements. To these unusual surroundings was added the unfamiliar movement of the ship, particularly towards the bow, and the horses were more or less continuously on the move just to remain steady on their long legs. To cap off their problem, we went straight out from Southampton into a terrific storm. Being an old ship without stabilizers, the movement, to say the least, certainly wasn't comfortable. This was my first trip to sea in a merchant ship, and my own welfare, health and stomach certainly weren't at their best!

There are certain areas of water around the world which are notorious for their bad weather or, more appropriately, their rough waters. The Bay of Biscay is one such notorious patch. Due to the contours of the ocean floor in this area, even mildly stormy weather can create exceptionally rough seas. In fairness, I must add that it's quite usual to travel across the Bay of Biscay and find it as calm as a mill pond, but as with the young lady from the catechism, 'When she was good she was very, very good, but when she was bad, she was horrid!' Anyhow, this was one of those days!

What little sympathy I had left over from catering to my own condition was in great demand amongst the five hundred or so passengers on board, but the poor horses also had to be considered. Apart from the terror which must have been caused by their incomprehensible, violent environment out there on the wildest area of the ship, the risk of injury to the animals was obviously tremendous. It took many dangerous, buffeted, turbulent hours of dedicated patience by the handlers to help calm the horses, and some rapidly improvised harnesses and tackle were devised to help restrain them and prevent injury.

What a very dramatic sight it was: a mixture of lightning, driving rain, great gushes of sea spray and water; the violent rocking and lurching of the deck, the piercing whinnying of the horses, the pounding of their hooves, the shouts of the handlers, the snapping of ropes, the creaking and cracking of the boxes, the clanking and grinding of the anchors and their chains, and the thudding and pounding of the ship as it drove in surges into the dark storm and huge waves ahead. On and on it went, for hour after hour: wet, frozen figures; the crushed, scraped, bruised and battered limbs of animals and men. It seemed the night would never end; the storm raged on and on.

Dawn came, and suddenly it was calm, and quiet, and peaceful: one of the many fascinating phenomena at sea which still continue to amaze me.

Patching up battered horses wasn't exactly what I had in mind when I set off on my jaunt as doctor at sea. Dogs and cats, on reflection, are somewhat easier! But even they can present a headache to the new recruit with nothing but a medical background and a veterinary manual. However, arriving eventually at the conclusion that cats and dogs are, in fact, only a variation of the human animal, life as an amateur vet is not so difficult as it would at first appear. Having said that, it's not the usual practice for a patient to express his feelings or disapproval by biting me on the leg, and neither is it customary to inform the doctor that he's found a tender spot by adorning his hand with scratch marks. Communication is achieved in many ways! Interpreter medicine has nothing on this!

On the assumption that pre-warned is pre-armed, upon receiving

31

a call from the kennel maids to attend a sick dog, it is always quite handy to know what size equipment to take and whether you'll be pinned to the wall by a Saint Bernard or nipped on the toe by a Chihuahua. When looking through the veterinary manual for the first time, I felt that I was on the right track by narrowing down the problem to the categories of big animals and small animals. Good, that's Saint Bernards and toy poodles, I thought; but no, it's not so easy. *Big* animals, are cows and elephants! *All* dogs are small animals! Try getting into a cage with a testy Great Dane, and telling yourself that! Small indeed!

I must admit, though, that however large, ugly or offensive our canine friends may be, few humans ever look quite so miserable as a seasick dog. Ignoring its food, lying cowed and curled up in the corner of its box rolling up big, sad, miserable eyes, looking for help and managing the occasional thin whimper, it's hard to think of a Doberman Pincher as a potential devourer of arms, and a seasick Spaniel could summon up sympathy even in Attila the Hun. For all lovers of animals – don't despair! The dogs respond to treatment in just the same way as humans, with an adjustment in dosage, of course.

The major problem, however, isn't which drug and how much to give, but establishing a diagnosis in the first place! The closest comparison which can be drawn in medicine is examining and diagnosing an ill baby. The history is very limited, and generalized observations of an anxious parent are often the only guide-lines. Manoeuvring ten big adult fingers around a four-week-old abdomen during the examination also limits the findings. In much the same way, there is an art in reading the signs and symptoms of an unwell animal, before even getting down to the treatment. I'm quite happy to leave all that to James Herriot, but I must admit, it's surprisingly gratifying to bring an ill animal back to health, however improvised and amateur the techniques.

Amongst other animals which are carried on the *QE2*, there are often an assortment of birds. These may include budgerigars, canaries, mynah birds or parrots. The exception to this conventional list of exotic feathered pets is occasionally encountered. The best examples are the pets of a certain princess from the near-Eastern regions, who had travelled with Cunard many times over the years on both the old *Queens* and the *QE2*. This sophisticated lady made a habit of always travelling first class, accompanied by her long-standing, treasured, close companions, her two pet birds. As eccentric as this may appear, one is even more surprised to discover that the birds were not parakeets, doves or birds of paradise, but a pigeon and a starling! Due to her long-standing association with Cunard and her frequency of travel, the management bowed to her eccentricity and allowed the birds to travel with her in her first-class accommodation, where they were intermittently let loose to enjoy the freedom and luxury of the surroundings of a first-class cabin on the world's greatest liner!

An incident concerning a bird caused my one and only contretemps between myself and a pet owner. On one occasion, *en route* from Southampton to New York on board *QE2*, we were carrying our usual cross-section of animals. Shortly after departure, I was in the operating theatre suturing a nasty laceration for one of our chefs, who had apparently mistaken his hand for one of the pork chops on the evening's menu. Ray, one of the medical attendants, came into the room and advised, 'Excuse me, doctor, but there's a lady on the phone who sounds rather distressed. She wants you to go to her cabin to discuss a problem.'

'Explain that I'm busy at the moment, and ask if the patient can come down here now, or come along to this evening's clinic if it's not urgent, Ray,' I told him.

After a couple of minutes Ray returned and said, 'The patient can't come to this evening's office, doctor.'

'Why? Is she too ill?'

'No, sir.'

'Well, why then?'

'Because it's a parrot!'

This was the start of what was to become a very strained relationship.

As it turned out, the parrot was the property of the wife of a very senior international political figure, who, it became evident, was obviously used to having her own way! When I saw her later, the lady gave me a long dissertation about her parrot, which was being accommodated up in the kennels. I'm not sure which was the more neurotic, the owner or the parrot. Apparently, the bird never thrived unless it was constantly with its owner, being talked to, given special attention, special food, patted and petted, oiled and pruned.

Over the next couple of days, I received a string of calls: the parrot wasn't eating well; its feathers didn't look right and were falling out; it wouldn't talk; it didn't know its owner, . . . and so on. On each occasion, I checked the parrot and spoke with the kennel maids, who assured me that it was doing fine, and it certainly appeared well, which I always think is relatively easy to tell because, believe me,

33

nothing looks sicker than a sick parrot! Not only I, but also the kennel maids, were being constantly harassed about this patient.

The final straw came when, in the depths of the night, I was woken by the duty night sister, who was unable to deal with the increasingly distressed owner, who was unable to sleep because she felt that the parrot was, believe it or not, 'deteriorating from lack of love and attention!' Being called from bed for an ill patient may not be a great way to spend a night, but it is, of course, always acceptable – if not always necessary. On the other hand, to receive an emergency night-call for a sick parrot – which, to make matters worse, is in fact very fit – does nothing to aid good humour or relationships. The owner was most offended when I concluded that the problem wasn't with the parrot but with herself, and suggested that she may benefit from a tranquillizer or night sedation. Unfortunately, this episode didn't curtail her continued pestering.

The following day Harry, the ship's baggage master, came to see me. On board *QE2*, one of the baggage master's responsibilities is the handling and documentation of the animals which we carry, and the preparation of the documentation ready to be presented to the local authorities, together with the animals, at our port of arrival and disembarkation. All the various certificates, forms and other required documents are checked on board, and then the baggage master presents them to the P.M.O. for rechecking, and countersigning if all is in order.

On this particular morning, Harry presented the usual fist-full of documents for the various animals.

'All in order?' I asked.

'All except one,' he replied.

'Which is that, and what's the problem?'

'Well, it's one of the birds, a parrot. The owner has lost the veterinary certificates,' Harry explained.

'Not Lady ——'s parrot?' I asked, not really wanting to hear the answer,

'That's it.'

'It would be!'

'Well, the authorities won't allow it to be landed without clearance, and I can't do that on board, it needs proper examination and certification by a qualified vet.'

'You'd better telex the New York office and explain the situation and see what they can arrange.'

Later that day, Harry returned. 'What do you think about that then?' he asked, and handed me a telex from New York.

The telex stated,

'A veterinary surgeon will visit the ship on arrival N.Y. and examine the parrot and issue the necessary documents. Fee for service will be $100.'

$100 for a house call on a parrot! (And that was 1980!)

I considered the telex.

'Well at least that seems to solve the problem,' I said, 'but I should think that she'll be a bit wild about the vet's fee.' Then I added, 'When you go up to see her, don't forget to let her know that the vet will cost $100. If she's not happy with the fee, tell her that the doctor is quite prepared to *strangle* the bloody thing for $5!'

There was an outcome to this story. Not realizing that there was such animosity regarding the parrot, Harry repeated what he thought was a good joke about the doctor's offer to the owner, whereupon she blew her top and complained to all and sundry about the dreadful attitude of the P.M.O.: 'If he is the designated ship's vet, he should have greater concern and feeling for the animals, and particularly my darling parrot!'

As I've said before, you can't win them all!

What the lady didn't know, was that I would have strangled the damned parrot for *nothing*!!

II
ALL AT SEA

A Different World

Quite obviously, the public at large are fascinated by the opulent lifestyle associated with cruising and transatlantic voyaging. Understandably, people are interested to learn how the other half lives, or in this case, probably the other one per cent – indeed, on a world-wide basis, we are in fact considering how a minute fraction of the earth's population enjoy this extremely privileged situation in life. Whether or not it is our desire to participate, it is entirely natural to wonder whether we're missing something special, the icing on life's cake, and if we are, we should at least be able to get an insight into whether the people fortunate enough to experience this luxury are in fact enjoying it.

A book such as this should provide an opportunity to take a peek through one of life's keyholes at situations which are not readily accessible to the world at large. Allow me to explain what I find enjoyable about working in these surroundings and amongst these people.

I have gone into the medical role of the ship's surgeon at some length, and as I've already discussed, I must say that the principal satisfaction of my position has to be the reward of addressing and meeting the medical challenges which are presented in an isolated, detached environment. Here, success or failure depends almost entirely on the skills of yourself and the small team around you. Working and winning – even on day-to-day problems – with an efficient, happy team, is a great kick. At the other end of the scale, I shall reveal to you later the very definite attraction of the social side of life on the QE2. However, in addition to the major considerations of work and play, there are obviously many other aspects of the job which influence our decision to stay at sea.

On board every ship on which I've worked, there has always been a strong and comforting family and team atmosphere: everyone on a ship is totally interdependent. It always fascinates me, as I walk quietly through the long carpeted corridors of the ship, to think that all around me, in very close proximity but mainly unseen, the team is working. In every corner of the ship, there is some function, some activity, the ship ticking on, always working! Even in the dead of night, down empty corridors, behind closed doors, the hive buzzes. When all have been wined, dined, entertained, danced to a standstill, have quietly retired to bed, and are being rocked in their sleep, the team is still at work . . . the ship goes on. Walking through the quiet corridors, you sense all of these people around you, working with you, for you, every one filling their role, every one taking care of all the others, every one depending on everyone else.

I am well aware that this form of interdependence exists on shore, in a large hotel for example, but think again: if you don't like the food, you can eat down the road. You can go home after work. If you don't like the doctor, or his opinion, you can find another, or go to another hospital, and so on. I don't think I'm over dramatizing the situation when I say that the degree of family atmosphere found on board is very rare in any other form of community.

What else attracts and keeps me at sea? People often wonder if I ever get bored. Does the travelling become mundane? Don't I miss the variety of working ashore? Whenever I come across these questions, I automatically think of the possible alternatives, which many 'normal' people live: starting the day by being jostled in an underground train, whilst travelling to work across London each morning of the working week, and after a hard day's work – probably in some small office, shop, or factory section – having to repeat the process for another hour back across the city, the only view available being an upside-down newspaper, the advertisements, the rows of blank staring eyes, and the dark walls of the tunnels through the windows, squeezed in amongst the smell of the unwashed masses, and the odours of last night's dinner – garlic from one end, curry from the other! I tried it once. No thanks!

Of course you could, as an alternative, consider the excitement and freedom of your own private transport, and the stimulating pleasure of creeping through central London, or the gloriously unattractive freeways of Los Angeles, during the joys of rush-hour traffic: hooting, snarling, swearing, crawling, frustrating, fender-bending, coronary engendering immobility for hours on end, to and from work, day after day, after week, after year. I must admit that the exhilaration of travel, the excitement of new ports, new countries, new continents, new people, and new experiences must

40

naturally diminish with repetition and familiarity, but believe me, it most certainly could never be described as boring.

There are many jobs available which entail travel, some more extensively than others; but I venture to say that living on board a ship is the most attractive and certainly the most convenient way of covering great distances and visiting multitudes of places – some of which, incidentally, are completely unapproachable by any other form of transport.

It is difficult perhaps for the non-seafarer to visualize or appreciate the simplicity of personal effort involved. All being well, the weather encountered during a voyage will not be too inclement, and hence the ship's movement will be comfortable, sometimes negligible, and occasionally hardly detectable. This means that, for the majority of the time, a ship – particularly one as large as the *QE2* – can be dashing over the ocean, and across the surface of the world, at speeds of around 29 knots, or approximately 34 m.p.h., with its inmates being totally unaware of movement from A to B. The normal activities of the day, therefore, usually proceed without interruption or distraction, and crew and passengers arise from bed each morning and proceed with the day's events in much the same way as if they were in an hotel ashore, and certainly in much the same way as they might if the ship were permanently tied up alongside the dock. But, as you get up, shower and get dressed, the ship ploughs onwards. You go in for breakfast, discuss the night's events, eat your eggs and bacon, read the daily newspaper, which is printed every day right there on the *QE2*, go down to work, get stuck into your various tasks, sort out the problems, and the ship still ploughs onwards. At the end of the morning you may meet some friends in a bar, have a chat, eat lunch . . . the ship continues to travel. You might write a few letters, read a book, sunbathe, go back to work, sort out the filing cabinet, wander back to your quarters, rest, shower, change for the evening, and still the ship presses on. There will be an evening of drinking, eating, dancing, entertainment, possibly romance – the ship hasn't stopped. You reach the end of another full day, and so to bed, and while you sleep the ship never ceases its onward travel, hour after hour, ceaselessly, day after day. Another day, another meal, another dance, and still the ship continues onwards.

I still find it fascinating to look out through my porthole, draw the curtains and go to bed in England, and after five intervening days of normal activity, awaken, draw the curtains, and see the New York skyline! Without any apparent effort or involvement I've changed my location to a spot not a quarter mile down the road, but a quarter of the way round the world! One day Miami, another day Rio, and another, Cape Town. All without any inconvenience: no packing of bags and baggage in between, no taxis, no waiting rooms, no transit lounges, no queues, no walking, pushing, sweating, no dashing for connecting trains, planes or buses, no cramped seats, bustling crowds, escalators or plastic meals. No porters, no unintelligible signs, no ruined luggage. And so to Sydney, and Bombay. Open the curtains again, and it's Hong Kong, Yokohama, Hawaii, Acapulco, the Panama Canal . . . and still no effort. Another breakfast, another day's work, and bingo, Naples. More meals, more dances . . . Bermuda.

How easy! It's almost as though the world is coming to *you*! And *that* sums up travel by ship – no other form of travel can compare.

Between the travel? Between the weeks of work without break? What then? Well, that's yet another attraction – the time off! Your reactions to a seafarer's holiday time, or leave allowance, may well be one of initial surprise and perhaps envy. In my case I am allowed 165 days per year as leave. This total is taken in a number of sections, which basically breaks down to approximately two months' work and one month's leave, with occasionally two months on and two months off, to balance the discrepancy. Superficially, this no doubt appears excessive, but in comparison, take the average man working ashore. To start with, he'll usually work a five-day week, and so just for basics, he'll have fifty-two weekends off, which, of course, is 104 days. Let's add the statutory holiday days to this, which in the UK may be up to ten days a year, including Christmas, Easter, New Year etc., and then three or four weeks paid holiday – as much as another twenty days. Without much effort we've accounted for about 135 days. Now think how many people you know who play golf one afternoon a week – that's another twenty-odd days. Bear in mind also that the seaman working on board ship is, in fact, never actually off duty – you certainly can't go home for the night. You're always available, and the vast majority of the jobs entail far more than ten hours' work a day. I make these points not in defence of my 165 days, but merely as an interesting illustration of the differences in working life on board ship of which you are perhaps not aware. You can no doubt deduce that two months of being continuously available for work requires a good break to recover.

From my point of view, I enjoy the arrangement. I enjoy being involved with the overall running and administration of the ship as a whole in addition of being in control of our own medical department over a period of months rather than on a day-to-day basis, then having a long break with sufficient time available to be involved in other aspects of life; to have enough time for other outlets and interests, to be involved with other businesses, or with something constructive, such as writing a book!

What other attractions are there to life at sea? Well, I don't think that anyone could dispute that on board *QE2* we have a most unusual and interesting variety of patients, and I'm confronted daily by a cross-section of characters, personalities, and celebrities to which few other practices around the world could be exposed.

You may consider it unfair that the patients on board the ship have no choice as to whom their doctor will be – or at best a choice of two. However, to counter this consideration I would reiterate that the circumstances and practicalities of providing additional doctors – or any crew members for that matter – are the restricting factors, and consequently we like to feel that we compensate for the lack of choice by offering a high level of quality. This, in fact, means that anyone becoming unwell on board ship must inevitably fall under our wing – except in the very rare circumstances when a passenger may be travelling with their own physician. However, even in these cases, the ultimate responsibility for the patient's welfare and health must lie with the Principal Medical Officer of the ship, and of course, all medical facilities fall unquestionably under his jurisdiction. Hence, prince and pauper alike are our responsibility.

I have to admit that from my very earliest days of medicine, it was an overwhelming experience to be responsible for the well-being and, for heaven's sake, the *life*, of another person! I have never ceased to respect the trust and confidence which a patient places in me when they consult with me for help. To be regarded in this manner is an extremely privileged position.

As we mature, we come to understand that all beings are equal; there are no supermen, immortals or supreme beings walking amongst us. However, it is a unique, disquieting and somewhat alarming experience to be initiated into the wider world beyond our home town, and to be confronted for the first time with the medical problems, psychological disturbances, and possibly mutilated anatomy of someone who, until now, may have been the screen idol of your youth, the oracle of your political opinions, the sculptor of your medical knowledge, the hero of your athletic ambitions, or a defender of your realm . . . and so it was, during my first days with the *QE2*.

It is now commonplace and relatively uneventful, for my 'next patient please' to be an explorer, a world-renowned politician, an astronaut, a World Champion athlete, a famous author, a film star, a TV personality, a great actor, a president, an ambassador, a great inventor or innovator, or even – probably among the most demanding and rewarding of confrontations – a pinnacle of my own profession, such as Dr Christiaan Barnard.

For princes, sheikhs, pop stars, industrialists, socialites, entrepreneurs, . . . illness, like death, is a great equalizer. Be they billionaires, bishops or bums, viruses or occluded arteries have no respect for status. So, generally speaking, the less dramatic moments of medicine on the *QE2* can be spiced by an assortment of interesting characters.

Interesting characters could, of course, include the likes of a refuse collector, who may have saved up for years to take his wife away on a once-in-a-lifetime cruise on the *QE2*. By striving for, and achieving his cruise, he has demonstrated his determination, his quest for achievement, and an aspect of his character which separates him from the ranks of his associates, who may be complacently satisfied with their lot. You can bet that the little old lady, or the secretary, or the school teacher who have saved up their cash to take a trip, are usually great company – and there is all the more reason to get them back on their feet to enjoy their holiday if they should become unwell!

And now, what about formal entertainment? Well, that's certainly a great attraction of the job. There are few work situations in the world where first-class entertainment is so easily available.

On board *QE2* there is a terrific assortment of pleasurable pursuits. At any one time, there are two big bands playing each night in the two main lounges, the Grand Lounge and the Queen's Room, including great names like the Joe Loss orchestra. A quartet might be playing in the nightclub, alternating with disco sounds. In the theatre bar, you may find a duo, or trio, or even a full blown jazz band. In the yacht club, a pianist might be tinkling the lunchtimes and evenings away; in the mid-ship's bar, possibly a harpist. In the restaurants, there may be a zither or perhaps a duo of violins to gently accompany the gastric tympani. On occasional afternoons or before the main film in the evening, there may be concert pianist John Biggs, or Max Jaffa on his violin, in the theatre. Music and good sounds are to be found everywhere.

Two decks directly above the Principal Medical Officer's cabin, which is situated on two deck adjacent to our passenger consulting rooms, is the nightclub, separated by perhaps fifteen to twenty feet. During the first fifteen years of the ship's life this used to be a relatively small, intimate room, the Q-4, with low lights and quiet corners, where you could drift along or shuffle around to the sounds of Edmundo Ross or even the fabulous Count Basie. Imagine being called to the hospital at 11 p.m. for some minor emergency: you finish the work, comfort the patient, write up the notes, wander back to your cabin, straighten your tie, walk up perhaps twenty-four stairs, and sit down comfortably to listen to the fantastic music of Count Basie: So *easy*, and so enjoyable!

In addition to being surrounded by musicians and dance floors, there are also the entertainers. Some of the greatest names in show business have trodden the *QE2* boards. Every night at sea, there's a different cabaret. Again, how convenient and enjoyable to share an evening meal with excellent company, quietly check the hospital patients, sort out the night sister's problems, have a pleasant chat, nip back to your cabin, brush your teeth, perhaps sit quietly and read for fifteen minutes to allow your food to settle, and then wander upstairs and watch Charles Aznavour, Jack Jones, Bill Cosby; alternatively, on a night off, to get together with a crowd for after-dinner drinks, set up a party, and then go into a really good cabaret with Burt Bacharach. When the show's over, you can all step onto the ballroom floor, then go off to the nightclub or the disco and probably join the entertainers for some lively fun.

If you're in a less energetic mood, perhaps you'd prefer an after-dinner concert recital, a one-act play from Jennifer Watts's live theatre company, a live performance of Gilbert and Sullivan, or just relax quietly in the cinema and watch a first-run movie – there's a different one every night.

If excitement is more your scene, perhaps you could sit shoulder to shoulder at the tables with Telly Savalas, George C. Scott, Rod Stewart or George Hamilton, and try winning your passage money back in the gaming casino, at blackjack or roulette.

On consideration, there are some very distinct advantages and pleasures to life at sea and particularly on board *QE2*. I think you might agree that it's all a bit different to general practice in Wigan, Woolloomooloo or Wyoming.

Life would really be rosy, wouldn't it, if we never experienced its disadvantages. Unfortunately, even the Garden of Eden had its snake. I'd say that, broadly speaking, if you find yourself in a situation in life where there are more pros than cons – you're onto a winner! Ship-board life is no exception, and I'm pleased to say that the balance has usually been tipped in my favour.

I suppose that the principal disadvantage of life at sea, working on board a ship, is the inability to walk away from your job at the end of the day. It really was a very new experience for me to live, eat, relax, sit at a bar, visit the cinema, or even just lie on deck, in the constant company of, and surrounded by, my patients for twenty-four hours a day. If you're winning and the patients are improving, that's one thing; but what if they're not getting better? What of the situation when I may be watching a show, and sitting in the next row is the husband of the lady down in the hospital. He's understandably of the opinion that the doctor should never relax until his wife is back to normal and enjoying herself, or at least out of the hospital. He thinks that all doctors should live in a library and read medical books when they're not working, which makes for a difficult situation.

It's all very well for a doctor ashore, in the anonymity of a dinner suit or a sports jacket, to chat to all the pretty girls at a cocktail party or have one too many and fall off his perch, but it's rather more delicate when everyone in the room knows that the man with red between the gold stripes is the ship's doctor, and as an added complication, you would be truly amazed how many cocktail party consultations ensue – an entire minor medical compendium of bad backs, chest pains, abdominal problems, rashes, bad feet, and other complaints.

Other than being on tap for two months without break, what are the other disadvantages of life as a ship's surgeon? Well, from my point of view as a single man, the problem of separation from wife and family doesn't exist. However, for those seafarers – including fifty per cent of Cunard's doctors – who are married, the wrench of leaving your family for long periods, several times a year, must for many be heartbreaking. I suppose that when a woman marries a seafarer, she's well aware of his lifestyle from the start. Their marriage is based on this relationship and restriction, and both wife and husband accept the situation. But what about the children? Growing up as a one-parent family for two-thirds of their lives must be bewildering for them.

One of our navigation officers was speaking to me one day about this problem. He had just returned from leave and had flown out to join the ship on the previous day. He wasn't looking very happy with the world, and I enquired how his leave had gone.

'Great,' he told me, 'but I got really upset yesterday.'

'Oh, what's the problem?' I asked.

'Well, my youngest boy is five years old,' he explained. 'He came to the airport with my wife to see me off. As I was saying goodbye and about to leave, he wrapped his arms around my neck and wouldn't let go. He was crying and said, "Please don't go away, Dad! Please don't leave us again!"'

The navigator sat quietly, almost with tears in his eyes. 'I didn't know what the hell to do,' he said, 'but I didn't have any choice!'

He was depressed for days afterwards.

To be fair, perhaps he didn't have any choice. If it had been myself, the decision would have been easy – as soon as a replacement was found, I'd be on the first plane back home, but it's far easier for me to say that than for a ship's navigator. If I leave the sea tomorrow, there will be a choice of a dozen jobs. It would be a far different decision for the navigator who has spent many years training to achieve his Master's ticket. This is the case, also, with the men down below who've specialized in marine engineering. It is not so simple in this day and age to switch careers, or start training all over again for another profession, when you have a home and family to maintain – particularly bearing in mind the present unemployment problem – even for trained personnel. Not an enviable decision to be faced with.

I was once present during a conversation between a fellow officer and his wife, when she challenged him with the statement, 'It's all right for you! You're never home to share the worries. You weren't there when young Alan fell and cut his head, nor when he had chicken-pox. You didn't have to change his nappies, wipe his nose, take him to school, sort out all his problems! You didn't have any of the burdens of bringing him up!'

Her husband paused for a while. 'No,' he admitted, 'and I wasn't there for a goodnight hug, or a good morning kiss. I wasn't there to watch him open his birthday and Christmas presents, nor win a prize at the school sports day, nor see his face when he passed his exams!'

There was no reply!

There are always two sides to a story. Life is always a balance.

As I've said, this aspect of seafaring fortunately doesn't apply to me, but even so, I find that spending a few months at sea and a short time at home creates a very fragmented life, which consequently lacks continuity. It is quite disorientating to have a few weeks of spring at home, then perhaps a short spell of a typically dreadful English summer, then a bit of miserable winter, mixed in confusingly with a couple of months of winter sunshine out in the Caribbean, or a red-hot spring down in the South Pacific. The body's seasonal clock takes quite a hammering! The dreadful secondary effect of this, of course, is that the years rush by so much quicker! Life goes by quite fast enough without speeding it up, thanks!

Are there any more problems? Trying to lead a normal life in a force 10 gale is difficult, to say the least, and of course if the seas are high enough, even the *QE2* can take a pounding. However, as a passenger, provided your seasickness is under control and you're feeling chirpy, it can be extremely exhilarating to sit comfortably and watch the forces of the ocean around you. During the winter in the North Atlantic, it's not unusual to see mountains of water pounding around the ship in waves fifty feet high, and – very occasionally – even eighty feet. Don't be in the least bit worried; this is exactly what a transatlantic liner is built for. I can assure you that if a little banana boat can sail safely through this type of weather, then the *QE2* has no trouble. However, I must confess that crossing the Atlantic on one of Cunard's smaller cruise ships, a few years ago in 1977, wasn't the same relatively comfortable experience.

The *Cunard Princess* had been built in Europe and fitted out in Northern Italy. The planned itinerary was for the ship to be based in New York for weekly cruises to Bermuda – which, incidentally, I consider to be my favourite island throughout the world. The ship had to be transferred from Italy to New York, where it had been arranged that she would be christened by Princess Grace of Monaco. This was a clever public relations move, based on the ship's name, *Princess*, and the fact that the anticipated market was American; it would be appropriate for an American-born Princess to perform the ceremony. In addition to this, she was a lovely lady for the ship to be associated with.

Being the end of April, the timing of the transatlantic crossing was possibly a little precarious, but we sailed out through the Straits of Gibraltar on our way to Madeira in absolutely ideal weather. The sun shone continuously, and the sea was flat calm. We were carrying around 180 passengers on this 'positioning' cruise. On board was the naval architect involved with its construction, Bill Harcus, a very likeable Scotsman who, being very personable, was asked if he would lecture to the passengers on the ship's planning and construction. This he did, the day before our arrival in Madeira.

During the lecture he stated that the ship, being intended for cruising, was of a particular design. In order for the ship to enter the shallow ports of the various small islands – around the Caribbean for example – it was necessary for it to be relatively flat-bottomed, and not very deep in the water. This meant, naturally, that the ship would be less stable than a transatlantic liner which was built for a different role. As the seas encountered around the Caribbean would never be as high as in deep-sea sailing, and also, as the ship would never be far from land, the lesser stability was acceptable. He also explained that a positioning cruise such as our present voyage was usually timed for the calmer periods of the year. Therefore, the risk had been calculated: our transatlantic crossing would be fine!

Talk about tempting fate. . . . The day after leaving Madeira, Neptune must have decided to use his jacuzzi – we hit one hell of a storm!

The ship was thrown around like a cork, the waves broke over the top of the bridge, and we rocked and rolled like crazy. To ease the discomfort, and for safer handling, the ship was 'hove-to'. This is a condition whereby the ship slows right down to a speed just sufficient to maintain steerage. The bow is pointed into the oncoming gale and the approaching waves, but doesn't drive hard into the sea. Therefore, instead of pounding ahead, the ship 'rides' the storm.

The storm went on and on and on, for four days solidly, during most of which time we were hove-to. The christening in New York was going to have to wait!

In the hands of our excellent captain, Peter Jackson, we were of course completely safe at all times, and the passengers were advised and reassured, but following the lecture two days previously, there were a whole bunch who weren't going to believe a word of it! It's difficult to eat with your life jacket on, and sleeping in one is an experience! Nonetheless, one or two of our passengers were damned if they were going to get out of them. I've no idea how they took a shower!

It was impossible to cook even bacon and eggs or steak and chips in the galley, and equally difficult to serve them or keep the plates and cutlery on the table to eat them. Consequently, for forty-eight hours we lived on sandwiches and mugs of soup – except for one meal when a fire extinguisher jumped off the wall in the galley and went off explosively, emptying its contents into the soup cauldrons. Then we were down to sandwiches only! Thank goodness someone had witnessed the incident: I don't think 'extinguisher soup' would have gone down too well!

Believe it or not, it was all good fun. After their initial fright, the passengers spent most of the time laughing at each other, and became very close friends.

Travelling with us on this assault course, was probably one of the youngest passengers we have ever carried, Danalee, a tiny baby only a few weeks' old, travelling with her mother, Donna, and her grandfather, Doug Greenidge, a great friend of mine from Barbados. Danalee was one of the few people who couldn't have cared less

49

about the storm, and she certainly had no complaints about the food. With a maritime baptism like that, she should grow up to be one heck of a good sailor!

A battered, messed-up *Cunard Princess* eventually sailed into New York three days late, and there was a mad dash to transform the ship and clean her up ready for the delayed christening ceremony. When Princess Grace crashed the bottle of champagne against the gleaming white hull of the ship the following day, little did the TV cameramen and newspaper photographers realize that they'd have seen a very different picture if they had gone round to the rusted, cracked and storm-torn paintwork on the other side of the ship!

The christening was a great success, and the storm well and truly forgotten. Accompanied by the number-one New Yorker, Mayor Koch, and unexpectedly joined later in the day by our surprise guest, Lord Louis Mountbatten, Princess Grace did indeed achieve all the anticipated news coverage – fortunately overshadowing the storm delay – and she was great company on board as she sailed on an overnight inaugural cruise with us, and amused her fellow passengers by playing the one-armed bandits with great enthusiasm for hours on end, while her lady-in-waiting quietly followed behind, carrying an endless supply of coins.

I suppose there's one final disadvantage which I've encountered since leaving England's fair shores and working at sea: litigation. Although doctors throughout all the Western countries of the world are always open to the risks of being sued if they should make a mistake, I'm afraid that America stands out way ahead of everyone else in the litigation stakes. I'm sorry if this should appear to be a put-down – it's certainly not intended to be – but let me merely illustrate the situation and the difference with a few figures. In the USA, as in Britain, all doctors are required to take out insurance against the possibility of being sued for malpractice. The premiums for this insurance vary enormously, but in broad terms the average general practitioner in America may be paying anywhere between £15,000 and £30,000 per year. In the speciality fields these premiums are much higher: the highest risk specialities, such as plastic surgery, neurosurgery or orthopaedics, could be paying from £75,000 upwards!

In startling contrast to these figures are the British premiums. I am insured through the Medical Defence Union of Great Britain. My cover is unlimited and extends to every circumstance and country in the world, except North America, and also excepted is any ship on which I serve which carries North American passengers!

With these exceptions, my otherwise total coverage is for a present premium of £500! I'm afraid the figures speak for themselves! So, what is the solution to my medical insurance problem? It is simply that I have to be insured as part and parcel of the ship and its other liabilities.

When I first went to sea, it was a new experience for me to be working under the constant threat of litigation. However, there has, in fact, only ever been one occasion when there was a serious suggestion of litigation against myself, and this indeed turned out to be nonsense. The story bears relating.

We were sailing on a long journey from America down to South Africa. We were carrying principally American passengers, amongst whom there was a very pleasant middle-aged lady, who throughout the journey befriended many of her fellow passengers and became a familiar face to the crew. She was not extrovert or intrusive, but happily involved in all the ship's activities. She was travelling alone, but was sharing a cabin with another single lady, whom she had not met prior to the cruise.

Towards the end of her journey she abruptly developed a change of character. Overnight she developed what I later diagnosed as an acute paranoid schizophrenia. This was obviously a most distressing situation for both herself and for all her new-found friends, particularly as she was such a charming and personable lady. Her problem unfortunately was not easily concealed, as she demonstrated increasing outbursts of rage, paranoid accusations, screaming and threats. These rapidly progressed from what appeared to be minor controllable temper tantrums to full-blown episodes of breaking up her cabin furniture, threats of suicide, and spells of locking herself in her cabin away from her 'enemies'.

In the first instance, she responded to medication, consultation and supervision. Unfortunately, her hallucinatory episodes and her activities increased to eventual culmination, when she almost destroyed a corner of the restaurant and – in retrospect, somewhat amusingly – pinned her neighbouring diners under their tables with a barrage of oysters and filet mignon. She was finally escorted from the restaurant by a number of bruised and battered crew members, with her legs and arms flailing, screaming for help, and calling out that she was, 'being taken away for execution'. An extremely unhappy development.

I gave instructions for the unfortunate lady to be taken to the hospital where her fury and her assaults continued until she eventually responded to an injection of sedative medication. Finally, she settled and was no longer a threat to her surroundings nor herself. Her condition was kept under control throughout the night, and she remained settled until the following morning, when she was due to disembark upon our arrival in Cape Town, where I contacted the port Health Authorities and arranged for the lady's admission to hospital for further assessment, opinion and treatment. She was subsequently admitted to a very good psychiatric unit, where the diagnosis was confirmed and she was retained for further treatment until she was eventually declared well enough for discharge and for her return home to America, by air – a very satisfactory outcome.

Several months later, following the ship's return and my arrival back in America, I was issued with a writ. I was to be prosecuted, unbelievably, for (1) assault and battery and (2) wrongful imprisonment. The writ went on to give an 'explanation'. The wrongful imprisonment referred to the occasion of our unfortunate patient having been admitted to hospital, and the 'assault and battery' referred to the administering of the sedative by intramuscular injection. I was dumbfounded.

Needless to say, these allegations were very rapidly batted out of court, but not without stress and a great deal of inconvenience to myself and considerable cost to the company preparing and acquiring statements from crew and passengers scattered all over North America, and around the world.

That's about the long and the short of the pros and cons of life at sea. As I've already said, the good times far outweigh the bad, as shown by my still remaining a doctor at sea after more than fourteen years before the mast.

The Crew

Late one morning I was sitting in the hospital of the *QE2*, writing up patients' records and chatting with Tommy, one of our medical attendants. Tommy hailed from Northern Ireland. He was a great character and a good friend, with all the blarney and humour of his countrymen. He was in his upper middle age, at a time when life's pace should be readjusted to allow a more gentle style, and exclude the adrenalin-induced surges of activity of younger men. Being a heavy smoker, his respiratory system wasn't at its peak, and intermittent dieting was needed to control his varying waistline. As was his custom, he was holding court with yet another of his amusing reminiscences, in his strong Northern Irish accent.

His story was interrupted by the telephone. The duty sister had been called to a cabin where a passenger had just developed cardiac distress. I immediately called the bridge and instructed the officer of the watch to initiate the '*starlight*' procedure, and gave him the cabin number. In rapid response, the 'starlight' code went out through the ship's communication system. Within seconds, all available medical staff were rushing to the scene of the emergency.

'Let's go!' I called to Tommy.

I grabbed the emergency case, defibrillator and portable oxygen supply, and dashed for the door. Behind me, Tommy snatched up an electro-cardiograph machine and a portable suction unit, and bolted after me. I was running up the stairs two to three at a time. Looking back, I saw Tommy poking at the lift call button. 'Come on, you lazy beggar, there's no time for that!' I shouted, and bounded off up the stairs again.

Behind me came the scuffling and pounding of footsteps on the stairs. One flight, two flights, three flights. . . . On the fifth flight I was starting to catch my breath and slow with the weight of the gear. Suddenly, from behind me and one flight down, there came a terrific gasp and a rasping cry of, 'Jaisus!' More gasps, then, 'Bloody hell!'

53

and a 'bump!' as my tobacco-ravaged friend came to an abrupt halt, and dropped down sharply onto his backside on the stairs, clutching his cases and sucking in great gulps of air with a wheeze to rival an accordion. Poised almost in mid-flight, I didn't know which way to run – which emergency was the greatest?

'Oh! Them bloody cigarettes!' he gasped, as he patriotically passed through the various colours of the Union Jack, red from exertion, white as he nearly passed out, and eventually blue from lack of oxygen. As his head sagged lower between his knees, I leaped back down the stairs, turned on the oxygen, and placed the mask over his face. After a few gulps, his breathing slowed and his colour started to return to normal.

'That's better! That's better!' he crooned.

Having quickly checked him over, I decided that he hadn't joined the coronary club and that he'd be OK.

'I'm off,' I said, and grabbed up the bags again. 'Make your way back to the hospital when you're up to it.'

'Don't worry, don't worry! I'll be all right!' he called back, 'I'm much better now, it just gave me a bit of a shock, I'll catch up with you shortly. I'll have a rest here for a minute, catch my breath, and have a cigarette.'

A *cigarette*!!! I could have throttled him.

I'm well aware that many of my recollections so far have related to the passengers we've carried. Obviously, total passenger numbers during a ship's life far exceed the crew, not only because of the daily passenger/crew ratio, but also because of the relatively enormous turnover of passengers within a twelve-month period. On average, the *QE2* might carry up to 50,000 passengers per year, and consequently there are considerably more of them to meet, and stories to relate.

The crew, on the other hand, are a relatively small but stable community, and for many, especially our old-timers, the *QE2* is virtually home. This doesn't mean that there is any shortage of crew stories worth recording, but usually it is we who observe a continuously unfolding cabaret put on by the passengers. This community is not only responsible for the running of the ship but also shapes the ship's entire character. Sea-faring produces an absolute host of interesting and sometimes fascinating people, all of them making the ship tick, all of them taking pride in their own areas of responsibility. What are these areas?

High above us all, up on the bridge, a seaman stands at the wheel, studying the compass, guiding the ship safely through the great oceans. The officer of the watch stares out over the waves, plotting the charts, scanning the radar, watching the skies and the weather maps, smelling the wind, 'feeling' the air, bringing us all unwittingly, and safely, to our destination.

In the depths of the ship, the engine rooms are throbbing. In the working areas, chains, wrenches, spanners and hammers are pounding and pulling. Valves, pistons, pipes and boilers are maintained and repaired, as they thunder along for hour after hour, day after day. The generators must be kept whirring, the air-conditioning units pumping, the heating blowing, the fresh water flowing, the sanitary water gushing. The propellers, the lights, the lifts, the radios, the stabilizers, are all constantly on the go, all powered and controlled from down here. Amongst this whining, pounding, hissing, clanking hubbub sits the tranquillity of the control room, where, at every minute of the day, someone is watching a myriad of dials, adjusting controls, keeping all the above functions working. Meanwhile, the ever-watchful eyes are also scanning for warnings in a thousand corners of the ship, checking fire door functions, water-tight integrity, or whatever else, on and on, with never a pause.

While these unseen men carry out their tasks, up in the kitchens the butcher is chopping a carcass, the fish chef is opening his oysters, the pastry chefs are baking bread and rolls, the salad chefs are slicing tomatoes. Chefs are cooking eggs, boiling cabbage, stirring huge cauldrons of soup. Dish washers are washing, plate stackers stacking, silver cleaners cleaning.

Out in the restaurant there's the scurry and bustle of dozens of waiters, carrying trays, taking orders, serving food, chatting pleasantly, clearing tables, laying cloths.

At the same time, further along, in the lounges, the bands are playing. The trumpeter with a split lip is wincing, comedians are cracking jokes, a young lady sings her heart out after hours of rehearsal, of making up, dressing up. The dancing troupe swirl, showing off a new routine, the girls leggy, beautiful and alluring.

In the bars, bottles are popping, ice is clinking, scotch, gin, rum, brandy and beer are poured by the bucketful.

Meanwhile, the plumbers are repairing a burst bathroom pipe. A gang are stripping out a flooded carpet, bringing out new furniture. The carpenters along the corridor are making a frame, changing a door, hanging a picture.

Down two decks, the printers are churning out another thousand menus for lunch, another thousand for dinner, then tomorrow's breakfast, lunch and dinner. Daily programmes, daily newspapers by the armful. The printer runs his ink-stained fingers through his hair.

In the shops, the assistants are showing off silk and perfumes, jewellery and gowns; selling chocolates and combs, radios and batteries, pearls and pins, plates and crystal; checking their stock, counting their cash.

Seated at their multitude of desks, the secretaries, rat-a-tat typing, reporting, writing; shorthand, longhand, and for the cheeky office boy, back hand!

The cinema operator untangles his film.

The golf instructor checks his clubs, watches a dreadful swing.

'Morning folks, and it's a lovely day on the *QE2*, out here in mid-Atlantic,' twitters the *QE2* radio disc-jockey.

In a dozen pantries, the bedroom stewards are dashing to answer red lights, green lights, buzzers. Vacuums buzz, beds are being made, tea being served, a smile, a joke . . . a cigarette.

The security man plods the corridors, checking doors, listening out, turning his key, keeping the peace.

'Manicure, sir?' asks the beautician.

'Nasty corn here,' says the chiropodist.

'Bit off the top?' says the barber.

The flip of a curl, the hint of a tint, from the hair stylist.

'What time is it in Oshkosh, Nebraska?' demands a mid-West twang of the bewildered operator, cooped up in her 6ft by 5ft telephone exchange.

In the dark room, humming to himself, one of the photographers inserts a roll of film into the automatic developer: another few dozen pictures for the show case.

In the flower shop, roses of England, are being arranged by a pretty English rose.

Out on deck, a deck hand paints the rail, another whistles lazily as he sweeps the boards and, beyond them, a deck steward straightens a lounge chair, lays out a cushion, adjusts an umbrella, serves a drink, gives out advice on world affairs, politics, cricket, baseball, space travel, geography, fishing and, inevitably, this morning's weather.

'This is *QE2* calling Portishead radio, do you receive me?' Along the boat deck, just back from the bridge, the radio room da-di-da's its ethereal tentacles around the globe. The machinery from Mr Morse's drawing-board sits cheek-by-jowl with the marvels of satellite communication. The radio officer sucks his pipe, twirls his whiskers, and communicates every few minutes with yet another line, thousands of miles away around the world.

In the boardrooms, committees are sitting, policies dictated, notes noted, rules created. Senior officers gather, scratching their heads, their chins, their. . . . Problems are discussed and resolved, the town council decides.

Up on the 'roof', below the funnel, the kennel maid gives 'Kitty' some more milk, combs a poodle and walks a Great Dane.

Behind their grills, the bankers count their cash, write their money orders, change pesetas, lire, francs, dollars. '1.41 to the pound today, sir,' says Sally, the clerk. The manager slams the safe door shut, rechecks his cheques, works on his sheets.

Past the bank strolls the linen steward, on his way to the laundry with yet another mountain of washing for the Chinese laundrymen below, where, in flip-flops, shorts and undershirts, they sort through stacks and stacks and stacks of sheets, towels, table cloths, serviettes, deck towels, bath mats, shirts, trousers, underwear, socks. Great machines turn, vibrate and spin amongst the ironing boards, stacking shelves, identification tags, and more identification tags, and rarely a mistake.

Flitting amongst the passengers, the cruise staff chat, help, direct, advise, entertain. Overhead, someone is working a spotlight; behind the stage, someone is working the sound. Out on deck, someone instructs the skeet shooters. On the floor, mingling with the crowds, men are dancing with the ladies.

And, of course, down in the hospital, a crying baby is being examined, a drunk being sewn up. A nurse is checking blood pressure and scanning the monitor of a frightened cardiac patient, giving soft words of comfort, straightening the bed, adjusting the pillows, checking the I.V. flow.

And so it goes along. Tommy is only one of this huge team and family, a family which includes very many old pals whose camaraderie and devotion helped shape the ship's history, its character and its spirit.

Whenever I think of family and camaraderie on board ship, a particular incident comes to mind.

Cruising gently around the Caribbean one calm, sun-drenched day on one of our cruise ships, I was sitting out on deck, the morning's work complete, enjoying the warmth, the company and the view of the tropical island of Martinique with its gleaming white margin of sand, out across the glistening waters. A light, cool breeze wafted over the decks. I was sitting with New York Mets baseball star Gary Carter and his wife Sandy. We were laughing and bantering about the great day that we'd had, together with that other king-sized Mets player, Daryl Strawberry and his wife, at my beach home in Barbados the day before, while the ship had been in port.

The relaxed atmosphere was abruptly shattered by the tannoy.
'Starlight . . . Starlight . . . hospital.'
I was up and running.

As I dashed inside the ship from the open decks and ran down the stairs, I descended into increasing darkness. The main lights were all out. Scattered throughout the darkness along the corridors and on the stairs were dull oases of light from the emergency bulbs. It didn't take a mechanical wizard to work out that there was an electrical failure – either the generators or the switchboard. Living on board ship for any length of time, it's surprising how quickly you become used to the constant drone of background noise, particularly the never-ending buzz of the air-conditioning system, blowing gently into every corner of the ship. It is usually only when the noise eventually stops that you're suddenly aware that it had been present in the first place.

On this particular occasion, both the lights and the air-conditioning were off. The corridors were darkened and strangely, almost eerily, quiet. I was aware of the sounds of my own breathing, my running footsteps on the carpet. Far off, I heard the noise of clinking cutlery in a pantry, a toilet being flushed, a drawer being closed, the light hubbub of conversation behind a cabin door – all sounds which are usually missed. I turned into the hospital corridor, dark and very quiet, no movement, and went in through the hospital doors, which were standing wide open. A dim light glowed in the foyer, which was empty. My eyes were now adjusting, after the fierce brightness of the sunlight on deck.

From the other side of an open door in the adjacent treatment room came a long, long moan. A second, pleading voice called urgently, 'Doc, quick!'

I dashed into the room. Being, as I was, highly charged with adrenalin, I was acutely aware of the minutest detail and movement. The scene in the treatment room created an instant, very detailed impression. A soft light bathed the corner of the room. On the couch were two shadowy figures. The silence pressed in like some unseen force. The air, which was still and already slightly warm, was full of the overwhelming smell of burning. I snatched a portable spot-light off the wall and shone it over the figures, both in oily, black overalls.

Twisted up into a pain-racked tangle, lying on the couch, was a completely unrecognizable figure; his face, hands and the exposed areas of his neck and wrists were totally blackened and scorched. His eyelashes and brows had been burnt away and the front of his hair singed a rusty brown. His eyes and mouth were shut tight in agony. His hands, already blistered and skinned, were held out from his body to prevent contact and further pain, like some grotesque sleep-walker. It was, unmistakably, a flash burn. The man had been working on a switchboard when it exploded, and he had taken the full extent of the flash, face on!

I am obviously delighted to report that, despite the severe and dreadful appearance of the burns, they in fact all responded excellently to treatment over the following weeks, but the point of my story is that it was not so much the patient's injuries which commanded my attention as the second figure, which in some way was more dramatic. The patient's head and shoulders were cradled in the arms and lap of the other engineer, a big, healthy, fit man, probably tough and gritty enough to punch a hole in the wall, who had stumbled and carried his mate up the steel steps of the engine room, struggled and panted through the silent darkness of the stairways, through fire doors and corridors, carrying, pulling, and desperately staggering to the hospital. Now he sat quietly, unspeak-ing, like a frozen figure from a sculpture, supporting and comforting his injured colleague; oil-streaked, sweating, black, he was looking down at the grizzly mess.

'Help him, doc, please help him!' he whispered. He raised his head to look pleadingly, almost helplessly, at me, and as big, tough and macho as he may have been, great tears rolled down his blackened cheeks.

This scene somehow epitomizes to me the closeness and in-terdependence which we know and come to rely upon aboard ship. Of course, this type of camaraderie exists in all walks of life – particularly in the services, and more particularly in war. But at sea, there always seems to be someone there. I sincerely hope that we all have such companions in times of need.

There is another story in particular that I feel summarizes this family atmosphere. As you may well imagine, the hairdressing and beauty salon on board *QE2* plays an important role in the daily life of many of our passengers, and it is consequently a large and very well staffed and equipped department.

During the early days of one world cruise, I visited the salon for a trim. How unisex salons have managed to survive, I'm not quite sure. Whenever I've been parked too close to a female client with her head sticking out of what appears to be a hole in a dust cover, devoid of make-up, with her hair wet and sticking up in an assortment of rollers, I've usually been given an 'if-looks-could-kill' stare for having dared witness the chrysalis stage of the female social butterfly, prior to her emergence in silks and satins a few hours later at a cocktail party. I must agree with their sentiments; if they're going to all this trouble to look beautiful for their male counterparts, then they certainly shouldn't have to tolerate a scattering of men intruding upon their domain and studying their very unflattering transition.

On this particular occasion, I was tucked away around the corner, in a quiet booth. The young man who came in to wield the clippers was a particularly pleasant lad whom I'd not seen before. He was very chatty, and obviously very happy. When he wasn't chatting, he was humming or whistling along to himself.

'I'm new on board,' he explained, 'I don't know who's who, as yet. What position do you hold?'

I explained that the red between the stripes indicated medical department, and that I was the Principal Medical Officer. He asked a string of questions about the department, the hospital, the facilities, the staff, the work-load, and showed great interest. He chattered on in a pleasant, light mood and I remarked, 'Well, you're obviously very pleased with your new life on board ship.'

'I'm over the moon,' he replied, 'I really can't get over how great it all is. I knew I was going to enjoy myself, but this beats all my expectations.' He was bubbling over.

He went on to tell me where he had worked prior to joining the ship, and it turned out that in fact his home was fairly near to mine, in the Midlands. 'Does your family all live around there?' I asked.

'Yes,' he said, 'and I must admit that I miss them a hell of a lot; but they're pleased that I'm here because they know I'm having a great time.'

'You keep them well posted then?'

'Yes, yes,' he replied enthusiastically, 'I write to them about everything, and they're having a great time reading it!' Then he went on, 'I wrote to my gran today, and I told her, "Guess what? I cut Joe Loss's hair yesterday". She won't believe it, she'll be so excited and proud. Joe Loss – the best band in all of Britain! My gran used to dance to him when she was younger. She always talks about him, she knew he'd be on the ship. She'll be thrilled!'

His enthusiasm, his happiness, his total and obvious *joie de vivre* were contagious. As he chatted on, I was mesmerized. I had rarely come across anyone with such effervescence, contentedness and pure happiness.

'My gran's the greatest,' he said. 'We've really been close all through my life.' He paused. 'Can I tell you something?' he asked. 'I don't talk about it to many people, but you being a doctor, you'll probably understand.'

'Yes, of course,' I replied, wondering what on earth he was about to say.

He continued in a more serious note, but in no way a depressed one, 'When I was a child, only six,' he continued combing, snipping, 'I had leukaemia.'

I went cold. My neck prickled. The thought of children and leukaemia devastates me. I looked up and caught his eyes in the mirror. They were reflective, but not at all sad.

'I was ever so ill, it was terrible. I was in hospital for months and months, it seemed for ever. You know how it is,' he said, 'you've seen lots of children like that I expect. I lost my hair with the treatment. I felt dreadful, really dreadful. I lost a load of weight, and I was too weak to move most of the time.'

I kept totally quiet. I knew just what he meant, I had witnessed these terrible, unfair catastrophes too many times. I had watched the suffering, the bleeding, the pain, the bruising, the swelling, the parents crying, questioning, 'Why?' The total heartache. He was right, I *had* seen it. At times I had been too close to it, cried deep inside, mourned with the parents, frustrated and helpless.

'My gran sat by my bedside day after day after day. She watched all the needles, the drips in my arm, the tubes, and all the rest,' he said, 'but she never let on that she was sad. She used to chat to me for hours. She'd tell me how I was going to get better. She never let up, always encouraging me, even though she must have known I was going to die and it must have been breaking her heart. We'd chat about everything, what I'd do when I got out of hospital, what I wanted to be when I grew up. I don't know why I decided on it, but I said I wanted to be a hairdresser. "That's what you'll be!" Gran said. "You'll get over this, you'll get better and you'll get out of here. You'll be a hairdresser one day, just like you want to." And I want to sail on a ship, Gran I told her. "Well, that's what you'll do as well," she said. "You'll make it! I promise you."

'I can't remember just how long it went on for, years and years it seemed, but she was always there, always there.' He was still very chirpy, although reflective. He smiled a smile a yard wide through the mirror.

'You know what they told me, doctor? In the hospital, I mean.'
'No. What was that?' I said.

'They told me that . . . I was the first child that they'd ever cured of leukaemia! I think that I was one of the first children in the world to be cured! How about that? Isn't that fantastic? That's why the world's so great, and that's why I'm so happy.' He paused, then chattered on.

'I can't believe it when people come in here with moans and groans all about little things . . . nothing! They wouldn't upset me! I can't get over how lucky I am, I just enjoy every minute that comes along. And look what happened, my gran said that I'd get well, that I'd be a hairdresser and sail on a ship, and just look, I got both! But even better, I'm a hairdresser on the greatest ship in the world! . . . And I cut Joe Loss's hair!! My gran won't believe it, she's going to be over the moon!'

I don't know how this young lad's story affects you, but I was bowled over! I went for a haircut, and came away with a great deal more. It is rare and superb to hear one of life's success stories, when fate, for once, was kind, and the receiver was so aware, and completely appreciative. I felt that in some way it would be terrific to add to this story. What if the lad could go to a party with Joe Loss and get some photographs to send home to his gran with his next letter? Joe Loss and his wife Mildred are very close friends, and I knew that unquestionably Joe and Mildred would be willing to help in any plans that I might arrange, but I thought it might be even better to go a stage further. Where easier to arrange a special surprise party than on the QE2? Where else could so many close friends and personalities be so readily accessible to join in, and happy to contribute to the event?

I sat down to draw up a list of who was sailing with us on the ship at that time, and whom I might call upon to attend a pre-dinner cocktail party in my quarters. Joe and Mildred Loss of course headed the list, together with Joe's singing personalities, Larry, Todd and Leslie Anne. The principal guest would naturally be the Master of the ship, Captain Robert Arnott, and his wife Joan. Captain Bob, as he was affectionately known by a vast number of passengers and old friends, was in fact master of the *QE2* for the majority of the ship's life up until his retirement in 1985. I am unable to pass his name without saying what a great character Bob Arnott was: one of shipping's more memorable captains, whose company I have been delighted to share over a number of years at sea. Many people were very sad indeed to see him retire, but his sea-faring life has fortunately been recorded in his own book, *Captain of the Queen*.

The ship's General Manager was Commodore Doug Ridley, and I knew that Doug would be more than pleased to help with the surprise. Of course I knew most, if not all, the entertainers on the ship. Many were TV personalities from Britain, including the immaculate Max Jaffa, with almost sixty years of superb violin playing and entertainment to his credit, Harry Secombe, one of my very favourite characters both on and off the stage, also Vince Hill, Paul Melba, Peter Gordeno, Jamie Michael Stewart, and from France, Lynda Gloria. I was sure that they would all attend.

Now, who was on the lecturers and passengers lists? I scanned the names. . . . Sitting with me at my restaurant table during that section of the cruise was a man who had travelled on board the *QE2* two years previously, under totally different circumstances, when he sailed down to the South Atlantic to take the role of commanding officer in the assault on Port Stanley in the Falklands war – Brigadier Tony Wilson, together with his wife Janet. They were both great party-goers, they would certainly join in. Dr Christiaan Barnard was also travelling with us. From our own time together I knew that he had a great joy and respect for living and the quality of life. He would enjoy this get-together, and his female companion would certainly add some glamour to the group.

Rod Stewart was to have joined us during the previous few days, and was possibly ensconced up in the penthouses. I had known Rod from previous visits to the ship. Although he didn't enjoy too much public attention while he was relaxing, perhaps he might like to join the gathering.

From the acting world, a very special man and his equally special wife were on board: possibly one of the greatest actors of our day, the star of *Ghandi* and a host of other roles, Ben Kingsley, and Alison. I find their company great, with or without an excuse for a party!

Other well known actors were sailing with us, too. From America, we had the screen and television star, Dom Deluise – one of life's wonderfully funny people, who is always able to portray a sense of happiness with the sensitivity of a greatly talented man. Also from the American entertainment world, Twiggy's co-star of stage and screen, the very talented Tommy Tune; and to add cream to the cake, George C. Scott was between films and enjoying a respite from the rigours of the Hollywood empire.

From the awesome and fascinating realm of space conquest, a truly remarkable man, who may well have splashed down in these very waters, in very different conditions, was also here – Scott Carpenter, the astronaut, who was relaxing in the serenity of an alternative form of travel!

Turning to the world of writing, a dear and very fondly remembered friend, Helen McInnes was on board – the lady who held the world spellbound with her writing talents and her superb thriller novels, in whose company I spent many pleasant hours. From a different area of the writing world, the beautiful Jeraldine Saunders – author of *The Love Boats*, from which the immensely successful TV series was created – had also joined the ship, with her husband. And yet another writer, in the person of Mary Allie Taylor, syndicated travel author from Memphis.

From France, the Ojeh family, mother and grown-up young, industrialists and oil magnates: the Ewings of France, frequent, and always welcome, guests of the ship.

From the halls of the English gentry, one of the ship's gifted lecturers was photographer and Peer of the Realm, Patrick Lichfield, another near neighbour of mine and our special guest from the Midlands.

A string of other good friends were also on board, including Mrs Anne Brookes, a great ambassador for her country, the United States. She, I knew well, would be delighted with this project.

Our unofficial photographers for the evening were two particularly close pals of mine, Mr Guitar, the all-time great: Bert Weedon, and his wife, Maggie.

Looking back now, we had the ingredients of a very memorable evening!

Invitations went out, and telephone calls were made. Obviously, due to previous commitments, and in some cases the demands of work, not all our guests were able to attend, but the turnout was impressive.

The party was under way when our young guest arrived. He was absorbed into the gathering quietly and without fuss, initially, I'm sure, not really aware of the identities of the other guests. He was introduced amongst his fellow party-goers and mixed well, in a way beyond his years. At the height of the party, I called for attention and explained:

'As you all know, it's not my usual routine to make speeches at a cocktail party, or to interrupt the proceedings in any way. However, I was fortunate enough, a few days ago, to hear a rather touching story, and as they're not too frequent in life, I thought I'd like to share it with you. We have amongst us a special guest who is completely unaware that I'm about to risk embarrassing him, but I hope not to spoil his evening. He is a young man who I was lucky to meet when he cut my hair and told me the following story.'

The room was quiet, the drinks lowered, everyone listened. I related briefly, and as best as I could, the details of our guest's history, his joy of life and his grandmother's dream and encouragement. I concluded by relating that his gran was expected to get a great kick when she read about Joe Loss in her letter. My final request was that perhaps we could all get together and make Gran even happier by sending her a whole bunch of souvenir photographs from the party, of her favourite grandson in his new home. There was a rush, and the young man was swamped and totally overjoyed. I imagine he had enough photographs for ten grans. I sincerely hope that they're both still very happy. Well done, Gran, to you and your grandson.

There is, in fact, a second side to this story: what no-one knew, until now, is that the occasion was a celebration of life which had great significance to myself for a more personal reason. At almost exactly the same time that Gran had sat, heart-broken but hopeful, at her grandson's bedside, only a few miles down the road, on the other side of the city of Birmingham, I had sat in similar circumstances at the bedside of my younger brother, who was twenty years older than the boy, but also suffering from the same dreadful disease – leukaemia. I did indeed know the desperate heart-ache and despair of being so close to this illness.

While my brother had eventually died, this young lad, only a short distance away, was winning his battle. It was a terrific compensation to witness one of life's successes, particularly for such an enormously appreciative recipient.

The following day I received this letter.

Dear Dr Roberts,

Thank you so much for a beautiful evening last night. You shouldn't have gone to so much trouble getting all these lovely people to come. I was so happy meeting everyone and having my photo taken with them all. I felt very honoured to meet them all, and I can honestly say you made yesterday the most happiest, most proud day of my life. Just being alive is enough, but fulfilling my wish of working on the QE2, and then meeting you and the other lovely people (which is something I know will stick with me the rest of my life) is something I thought would never happen.

I can't wait to tell my family about it, I bet they won't believe it. Wait till I show them the photos. It really is a dream come true, they'll be so happy.

Thank you once again,

Very best wishes

III
HIGH SEAS SOCIETY

A Floating Party

The life of a doctor at sea is not all work and no play! Quite obviously, if the work-load is heavy or if an emergency situation arises, then the social life of the ship's doctor – in exactly the same way as that of a doctor in any other field – takes a very secondary role, or doesn't exist at all. However, for a good proportion of the week, the work-load does indeed allow time for socializing, and possibly romance.

Inevitably, through various media, the vast majority of the Western populace will have encountered some form of exposure to the world of sailing and cruising – whether it be advertising material in brochures or television travelogue spots, women's magazines or some of the better-known novels and television series such as *Doctor at Sea*, based on the book by Richard Gordon, and the American TV series, *The Love Boats*, based on the book by Jeraldine Saunders. Mainly, the impressions will be of glamour, romance, and exciting holiday affairs. It would be more than excusable to believe that the 'pulp' magazines are the appropriate and only place for these fantasies and that it is a world of clichés and exaggeration. However, no matter how repetitive the stories, how over-used the clichés, how corny the whole business may appear, believe me, having wined, dined and gently swayed with your partner on the dance floor, if you then stand out on deck at the aft rail in the warm night air, with the ship slipping slowly through the calm of the Caribbean, a gentle breeze blowing across the decks, the silver reflection of the moon and a host of brilliant stars set in a jet-black sky glimmering in the wake of the ship, the silhouette of a tropical island on the horizon, the lights of a passing ship, the smell of the sea and distant tropical flowers, the low strains of a soft melody from the band playing inside, and the partner of your choice resting against your shoulder, then I guarantee you that, no matter how sceptical you may have become from over-exposure to so many similar descriptions, every last ounce of your dream will be there. I promise you that you'll find it difficult to believe that it can be true, and that the myth really exists, that life can be this exhilarating and at the same time tranquillizing and contenting.

Some time ago, during a radio interview in America concerning the medical department on board *QE2*, the interviewer asked, 'What do you consider to be the principal social attraction of a doctor's life at sea?'

The answer, which was meant to be tongue in cheek, was possibly too candid: 'Working on the *QE2* during a series of transatlantic crossings is the only situation I've ever encountered where I can be sure that both the bed sheets and the women will be changed every five days!'

The perplexed interviewer, having perhaps bitten off more than she could chew, was unsure how to react to the statement, but I'm quite certain that it summarizes the average person's impression of life on the cruise liners. Whether this impression is valid, I'll leave unanswered, but the opportunity is certainly there!

Despite having been at sea for a considerable length of time, I'm still quite amazed, when observing relationships develop and mature, how much the whole process is speeded up when the people involved are brought together on a ship. The situation can almost be compared to nurturing plants in a grow-bag. A multitude of all the correct ingredients are brought together within the confines of the ship, the seeds are planted, and relationships pop up all over the place, just like forced geraniums.

The 'grow-bag' of ship's life has many ingredients. Nearly everyone setting out for a holiday is looking forward to making new acquaintances. The majority of single people anticipate finding a partner, to the extent that their holiday is less enjoyable, or even ruined, if they don't. In the holiday atmosphere, the singles unknowingly make themselves more available to approaches, or are more likely to initiate contact, than in their home environment. If this applies to all holidays, then it applies even more to cruising, where the preconceived images and expectations of romance are promoted so much by the media. So, relationships get off to a much easier start.

In the evenings the ship takes over, and provides the perfect setting for new couples to become closer. They can enjoy a meal together, with good food, wine, and happy, smiling service, spend a relaxing or fun-filled hour together watching an after-dinner show, enjoy a few hectic moments on the discotheque dance-floor, and then drift along to the quiet gentle music of the nightclub, with the lights turned low, the ship gently swaying, holding each other tight. Then they can go out onto the open deck, with the moonlight and warm breezes. From here on, it really doesn't need a Robert Redford to make the grade!

There is an additional factor in the grow-bag which has a strong influence on the situation and which, to the chagrin of the unattached male passengers, gives an unfair and distinct advantage to the officers and crew: for whatever reason, a surprising number of females are attracted towards a man in uniform. Psychologists have many explanations: perhaps it represents authority, reliability or a degree of power; maybe it's the macho image; or perhaps many men look smarter and more attractive in a uniform, which, in addition, may be better cut than average off-the-peg clothes. Maybe the wearer is simply more noticeable and stands out in a crowd in which he would otherwise be merely another face. It could also be understood, of course, that anyone wearing a uniform is part of the establishment, and as such, is a passport to whatever private social events or parties may be in the offing. Irrespective of the psychology of the situation, this 'boost' brings a regular smile to the faces of many an officer who might otherwise have been left on the side-lines.

As you can imagine, there is no lack of inclination to take advantage of this female tendency, and most voyages aren't many hours old before some smart wolf, adorned with bow-tie and white mess-jacket, swoops amongst the wide-eyed, unsure and unwary young innocents and takes them comfortably under the protection of his secure, caring, uniformed wing.

Some proponents of this routine of 'maritime mesmerism' are more blatant, unashamedly emotional and calculatingly callous than others. Taking total advantage of all the seductive circum-stances which I've mentioned above, they sweep the overawed innocents off their delighted feet, in an absolutely overwhelming storm of torrid and intense emotion, with vows of total commitment, floods of tears, gusts of heavy breathing and complete conviction in their romantic intentions . . . which terminate at 8.05 a.m. on the quay-side at the end of each cruise, accompanied by weeping and wailing, calling out injustices to the heavens, holding on tightly, so tightly! All kinds of promises are made with, of course, an occasional glance over the tear-drenched shoulder of the departing love of their life, just in case another good-looking lady should slip by unnoticed, up the gangway and onto the ship! Finally, there is the last tearful

71

kiss . . . 'Goodbye . . . I love you . . . I love you . . .!' and then it's off for pizza and french fries in the crew mess, a quick beer in the bar over the road, a trip to buy a couple of pairs of socks and a tube of toothpaste and then back onto the ship to pick up the laundry, shower, get into uniform and prepare for the next chapter at 6 p.m., when the ship sails with a new complement of passengers. Full circle. Sorry ladies!

There have been many incidents and associations which have peppered my years at sea, a host of romantic, sad and happy stories; many friends have come and gone, and are now scattered all over the world. Sitting now and considering the past years, one incident occurs to me which typifies the unexpected and precipitous aspects of ship affairs.

I was sailing with *QE2* from America on a world cruise and we were travelling south to Australia from Los Angeles, via Hawaii and the South Pacific islands, a journey which entails several long periods at sea, and usually long, quiet afternoons in the sunshine out on deck for the passengers. In Hawaii, we picked up extra passengers who were taking a section of the cruise. Amongst these new passengers was a particularly beautiful woman in her late thirties, whose face is known on the cinema screens throughout the world. She was accompanied by her two daughters, both equally striking young ladies in their teens. Whereas the girls were extremely open, extrovert, happy and very friendly, their mother was elegant, quiet, sophisticated, and very reserved. She enjoyed her own and her daughters' company, and other than this, spent time only with her table companions and two couples she had met during the first few days. She caught everyone's eye, but kept conversations light, interesting, and brief. She enjoyed this limited company during the evenings, graciously declining invitations to dance from outsiders. As the days progressed, the two daughters befriended increasing circles of people and became popular throughout the ship.

Sitting in the Queen's Room with friends one day, I was approached by the eldest daughter who asked if she could sit and have a chat. During our conversation, she proceeded to fill me in on her family's details, about herself, her sister and mother, who were all travelling to Australia. Our young lady, who we will call Susan, was studying at school with the hope and intention of taking up a career in medicine in later years. She had a favour to ask. As we had been at sea for so many days during the journey, she'd found herself with time on her hands, and was enquiring whether there were any problems or jobs in and around the hospital which she could perhaps help out with. I thanked her for her offer, but advised her that unfortunately this wasn't a practical idea.

'Thanks anyhow,' she said, and then added, 'I wonder if you'd mind my borrowing a medical book or two, that I can read while we're at sea?'

'Of course you can,' I said. 'In fact, I've got some in my cabin and you can collect one now if you like.'

In my cabin, I selected one of the more simple basic medical text books, which Susan took, and went on her way.

The following day, I returned to my cabin after lunch; lying, sprawled across the floor of my day-room, surrounded by a collection of medical books, was young Susan.

'I hope you don't mind,' she said, 'but I came down to ask for some more books and I found your door open, so I thought I'd read them here.' She looked up, bright-eyed and innocent.

'OK, Susan,' I replied, 'I'm off to the hospital to see a patient; close the door when you leave.'

Over the following couple of days, Susan's visits continued and it became increasingly obvious that her interest in me had passed well beyond my use as a medical library. In the public rooms, I'd become aware of her presence nearby and would look up to find her staring at me from the shadows. She found many and varied excuses to approach me in company and ask questions or start to chat. Her attentions were soon noticed by other officers, and every now and then a slanted comment could be picked up, particularly concerning Susan's visits to my cabin. Trying not to cause offence or disillusion-ment, I delicately suggested that she borrow whatever medical books she might like and read them in her own cabin or elsewhere, and coaxed her to perhaps spend more time with the few other young people who were on board. Her visits to my cabin stopped, but her continued presence nearby, around the ship, continued.

Sitting quietly on deck in the sunshine a day later, I looked up to gaze at a striking, curvaceous female silhouette against the sky.

'Hello, I'm Susan's mother,' she said.

'Yes,' I replied, 'we've met briefly.'

She went on to inform me that she'd like to have a private and very serious word with me. I told her that I'd be going down to my cabin shortly to change, and anticipating a misinformed and embarrassing confrontation, invited her to visit my cabin in half an hour. In precisely that time, she knocked at my door, entered, and accepted the proffered seat but declined a drink. She sat before me, a very beautiful but extremely serious lady, who had possibly filled the fantasies of millions of film-goers.

She considered carefully for a moment, and then stated, 'Dr Roberts, you realize, don't you, that my daughter has become infatuated with you?' It was a statement rather than a question.

'Yes, I'm aware of that,' I replied.

She paused. . . . 'I know that she's visited your cabin a number of times.' Again a flat statement, no emotion. I was about to become indignant, defensive, but she continued, 'This has caused some considerable apprehension on my behalf. . . .' A further pause; her dark eyes were penetrating. 'I've given the situation a great deal of serious thought.'

The room was still quiet, except for the gentle hum of air blowing through the ventilators. The atmosphere was tense. The circumstances left me with very little credible defence; however, I held my comments, awaiting her accusation.

She cleared her throat. 'In the circumstances,' she stated in measured tones, 'I have decided that if any member of my family attempts, or succeeds, in seducing you' – she paused for effect – 'it's going to be *me*!'

Yes, I'm sure you'd like to know!

Having illustrated the more superficial aspects of the social benefits of ship-board life and romance within the medical department, it's equally true to say that our department has experienced its fair share of more serious encounters, and in this respect we can't forget our dental colleagues.

In *QE2*'s earlier days, the dental department quickly developed a reputation not only for a high standard of professionalism and practical ability, but also as a breeding ground for ship's characters. There was a succession of New Zealand dental officers who were renowned for their very popular, extroverted characters, and who in no minor way left their mark on the social scene and, equally, their stamp on the ship. Work, wine, women and song was their motto, all approached with equal enthusiasm. Their reputations for hard work and hard play endeared them, throughout the ship, to passengers and crew alike.

When the last had left, in stepped a new image: shapely legs, high heeled shoes, long hair, short skirts and elegant dresses – a very attractive female dentist. Gone was the nasal twang of the South Pacific; here were the lilting chords of a Lancashire lass. If a shy, retiring, non-socializing workaholic was expected, this wasn't to be the case. To accompany the good looks, an effervescent personality was soon to reveal itself, with the inevitable result that a string of admirers, and a long line of hopeful suitors, were competing for dental appointments. From this varied array of flashing incisors, one major suitor emerged.

Armed with a dulcet set of vocal chords and a twelve-string guitar, one of the ship's musicians obviously hit the right note, and with the magic ingredients of ship and sea to speed events along, in no time at all she was swept away on a whirlwind wave of romance. This is by no means a one-sided love story; with equal effectiveness, retaliating with dental drill, Lancashire lilt and twinkling eye, she worked her way past his gnashers and into his heart. The continuing sequence of events reached their climax in Honolulu.

Following an eastbound voyage from Japan to Hawaii, which entailed a six-day sojourn on the Pacific Ocean, with all the benefits of the *QE2* and a world cruise, the ship sailed into Honolulu, past the enchanting vision of Diamond Head mountain, the lapping shores of Waikiki beach, and into the heady atmosphere of Frangipani scent, swaying grass skirts and the strumming of Hawaiian guitars. With these magic ingredients, Cupid plucked his final bow as our misty-eyed couple descended the gangway to set off on a day of sight-seeing. Stepping into a waiting taxi, they were asked: 'Where to?' to which they both dreamily and spontaneously replied, 'We'd like to find a place where we can get married this morning.'

Not without reason does Hawaii hold its romantic reputation: our taxi driver entered the spirit of the story, feet first! With enormous enthusiasm, taking the love-birds at their word, the driver rushed his living fantasy around the city, first to a medical laboratory to eliminate the very down-to-earth, practical requirements of American law, which demands blood investigations before vows. Then, back in cloud-nine mood, the trio dashed to the driver's home to borrow his wife's wedding ring to use in the ceremony and then off to the local registry office where, touched by the spontaneity of the proceedings, and before they could change their minds, they were whisked to the head of the queue. With a watery-eyed taxi driver as a witness to their betrothal, the deed was done! To the amazement of all on board, including themselves, our two fellow crew members, who had stepped briefly ashore on a simple sight-seeing tour of the land of the Lei, came back 'as one'. And they say that these stories only happen in fiction.

Throughout the ship and throughout the years, stories like these recur and are part of our lives at sea. Very few of these relationships, of course, end in matrimonial bliss; a cruise marriage for the duration of the voyage is more the rule, at the end of which time a great many tears are shed, addresses exchanged and promises made. With the sincerest of intentions, the partners disappear back into their own corners of the globe, separated sometimes by thousands of miles, joined delicately by the thin thread of the memories of a cruise romance, supported for a short time by postal services and telephone, until sadly, but usually inevitably, the flame dies.

One of the stronger images the public has of the social life on board a luxury cruise liner is that it revolves around champagne parties, seductive encounters and wild orgies, and that sex and sexual pursuits constitute the major – if not entire – attraction of life at sea! It would be true to say that where you have a large group of pre-conditioned holiday-makers with their varying concepts and desires coming together in a floating 'catalytic-converter', then unquestionably *any*thing goes! However, I can assure you that the true-life picture usually has a few blurred edges when compared to the image.

Generally, the image of life at sea is of a blend of the adventure and romance of travelling on a cruise ship. This is mixed together with the excitement of the prospects of foreign ports and their associated experiences. On the other hand, the image of medicine is principally of drama, blended with a myriad of other concepts created by television series, novels and movies. When you mix these two impressions together, the final image of the doctor's life at sea is one of excitement, adventure, romance and drama. This is *not* always so! It is sometimes, certainly. And if you're lucky, then it may be the case more often than not. But there's definitely a second side to the coin! Variations do sometimes occur, for example, in the scenario of the doctor's involvement with beautiful women and torrid romance.

It would be impossible to keep track of the number of occasions when, on being introduced to one of Cinderella's sisters, the handshake becomes of a more personal nature, and is held for an excessive period; there's a lowering of the shoulder, a tilt of the head, a narrowing of the eyes, accompanied by a flickering, slightly crooked knowing smile, and a slow husky, 'Oh yes? . . . the ship's doctor!'

'How do you do,' I reply.
'So you're the ship's doctor?'
'Yes, that's right.'

The eyes wander slowly down and back up to meet mine, giving me the once-over to see if I fit the image.

'I know all about ship's doctors!' still husky, suggestive, giving me the come-on.

'Oh, you've obviously travelled before, then?'

'No, but I've heard all the stories.' Another knowing smile, and a half wink.

'You shouldn't be too misled by all the *Love Boat* and *Doctor at Sea* stories you know.'

'No, no . . . of course not,' totally unconvinced, her image firmly imprinted. 'I hope I manage to see *more* of you during the cruise, doctor!' The innuendo is heavily underlined by further amateurish vamping movements and puckered lips.

This whole scene could be taken straight out of a fourth-rate play or a schoolgirl magazine, but, undaunted by the blatant corniness of the routine, successions of optimistic ladies aspire to investigate and confirm their images. The majority of these approaches are usually light-hearted and fun and not at all unwelcome, but believe me, the offerings come in every shape, size, appearance and age. To say the least, fighting off a hormone-activated, amorous mammoth, whose media-created image of cruises and doctors isn't to be shattered, is definitely not the stuff of romance magazines!

Ladies' Invitation Nights are prime time for the occurrence of some of these disquieting encounters. Throughout the cruise there are various theme nights arranged in the restaurants and entertainment areas in order to spice up the evenings, create a common interest and provide more of a party spirit. This hopefully encourages the passengers to mix more easily and adds to the evening's enjoyment. These events don't usually include all the public rooms, as there are passengers who prefer not to be organized, or coerced into mixing and joining the party atmosphere. Some people prefer to either sit quietly, or make their own entertainment by dancing, watching a show, or playing bridge; they can find plenty of scope for alternatives.

Meanwhile, a Ladies' Invitation Night is a theme often used. On these nights the social sexual roles are reversed. There are many who don't need the excuse, but on Ladies' Night the females are invited to take the lead. They are encouraged to open the doors for the men, light their cigarettes, seat them at table, order their meals, and if they feel extravagant enough, buy their drinks. Principally, however, it becomes the ladies' prerogative to invite the gentlemen to dance.

I have frequently been on the receiving end of these invitations.

The dance and conversation is usually pleasant and rounds off with a flourish from the band. The lady is returned to her table.

'You've made my evening, thank you, doctor . . . thank you very much.'

'My pleasure, thank you for the invitation.'

Another pleasant social encounter.

However, there is a variation. This social pleasantry often takes a different route.

I recall one of these evenings particularly. Sitting at a table with friends, I'd noticed in the distance a couple of elderly ladies huddled together, whispering and pointing in our direction, laughing and giggling like schoolgirls, caught up in the atmosphere, and no doubt encouraged by their images of the ship's officers and of the ship's doctor. It's not only the privilege of the young to harbour images of romance. I can assure you that seventy- and eighty-year-old ladies can have equally vivid imaginations – and aspirations!

From the behaviour of the two ladies, it was apparent that one was goading the other to take advantage of the Ladies' Night theme to request a dance. After several minutes, and perhaps a couple of drinks one of our ladies arose and made a shy, tentative approach. With nervous movements and a giggle, she hesitated half-way and turned to go back. She looked towards her friend who vigorously waved her onwards, and finally arrived at the table.

'Hello, doctor.'

'Good evening.'

'I hope you don't mind . . . I . . . as it's Ladies' Invitation . . . I've never asked a man before . . . would you mind if I . . . asked you for a dance?'

'My word, of course not; thank you for the compliment.' I got up and we moved off towards the floor.

'My name's Nigel Roberts, your name is . . .?'

'Hilda . . . Hilda Rogers.'

The dance-floor conversation was light and friendly – home town, cruise, ports of call, ships, family – no husband, dead – England, officers, ship's medicine. As the ship ploughed on through the sea, a gentle rocking added a little activity to the dance-floor.

The first time that the floor tilted slightly, the pleasant, grey-haired lady hung on a little tighter to keep her balance, laughed and joked about the ship's movement. The dance carried on. The ship rocked again. Her hold retightened and her hand gripped a little more securely. Was it my imagination, or was the hold tighter than before? With the next minor movement, my doubt increased; the grip *was* tighter, her right hand dropped lower from the shoulder, and her body came closer. I looked down and she stared into my eyes. The conversation continued, but now she was wearing a half smile. As the floor continued to move gently, her right hand had now reached my lower back. There had been a subtle repositioning of her body as she moved across and nearer to me, and then the pressure increased!

Now she didn't need the ship's rocking for excuses or help. I looked down, her eyes were still staring, glued to my face, trying to hold my gaze. Her eyebrows raised marginally, her eyelids widened and narrowed, her smile was now full and fixed, awaiting my response. This delightful little lady had passed through the looking glass, and had entered the world of her image! Her head dropped onto my chest and she drifted off into her world of fantasy. Just another of the many aspects of the 'romance of the sea'.

The Doctor's Table

Meeting such an incredibly variable cross-section of people is the aspect of my life at sea which I enjoy the most, and what better opportunity could anyone be given – or contrive – to meet people on a more intimate basis than to sit comfortably and share a meal with them. This I do regularly.

I'm sure that most people with a little knowledge of passenger ships will know of the Captain's Table. On all ships, the captain traditionally dines in the principal restaurant each evening at sea, unless work circumstances dictate otherwise on any particular night. His table will usually be fairly large and will seat eight or ten people. His dinner companions will be a selection of passengers who are invited to join him at his table, which is, of course, considered to be a privilege, and possibly one of the highlights of the voyage. However, this may not always be regarded as such, as evidenced by one lady's reply when requested if she would care to join the captain at his table for dinner. 'Young man,' she stated haughtily to the maitre d', 'I did not spend an inordinate amount of money to travel first class on this ship in order to eat with the crew!' This comment aside, you can be sure that most people are delighted by the invitation.

A lesser known aspect of this tradition is that most ships have several officers' or entertaining tables. All established or senior cruise lines will have four principal officers' tables within the restaurant. These will be the Captain's Table, the Chief Engineer's Table, the Hotel Manager or Purser's Table and the Doctor's Table. This means that on each voyage I have the excellent opportunity to meet around eight new people, and share their company for a sufficient amount of time to become far more than just bar-side acquaintances. The intimate atmosphere of a ship requires little aid to create close associations, and therefore dining for several nights with the same pleasant company creates a particularly convivial atmosphere and relationship between the people involved. Many close and lasting friendships have arisen from my table companions over the years.

I've often been challenged with the statement that I must find it very boring dining with the same people night after night; surely it must be tiresome to have to eat with the passengers regularly? I can quite honestly say that this has only very rarely ever been the case. Obviously there are going to be occasions when the day's work has been particularly heavy, and it's just too demanding to make the effort of dining and socializing. In these circumstances, the maitre d' will pass on my compliments and apologies, and not only will the guests hopefully miss my presence, and understand the circumstances, but in addition I'll invariably receive their sympathies. If all my dinner companions really were absolutely dreadful – a situation which in many years at sea I've fortunately never experienced – then I suppose that I'd just have to be 'busy' in the hospital every night of the week. Of course – as may occasionally occur – if a particular person or couple at the table were embarrassing, rude, undesirable, or anti-social in any way, then I'd advise the maitre d', and he'd politely suggest that they may prefer a quiet table for two elsewhere in the restaurant.

All in all, these situations are rare. Generally speaking, after a full day's work, a short rest, a shower and pre-dinner cocktail, I find it the most pleasurable time of the day. To sit down to good food, well served, together with excellent wines and, most of all, good company and conversation takes some beating. In actual fact, if I were to state my preference for a good evening's entertainment and enjoyment while ashore, this would be it.

While we're on the subject of good food and excellent wines a few statistics may be of interest. During the first ten years of the *QE2*'s life, the executive chef and his teams produced at least twenty-one million meals for the passengers and another nine and a half million for the crew! *QE2* is the world's largest single consumer of caviar, at one time quoted as using a fifth of the world's total annual production. In order to serve lobster, avocados or strawberries to our passengers we would require at least 1600 lbs of lobster, 1500 avocados and 600 lbs of strawberries. Each of these items would of course merely be one of several choices, on one of several courses, of one of three main meals of only one day of a cruise! On every single day of the year the chefs will crack well over ten thousand eggs!

Amongst a staggering shopping list at the commencement of a world cruise, the ship will take on 180 thousand pounds of beef. During the course of one world cruise alone, the ship consumed 2850 tins of Portuguese sardines, 11,000 lbs of salt, 15,000 gallons of milk, 15,500 lbs of turkey, 25,000 lbs of butter and 95,000 lbs of tomatoes. As the ship voyages around the world, it must replenish its stocks, and ship's chandlers must be capable of handling enormous orders: in Cape Town on one visit, we took on 14,500 lbs of fresh fish, 25,000 litres of milk, 11,000 cups of yoghurt, 6,500 litres of cream, 40 tonnes of canned Cape fruit, 1,000 lbs of kippers, 2,000 lbs of iceberg lettuce and 12.5 tonnes of potatoes, all as part of just one order!

The world cruise order, in addition to being staggering, is an imbiber's paradise: 10,000 bottles of champagne, 27,000 bottles of still wine, 16,500 bottles of spirits, 5,000 bottles of port, sherry and liqueurs and 45,000 cans and bottles of beer. Way down below, draught beer is kept in 27 stainless steel tanks with a capacity of about 13,500 gallons! As you can see, a tremendous amount of forethought and preparation precedes the dishes which appear at a multitude of meals.

Returning to the subject of the Doctor's Table, there is no set formula dictating who should be invited as guests. Obviously, if there were any close or old friends aboard, they would be a natural selection. On some occasions, requests will be made by my relatives or friends ashore to take care of their pals who may be travelling on the ship. Alternatively, there may be names on the passenger lists whom it would be either interesting or enjoyable to meet. At other times, the maitre d' may be inundated with forward requests – sometimes made months ahead – to sit at the Captain's Table, the Doctor's Table or any entertaining officer's table, or perhaps specifically *not* to be seated at any of the above. Often, however, the decision as to who will dine at a particular table will be left to the maitre d', who, if he's worth his salt, will have sufficient experience in the people business to select an interesting and compatible group of guests to dine together.

One of the principal priorities of a good table at sea, just as it is at home, is of course to balance the table with an equal number of men and women. If the maitre d' is smart enough to match up numbers by pairing the doctor, or host, with an attractive, unaccompanied young lady, then who's going to complain? From the shipping company's point of view, the officers' tables give an excellent opportunity for good public relations. The guests unquestionably enjoy themselves more on an officer's table, particularly if the mix is correct. Therefore, there is all the more reason to employ maitre d's who know their jobs and people, as this is an opportunity to send a significant number of passengers home who have enjoyed pleasant companionship, an important ingredient for a memorable holiday, which they'll inevitably recommend to their friends – the very best form of advertising.

So, with the tremendous variety of characters on *QE2*, think what a great opportunity the table affords for meeting and getting to know people from a very wide cross-section of life: people of every nationality, of all religious and political beliefs, from secretaries to playwrights, from bank clerks to bankers, from Mr and Mrs to belted earls. The evening's conversation may be amusing, serious, entertaining, controversial, but always educational in one way or another. Dinner conversation affords the opportunity for an in-depth insight into people, their work, their opinions, their homes, their countries, and many other aspects of their lives.

The social role of my position as ship's doctor and table host has inevitably not always run smoothly; the early days, to say the least, had their traumatic moments.

Having taken up my very first Merchant Marine appointment aboard the ancient but graceful *Edinburgh Castle* of the now defunct Union Castle line, I can easily recall the difficulty and discomfort of the settling-in period which I endured in this totally new environment with its equally unknown routines. The every-day task of making the very rapid transfer from working doctor to social host, sometimes with only fifteen to twenty minutes to make the transition, was a new experience, particularly as in those days I was still learning the very basics, such as what to wear and when.

Ironically, my first voyage was probably the busiest period I've ever known during my time at sea. Each time I sat at the dining table, I was approached discreetly and apologetically by the maitre d': 'Sorry sir, but you're wanted on the phone,' or 'in the hospital'. I was bobbing up and down like a yo-yo. Every time I managed to say, 'Hello, I'm Doctor Nigel Roberts, you are?', the phone would ring and I'd be gone! It was as though I were caught up in some nonsensical game called 'Beat the Bell'!

Apart from not making much of an impression on my guests, I was starving. I'd be sipping a spoonful of soup, and 'ring'! Or approaching a piece of fish . . . 'ring'! Cutting into a nice juicy steak . . . 'ring, ring, ring'! I eventually spent enough time at the table to at least recognize my companions if we met elsewhere!

This particular ship was unusual, in that it retained an old tradition of dinner-dances which, in the days of the great liners, was standard, and has recently been reintroduced on *QE2*. Every few nights, a dinner-dance would be held. Having at last become barely acquainted with my dinner companions, I was attempting to catch up on lost time and make a favourable impression. Tonight was a dinner-dance.

Amongst the guests at my table were an elderly couple, who were very pleasant company. The husband, I'd noticed, had a problem with his knees and, being unable to walk well, hadn't asked his wife to dance. She was full of vim and vigour, tapping her toes and drumming her fingers in time to the music, all ready to go despite her great age. A slow waltz was playing.

I leaned across and asked, 'Do you mind if I ask your wife for a dance?'

'Please do,' replied the husband, 'it will ease my conscience.'

'May I have this dance?' I asked the lady.

'Would you mind waiting for a fast dance, doctor?' she suggested in reply.

'Yes, of course,' I answered in mild surprise, 'whenever you're ready.'

The band played on, and eventually changed tempo.

'Ladies and gentlemen, please take your partners for a quickstep.'

'This will be lovely,' stated the wife, jumping up. I was amazed at her agility as she could well have been a great-grandmother.

Out on the dance area, the floor was none too steady! For the first time ever, I was trying to work out how to fit a 'slow, slow, quick, quick, slow' around a 'shuffle, stumble, shuffle, rock, tumble'! – not easy at sea, especially if you're no expert on solid land.

They were a lively band, with plenty of rhythm, and the floor was full.

We hadn't been dancing for more than a couple of circuits, when my partner looked up at me with a girlish sparkle and asked, 'Do you know how to jive?'

'Pardon?' I said in disbelief, thinking of her frail old legs and being, admittedly, a little aware of the possible spectacle and image. 'Yes . . . yes I can. That's more in my line, in fact,' I went on.

'Come on, then,' she said, and gave me a shove.

Well, she must have been saving up the energy for some time! With arms and legs waving, she soon cleared space on the floor and like an old Ginger Rogers and a young Fred Astaire we 'tripped the wild fantastic'. I choose these words intentionally, as a foreboding of events to come. Grabbing my hand she twirled and spun, around the back, under the arm and around again. There was no slowing her down. Dancers and diners alike were watching the act – probably wondering if they could get a supply of whatever the doctor had given the old lady.

In mid-manoeuvre, my whirling partner was completing a turn. Both of us were leaning outwards, and she reached forward to grasp my outstretched hand – a moment of vulnerability which fate was quick to seize. The ship gave a lurch, not a big one, but enough to cause a hiccup in our antics. My partner didn't quite reach my hand! Without stabilizing restraint, our individual momentum in opposite directions took charge, and as the roll of the ship was in her direction, the old lady commenced a slow backwards march, increasing speed with each step. I reached out. . . . Unfortunately, being caught on the wrong foot, my progress didn't match her regress! In what appeared to be the slowest of slow motion, we stretched further out as in the closing scenes of *Bonnie and Clyde*, and as was their fate, we never managed to touch. With gathering speed she shot off backwards, displaying the neatest piece of reverse footwork I'd ever witnessed on a dance floor. In admiration of what they mistakenly felt was a truly professional exhibition, the other dancers courteously stepped aside to make room for her frantic flight.

In the distance, beyond my partner, I was suddenly struck by the sight of the drummer who, having watched many a ship-board dance routine, was obviously able to recognize the difference between controlled flight and desperate plight! With growing alarm showing on his face, almost matching that of my partner, he unconsciously struck a roll of increasing crescendo until the final second before the inevitable impact, at which point his drum sticks flew into the air and he dived for cover. With a last desperate flourish of arms and legs, the whirling dervish tripped on the edge of the stage, and flew backwards through the middle of the drum kit. Accompanied by a final crash of the symbols, the dancing disaster came to rest and the music to an end.

Aghast at this demonstration of human ten-pin bowling, I dashed across the floor, trying to calculate how many broken bones you might need for a 'strike'. I knelt down to pick up the pieces. Amazingly, a large smile greeted me.

'My word, that was good fun!' she chirped, 'shall we go again?'

What an incredible old lady, and what a sport! My embarrassment was far greater than hers.

'I think I can safely say that the last routine deserves a rest,' I gasped, breathing an enormous sigh of relief.

I escorted her back to the table, where I poured out apologies to both my partner and her husband.

'She does it all the time,' he said, 'I could never keep up with her!'
I presumed he was talking about the jiving and not the drum trick.

This may not have been the best way for me to be broken in to my new role of table host! Things could only improve, and I think that it's true to say that over the years they have. However, the people remain just as fascinating, and forever unpredictable!

Generally speaking, travellers are fairly sophisticated people, especially on the *QE2*, but this isn't always so. On one occasion, during a four-day truckers' convention on board *QE2*, having ordered 'double everything' including caviar and smoked salmon, one of the guests at my table called for the wine steward.

'Yes sir, would you care to see the wine list?' the steward enquired.

'No, just give me a coupl'a cans'a cold Buds,' he instructed with a heavy Bronx accent straight out of a *Bowery Boys* movie.

'Yes sir!' said the steward with eyebrows raised.

Returning with the Budweiser beers, the steward started to pour one out into a glass.

'Just stick them down there!' he was ordered.

There, at the Doctor's Table in the first-class restaurant of the world's greatest ship, our friend swilled back his £200-a-pound Belluga caviar with cold beer from the can! It takes all kinds.

As you can imagine, it's sometimes difficult not to be impolite or to keep a straight face when you feel like bursting out laughing. It tickles me to recall the look on the maitre d's face on one particular occasion. On this evening he approached our table during dinner and asked if anyone would care for crêpes Suzette. Sitting at the table were a very affable couple from New Jersey, who had never ventured outside their state until their children had treated them to this cruise as a silver wedding anniversary present. I'll call them Dave and Iris. They were enjoying themselves immensely, despite initially feeling somewhat overawed by the entire experience and setting.

'Crayps? . . . Crayps? . . . What's "crayps" Dave?' demanded Iris of her spouse in a broad New Jersey accent.

'You've had "crayps" before, Iris,' he replied. 'You know, cheese "crayps", ham "crayps" . . .'

I leaned quietly over to them and explained that the maitre d' was referring to crêpes Suzette, very thin pancakes, impregnated with a sauce of mainly orange juice, liqueurs and brandy and then flamed. 'If you haven't tasted them before, give them a try,' I said, 'you'll like them.'

'OK, doc, yeah. Let's try them, Iris,' said Dave.

The maitre d', standing aloof throughout this interchange, went away and returned with his trolley.

Being of Latin descent, he took great pride in his skill and presentation, and he made the preparations to impress his audience with his well practised exhibition. As the main course progressed, the maitre d' went through his act with flourish. The routine went on for ten minutes, fifteen minutes, maybe even twenty minutes. The crêpes were soaked, the liqueur warmed, the brandy heated and added. The more Dave and Iris got involved with their sirloin steaks, the more determined the maitre d' became to catch their eye. If they were impressed they didn't show it. The maitre d' was confident that he would succeed with his *pièce de résistance* . . . whooosh! He lit the sauce and the flames leaped up. There was perhaps a flicker of interest from Iris, or was it concern at the height of the flame?

The crêpes were served and eaten, and were delicious. The maitre d' stood close by, studying their response. After this extra show, he awaited his anticipated praise.

Iris called to the waiter.

'Yes ma'am?' he enquired.

'Let me have the menu, would you,' she instructed.

'Would you like the cheese board, madam?' suggested the waiter.

'No, I want to see the desserts,' replied Iris.

The waiter was confused. 'But . . . but madam, you just ate the dessert.'

'What?' she almost shouted in surprise.

She turned slowly and deliberately towards the maitre d' who was still awaiting his acclaim for the skill which he had so admirably demonstrated.

'Dave!' she exclaimed, jabbing her finger at the maitre d', 'HE JUST RIPPED US OFF FOR A DESSERT!!'

The maitre d's face was an absolute picture.

A short time later, I was sitting with the captain, Lawrence Portet, and his wife, Anne, recounting this story and laughing at the memory. As I've said, it would have been impolite to do so at the time. We laughed together, and Anne then said, 'I don't wish to out-do your story, Nigel, but I think that we can top that!

'At our table, a short time ago,' she continued – referring of course to the Captain's Table – 'a lady called the waiter over and asked, "tell me, what's this cav-eye-ar, waiter?" The waiter replied, "Excuse me, madam, but it's pronounced caviar." "Yes, OK," she said, "but what is it?" The waiter wasn't too sure how to describe it,' Anne went on, 'and he sought about for the words. "It's, uh . . . it's er

. . . er, they're fish eggs," he eventually explained. "Oh, OK," said the lady, "well then . . . I'll have two . . . . *poached*!!" '

There are numerous similar stories, and there's certainly never any shortage of amusement!

Not wishing to detract from the excellent companionship of the vast majority of the past guests of the Doctor's Table, it would be unfair to dwell too long on the subject of the odd minority, but perhaps before leaving the subject I should illustrate just how difficult it can be to be host and balance a table made up sometimes totally at random, bringing together in one group characters from different walks of life, who in other circumstances would probably never dream of keeping each others' company.

The Columbia restaurant on the *QE2*. A transatlantic voyage, the first night out from New York. We had, as usual, entertained all the first-class passengers who were dining in the Queen's Grill, the Princess Grill and the Columbia restaurant, at the captain's welcome-aboard cocktail party in the Queen's Room, always held on this particular night. The weather was good, the sea calm, the drinks had been flowing and everybody was in a convivial mood. These are, of course, the ideal circumstances in which to meet the guests at your table for the first time.

Earlier in the evening a typed sheet had been placed in my cabin, listing the names and cabins of the various guests at all the entertaining officers' tables. I had read down the lists and noted that my table would be balanced, there being four ladies, three male guests and myself. I knew none of the names from the past.

The maitre d' had assembled the group. At that time there was a stand-in maitre d', and with more concern than usual, I hoped that he'd managed to mix a good table. I noticed that my table guests included a judge and his wife, a Mr and Mrs, a reverend, and two unaccompanied ladies.

Having allowed sufficient time for their guests to settle, the various entertaining officers entered the restaurant and joined their tables. In my usual custom, I introduced myself around the table before taking my seat, trying, as I did so, to get some impression of the people with whom I'd be dining over the next few days. The reverend was easy to spot in his 'uniform'. He was a very open, immediately friendly man, with the self-assured, confident manner of someone used to dealing with people. The very young couple sitting on my side of the table would be the Mr and Mrs – too young to be the judge – which meant that the stern, very sober and formal looking gentleman, who responded to my greeting with the briefest of nods, would have to be the judge, accompanied by his equally reserved wife. Sitting opposite me, between the Reverend and the young man, was a hearty, American lady with a loud voice and an engaging smile. She was obviously here to enjoy herself and the whole world was her friend. Finally, sitting to my right was an extremely upright, prim and proper lady, buttons and lace all over the place, her dress closed up to her neck in turn-of-the-century style. Thin lipped, owlish spectacles and little, if any, make-up.

'Well, this could be a challenge!' I thought.

I engaged in conversation with the individual guests and soon found out that the young couple holding hands under the table were newly-weds on their honeymoon. They were gauche and somewhat embarrassed, but bubbled over with enthusiasm and details of their wedding, in between episodes when they gazed at each other, smiling almost inanely. The prim lady on my right observed them with a positively disapproving manner, finding it difficult to smile. She was a very English spinster and the retired headmistress of a girl's school.

How interesting and unusual it was that the external appearance of everyone at the table should so accurately reflect the standard image of their backgrounds and situations.

I chatted as pleasantly as I could with the headmistress. She was polite enough, but utterly humourless, and so unfortunately were the judge and his good lady. Their answers to my attempts at conversation were clipped and difficult to draw out.

The wine steward approached and offered the wines which I'd ordered. The legal and teaching brigades abstained, the church and newly-weds enthused and so did our unaccompanied American lady with whom I hadn't yet had a chance to chat.

A toast: 'Calm seas and a good crossing, and many years of happy marriage to the newly-weds!'

The glasses clinked and the meal continued.

'BANGKOK!' called the American lady suddenly to me across the table.

'Sorry,' I answered, 'what were you referring to?'

'Bangkok,' she repeated, 'that's where I live, Bangkok.' Her voice was loud, sharp and intrusive.

The polite chatting around the table stopped.

'Oh really?' I said. 'You live in Thailand?'

She continued over my comments, almost without pausing, 'Yep! That's where they cut your cock off if you fool around!'

A small gasp came from the reverend and he paused with his mouth wide open, not quite sure of what he'd heard. Neither was I!

89

She went on.

'Out there, if a married man fools around with another woman, his wife gets a knife and cuts his cock off!'

I hadn't misheard! She *had* said that!

The reverend, facing directly towards me, developed a glazed look in his eyes, his mouth still open. 'Ooohh!' exclaimed Mrs Judge, and poured her Perrier water into her lap. The judge sat even further erect, if possible, and merely coughed. The bride's colour now matched that of the red rose placed lovingly by her husband beside her plate. There was a small moan from my right and I turned to see that teacher had stuck herself in the nose with her fork! Everyone had stopped eating, and was frozen, except for the narrator who, munching away, carried on, apparently totally unaware of the impact.

'Oh really?' I said, for once lost for words and desperately thinking of some way to divert the subject. Before I could say more, she ploughed on with her information.

'Just last week,' she said, 'some guy got his cock cut off, and his wife threw it out of the window!'

She was almost shouting, and the people at the neighbouring tables, having picked up a few key words, were beginning to pay attention.

'That's a very interesting medical problem,' I tried to joke, 'perhaps we can talk about it after dinner?'

If she heard, she didn't show it, she just carried straight on.

'He dashed down to the hospital to see if they could help him, and they asked, "Where's your cock?" "It went out the window," he told them. "Well go and get it!" they said.'

The reverend had forsaken his meal. He sat with his hands clasped, his eyes turned towards heaven, probably hoping for guidance. The newly-weds were giggling and nudging each other and Mr and Mrs Judge had resumed eating furiously, having totally dissociated themselves from our lady, myself, the table, the restaurant and, from all appearances, the entire world! Teacher was coughing, gently at first, and then more explosively, having tried to eat her fork with her steak. I tapped her lightly on the back, mainly for reassurance; she jumped so convulsively she nearly flew out of her seat. This time, Mrs Judge's Perrier drowned the judge's *sole bon femme*.

'He dashed back home,' resumed the cry from the opposite side of the table, even louder, as she worked up to her punch line. 'And what do you think happened?' she yelled, slapping the table and making the cutlery rattle. She began to guffaw out loud. Nobody replied – I didn't dare!

'The *ducks* had *eaten* it!' she exploded.

Well I don't think that I've ever seen a table quite so devastated before. The newly-weds burst into unrestrained laughter, the reverend sat with a half devilish, half angelic smile on his face, the judge and his wife did excellent impersonations of stone-faced Harold Lloyd, and the headmistress, in an apoplectic seizure, could say no more than, 'Oh dear . . . Oh dear . . . Oh dear.'

To cap her story, the lady dug into her handbag and threw a newspaper cutting on the table. 'If you don't believe me,' she stated, 'there's the story in the newspaper!'

As you can imagine, no-one picked up the cutting!

Now, if you were in my seat, how would *you* have handled the next hour?

This kind of thing is all part of the job – and in a perverse way, the enjoyment!

Happy Hours

Cocktail parties may be regarded as the most important and usually most enjoyable aspect of social life on any ship, especially the *QE2*.

Out on the ocean there are very few, if any, hours of the day which don't qualify as drinking time. However, in order not to be regarded as alcoholics, most people will – outwardly at least – restrict their drinking sessions to the four socially acceptable periods of imbibing; one questionable advantage of being on holiday is that you're allowed the liberty of a morning starter, to get the day going and help remedy yesterday's damage. The kick-start is therefore the first accepted session of the day. Session number two is the lunchtime drink – an established fortress of the boozer's domain. Next? Society naturally accepts the pre-dinner cocktail party as one of the principal aspects of social behaviour in the civilized world, hence session number three. And finally, only an oaf would doubt the necessity of an after dinner drink – session number four. And, of course, perish the thought of a meal without wine!

And so, our potentially gin-soaked holidaymaker finds no end of excuses to indulge his alcoholic inclinations, and the fact that these various sessions run amazingly easily from one into the other can for him only be an encouraging sign from above!

The most widely attended and socially acceptable of these occasions is the cocktail party. On board ships, we are experts at entertaining and socializing; on the *QE2* we excel! The *raison d'être* for a majority of the ship's company is to play hosts to our guests. What better way to accomplish this than with a cocktail party?

During the course of a cruise or transatlantic voyage, there are always a considerable number of cocktail parties to be thrown or to attend. The principal party of the cruise is, as you may guess, the captain's welcome-aboard party, and on the *QE2* the huge number of passengers necessitates two parties being thrown on consecutive nights. On these occasions, every passenger on the ship has the opportunity to meet the captain as he greets them individually with a handshake at the door of the main lounge, having been announced in a loud, clipped, formal voice, by Ronnie, the chief steward.

'Count and Countess Herbert Von. . . . Mr and Mrs John Smith, Sir George and Lady Alderbury, Miss Connie Rowbotham, Mr Alf Mic . . . Miczano . . . Miczo . . . Mozinco . . . uh . . . uh . . .' Too late! The captain gets through yet another 1500 handshakes, sometimes more, and sometimes as often as every five days.

The photographers, positioned neatly amongst the surrounding foliage and conveniently close to a tray of champagne, capture the occasion with a vision-blurring flash, for the world and his dog to view in the display cabinets next morning. Then, it's on to the alcohol, and the gathered assembly.

She who has neglected the opportunity to produce her most glittering, or alternatively most complimentary, most sexy garment for the evening, will rarely find a more suitable occasion. Here, in the Queen's Room, are assembled the choice of the designer stores' shelves – and anything goes, from silks to sack-cloth, from ostrich to rabbit, hair up, hair down, hair green, hair gone! Spikes and curls, diamonds and pearls. This really is the place for people-watching: dowagers, nymphs, machos and limp wrists. Pick a style, and you've got it here.

This is the first real occasion to see who's on board; to view your fellow shipmates, to renew old acquaintances and to make new friends. To mix with the Joneses and the celebrities. With a combination of excitement and curiosity, the passengers observe their associates.

'Who's that over there?' . . . 'It's Lady Bird-Johnston!'

'Oh! who is she talking with?' . . . 'That's Sir Nigel Broakes, the chairman of Trafalgar House, the parent company of Cunard Lines.'

'And look there! There's Peter Ustinov . . . and there's Sir John Mills!'

Sure enough, to the delight of their fellow passengers, they are indeed there; rubbing shoulders, chatting, socializing and drinking in an all-seafarers-together gathering.

As the alcohol flows and more people meet, the conversations get under way and the atmosphere becomes more convivial; a room full of elegance on parade. *Da-raaaaah*, goes the band, and up pops the cruise director, to quieten the gathering.

'Ladies and gentlemen! Your attention please!'

The hubbub reduces.

'I'd like to introduce you to the senior officers, who are in charge of your voyage to ——.'

One by one the heads of department parade out onto the stage, to the less than tumultuous applause of the gathered crowds, who are trying their best to clap with a glass of champagne in one hand and a caviar canapé in the other: the Chief Engineer, the Hotel Manager, the Chief Radio Officer, the Staff Captain, the man responsible for making you fat – the food and beverage manager, the Purser, and included in the line-up, 'The team we hope you will only meet socially, headed by our Principal Medical Officer. . . .' A cheer goes up from the patients we've cured, together with friends and admirers, and no doubt some on-board members of the society of hypochondriacs! Finally, to the accompaniment of a blur of flashbulbs simultaneously recording the completed line-up, 'The gentleman you met at the door, your host for this evening, and for the remainder of the voyage, Captain ——!'

'Welcome aboard' . . . and back to your champers.

Not all the cocktail parties are enormous affairs. As the week progresses there are smaller, more intimate and, I feel, more enjoyable gatherings. Once the cruise has settled, the dining tables and dinner companions have become established, and we've become acquainted with the new set of passengers, then the entertaining officers of the four principal tables in the restaurant traditionally hold a pre-dinner cocktail party for their table companions, together with a mixture of VIPs, friends, previous travellers and selected guests. I enjoy very much drawing up the list of guests and blending a gathering which I anticipate will mix well, enjoy each other's company and have a memorable party. Having completed the list, Pauline Sleigh, our ever patient, efficient General Manager's, Captain's, and Medical secretary, takes over the organization.

Obviously, to be a good host, you must enjoy people and be sufficiently outgoing, or extrovert, to mix and socialize – I don't think there's much doubt that most, if not all, ship's doctors tend to fit this description.

I can remember only one occasion when I was upstaged as a host, and that was when John Lindsey, the ex-Mayor of New York, was a guest at one of my medical parties. He was such an outgoing personality, and obviously so accustomed to mixing and socializing, that he was presumably unable to turn off and relax at someone else's gathering. He covered more territory, and expended more energy during that party, than I could hope to muster. He was a man of great charm and magnetism. He met everyone in the room, and they were delighted to meet him.

Personalities and celebrities naturally add a little spice to any gathering and of course it's always interesting to meet them yourself on home territory, as a guest at your own party. Some, of course, are ships that pass in the night: we share an hour of company and mutual enjoyment; perhaps the immaculate George Hamilton, the memorable Billy Ekstine, Miss America, Miss World, Miss Bluebell and her dancers. And, of course, this is their holiday, they're not on show and nobody on the *QE2* is likely to hassle them, and certainly not at one of our private parties. So the occasions are all the more pleasant.

Other guests return over the years and become regular acquaintances and, in some cases, old friends. It's always great to meet up again with vivacious characters like Harry Secombe, Bob Monkhouse or Jimmy Saville; or celebrate St Patrick's Day with that sparkling Irish leprechaun, James Galway; to find out from old pal Harry Nilsen how a mutual friend's wedding went in California, or how *Ghandi* star, Ben Kingsley, made out on his visit to a Red Indian reservation with his wife, Alison; or to see other friends return, like the late Sir William Lyons, who having built a motorbike sidecar in his garage, watched his business grow into the Jaguar Empire. It was fascinating to share his memories, and those of his truly lovely wife, of those early days of the motor industry. And, of course, there are the many other pals mentioned throughout this book.

Not all our parties are uneventful and totally pleasurable. There are the obvious occasions when an emergency medical call will rob the party of their hosts, and the guests must be left in the good care of the barmen and waiters; but there are very few situations, which our regular and dependable foursome can't handle – Dennis, Bob, Ronnie and Gary, whom regular passengers on *QE2* will know well, are great ship's characters and very experienced hosts in their own right.

Occasional incidents have caused hiccups, but there was one party, which I recall particularly, which was rather embarrassing. Fortunately, only myself and the person concerned were aware of it.

First of all, let me explain the background, which involves the complexities of the plumbing aboard ships. The majority of ships sailing around the oceans – and probably all modern ships – have two separate water supplies. The first is a fresh water system. This supplies the drinking taps, hand-wash basins, cooking areas, cleaning and laundry facilities, bath tubs and showers, and mountains of ice. The second system uses sea water. This system supplies water for the swimming pools, for washing down the decks, the pressure system for the fire sprinklers, and last but not least the water to flush the toilets. As the source of the sea water is much lower than the outlets, it is pumped up through the system under pressure.

In order to flush a toilet, the handle is depressed; this opens a valve which allows a controlled gush of pressurized water to escape into the bowl. Occasionally, the compressors are out of action and when this happens the sanitary water is, of course, shut down. If the toilet handle is depressed, nothing comes out. In fact, because of the lack of pressure, with the valve open the water is allowed to fall back down the pipe a short distance, and air is drawn in through the open valve. When the valve is released, the air which has been drawn in is trapped. When the compressors are restarted, the water again comes under pressure, and so does the trapped air. To the amazement and distress of the unsuspecting visitor to the lavatory, when the lever is depressed, he is startled by a *Whoooooosssh* of explosively escaping, compressed air – which sounds like the roar of a carbon dioxide fire extinguisher, only much louder! The rapidly expanding air strikes the water in the bowl and the 'whoosh' is immediately followed by a terrific blasting cascade of the bowl's contents, which engulf the user before they can even blink an eye. Stencilled on the wall of the bathroom is the shape of the unwary figure, who hasn't even had enough time to raise his hands in exclamation . . . or self defence. Once bitten, twice shy, I can assure you! If he's aware that the pressure has recently been turned on, the clever seafarer, having been caught on a previous occasion, isn't to be fooled again! He lowers the toilet lid before depressing the handle! *Whoooosh* goes the air, and a cascade of water bursts outwards through the gap between the pan and the closed lid, and decorates his knees!

Inelegant or otherwise, if you know it's going to happen, the only foolproof means of escape would be to stand on the lid. So, now you have the picture.

One of our doctors' parties was under way and in full swing, The guests had all arrived, had been introduced, and were chatting and laughing in groups around the room. It seemed to be another successful gathering.

I was standing with one group discussing some current topic, when I felt a hand on my arm. I turned to see that it was one of our guests, a very senior and well-known American politician – whose name I obviously can't disclose, in order to avoid embarrassment. He was dressed expensively and immaculately – not a crease, not a hair out of place. His suit was perfectly cut, he wore a silk shirt, satin evening shoes – looked almost as if he'd stepped out of a fashion magazine.

'Excuse me, Dr Roberts,' he said quietly, 'I wonder if I can trouble you. I'm afraid that I've been caught a little short, and as my cabin is up in the penthouses, I wonder if you'd mind if I used your bathroom?'

'But of course,' I replied. 'Through this way, the door on the left,' I directed him.

'Thanks.'

I turned and started chatting with a group of guests. 'I caught your lecture this afternoon . . .' pleasant, light conversation which turned into an interesting discussion.

Suddenly, I stopped, my head slightly turned and my ears pricked up. Through the conversation, I heard only a distant sound, but it was unmistakable to the experienced ear . . . I knew that I'd heard a WHOOOOOOSSSH!!!

'Oh, bloody hell!' I groaned, immediately visualizing the silk shirt, the tailored suit, the immaculate presentation . . . the silhouette on the bathroom wall!

'Oh, dear!' I said aloud.

The bathroom door stayed closed. A while later, it was still closed; and even later.

'Excuse me, Dr Roberts.' The politician's wife stood before me. 'Did you by any chance see where my husband went?'

'He . . . er . . . Yes, I . . . I believe . . . he just nipped out for a moment, he shouldn't be long,' I replied, hopefully.

97

But he was! He was gone for a very long time!

The party continued and the guests began to depart. Eventually, the bathroom door opened. Out stepped a decidedly more crumpled figure than had entered: bow-tie slightly askew, bits of fluffy towelling on the jet-black suit, hair slicked back and face flushed. I walked the other way and pretended not to notice. Eventually, I bumped into him.

'Ah, there you are. I thought you'd left while I was busy,' I exclaimed.

'No . . . no, no. I was just . . . uh . . . just . . . cleaning up a little,' he replied, in what must have been the greatest understatement of his entire career!

'Darling, where on earth have you been?' called his wife as she approached.

He adopted a fixed Cheshire-cat, public relations smile, and talking through clenched teeth like a ventriloquist, he said stiffly and quietly, 'My dear, you wouldn't believe me if I told you!'

I still have to laugh when I picture the antics which must have gone on behind that door. One thing I can say for sure – I had a very clean bathroom afterwards!

Another of the more selective and enjoyable cocktail parties of a cruise is held in the Wardroom – the officers' club. This prestigious gathering is held towards the end of each cruise, and consists only of friends and the closer acquaintances of the various officers, for whom the Wardroom is home. In addition to these guests, there is a cross-section of VIPs, selected by the Wardroom President. Through these doors, over the years, have passed some of the more esteemed personages from every country in the world, notably, our own royalty. Also, foreign royalty such as the Sultan of Selangor, presidents, leaders of nations, and a dazzling parade of celebrities from every field, from every nation. This very exclusive club, on the greatest ship in the world, has played host to an extremely impressive list of guests. The visitors' book must be worth a mint!

Here, in a relaxed atmosphere, the guests may pass the time with princes and princesses, or spend a raucous half-hour with a fire-ball of a character such as Shelley Winters. The ladies can swoon over superstars like Elton John, and the aspiring starlets can flirt with film directors or television producers such as Aaron Spelling of *Dynasty*, *Charlie's Angels* and *Vegas* fame – who, as the producer also of the American *Love Boats* television series, has made his own contribution to the magic image of life at sea.

The privilege of throwing cocktail parties is by no means limited to the ship's personnel. Many of the passengers get in on the act. On the longer cruises, and particularly on world cruises, it can be a pleasurable but demanding pastime keeping up with the numerous invitations. With the expert assistance of the ship's staff to organize and run parties for the various hosts, drinks, music, canapés, and good company are gathered together in cabins and lounges throughout the ship, in groups of tens, twenties, fifties or whatever.

What if your preference is non-alcoholic? Fear not, you're not forgotten! Soft drinks are always available, and – despite the preponderance of people trying to enter the alcoholic section of the *Guinness Book of Records* – you certainly won't be alone if you're teetotal.

For the fitness fanatics? The 'Golden Door' spa at sea will gather together its fit, but often weary members from the health centre, the gymnasium, the aerobics classes, and revitalize them with a shot of carrot juice at their regular 'Juicetail' parties! True to the ship's form however, you can get a glass of wine here as well!

For the Kids? *Coke*tail parties, of course! *No*-one is left out of the swinging, happy business of socializing and party-going!

Very Important Passengers

A very significant facet of ship-board life peculiar to the *QE2*, is the very high proportion of celebrities and personalities who sail with the ship. I have already made frequent references to the various world-wide celebrities I've known; some have become acquaintances, many have been patients, some are confidants; and there is a very enjoyable cross-section I'm pleased to number amongst my friends.

It has always been my contention that our own characters and personalities are influenced by everyone we meet. Our knowledge, beliefs and attitudes are enlarged or moulded by every contact. Those who have come to the forefront of society, in whatever field, have a great deal to contribute, but being a well known personality doesn't by any means necessarily make the person either pleasant or memorable. There are enormous crowd-pullers whom I find offensive and characterless, and I'd never wish to meet again; nevertheless, one has to accept that the experiences of even these people are, in one way or another, mind-expanding.

'What do they do? What do they say?' everyone asks, including newspaper and TV interviewers. I can promise you that, away from the limelight, what the vast majority of these celebrities 'do' really isn't extraordinary at all. Their pleasures and pastimes are frequently simple, rarely dramatic, and Rod Stewart's tonsils are just as normal as many millions of others. The interesting thing which all have in common is that a quiet drink, a day on the beach, a good meal and pleasant company is as important to them as to everyone. Away from the front line, most celebrities enjoy the simple, basic everyday events of life which the rest of the world takes so much for granted. This is so much easier on board *QE2*, where the celebrities themselves are part of everyday life, where they can be absorbed into the 'family', and proceed with their daily routines without having to maintain a status, away from intruders and pestering.

And so, Rod Stewart can cheer and shout as we take a beer together and watch Manchester United win the F.A. cup on television, as we sail along the south-coast of England; and, sharing a drink in my cabin, Boy George can discard his public image, and become again, plain, unpretentious George O'Dowd, and enjoy an evening of simple relaxation, while hypnotist Nigel Ellery demonstrates his mystic powers to us all.

It isn't my intention to create what could be a very extensive list, nor to risk offence by keeping it short but a few really memorable people I have known amongst this enormous variety of characters, who were not just personalities but made an impact when I met them, spring easily to mind.

When you grow up with a name which was always a household word from your earliest days, that name inevitably becomes deeply imprinted. When the personality behind the name continues to grow, and the name lives on into further generations it may become a legend. I doubt whether many of us would dispute that this is the case with James Cagney.

James Cagney was one of my first encounters with the apparently inaccessible, a legend so distant that a meeting is unimaginable. I'm sure that we all have a multitude of similar examples of the unattainable. James Cagney travelled with us on board *QE2* in the early 1980s – also his early eighties – together with another great Hollywood name, Pat O'Brien, and their respective wives. Of course, it is a surprising experience to be confronted with an ageing version of an image, but equally surprising how quickly the significance of the appearance diminishes as the underlying personality exerts itself. I am not shy to admit that I was literally thrilled to share a period of time in their company – quietly, informally, in their cabin away from the rest of the world – a private audience! I can't honestly remember our conversation; it doesn't matter, it doesn't detract from the pleasure of the memory of being with this surprisingly gentle, delightful man, and his equally delightful pal. I recall being struck by the closeness, the unity, of man and wife – a wife who after their many years together must have become a very significant part of this man's character and personality, a character so apparently well-known to us all. I was also struck by his closeness to his obviously dear pal, Pat O'Brien, with whom he had grown up, and grown old, in this world. Two very wise, experienced old men who had 'been there' over the years. Incidentally, not content with all their past adventures, they were travelling to London to take part in yet another film!

101

In a somewhat similar vein, as most of my generation will immediately agree, I grew up with another legendary name – Al Jolson. Some of my earliest memories were of the films *The Jolson Story* and *Jolson Sings Again*. Unfortunately, I didn't meet Al Jolson, but I found it almost equally as surprising and intriguing to meet with the woman who shared his life, Ruby Keeler, very much a star in her own right. To sit for long spells – as I have on many occasions – and chat with Ruby about Al Jolson and their fascinating experiences of the past, and, despite fate being so unkind as to have afflicted her with an illness which limits her movements, to dance slowly around the ballroom floor with the partner of a childhood legend is, to say the least, unforgettable.

Another name I grew up with was George Burns. A small, slightly built and frail man of enormous character; a witty, vivacious man who remains full of devilment, with a permanent gleam in his steady eye, and a pretty girl on his arm. I was amazed to find how alert, fit and well-presented he has remained – and his act is a delight! Whenever I chatted with him, I noticed he had an almost permanent half-smile, a knowing look as though he were inwardly enjoying some secret joke at life's expense.

On a sadder note, I recall another familiar name with great affection. He was a star of the silent movie era, who went on to become an actor and producer in the talking picture industry, a Hollywood mogul, the man associated with the rise to fame of both Jean Harlow and Marilyn Monroe. This man eventually became a household word in the post-war years of Britain, when each Sunday lunchtime, nearly every family in the country tuned in their radios to listen to, and share, the family fun and experience of *Life with the Lyons*. Ben Lyon. Through the radio waves, we became intimate friends with his family – Bebe Daniels, his first wife before her death, his children, Richard and Barbara. Over the radio, their voices became part of our lives. To me, as a child, he became almost a favourite uncle. Imagine, then, after so many years of apparent closeness, eventually meeting this man, and finding him to be every bit as pleasant as you envisaged. I really used to enjoy sitting and chatting with Ben and his lovely second wife about the incredible early days of Hollywood.

What a very romantic story he related to me one day. In his youth, he had met a young woman and fallen deeply in love. Fearing that his love was unrequited he had never expressed his feelings. Due to various commitments, they drifted apart. Later, Ben met, loved, married and eventually lost, his dear Bebe Daniels. The love of his youth had meanwhile fortunately met and married an equally cherished partner. When Bebe died, Ben was totally heart-broken. Shortly afterwards he met, of all people, his former love, who had unfortunately also lost her husband and was also heart-broken. They shared time together, comforted each other, and looked back across the years to their earlier days. Ben finally revealed that, all those years ago, he had been deeply in love with her, but had never expressed his feelings. In amazement, she heard his story and devastated Ben by making a similar revelation. Needless to say, their relationship developed from there, and became a fairy-tale marriage.

Some months later, Ben was making a return visit to the ship. One evening, I was in the Wardroom – the officers' club. We were putting on the 'Wardroom Show', whereby a number of the officers tie together various acts – singing, instrumental, comic, revue sketches and whatever else can be concocted for the entertainment of their fellow officers and a few select passengers. I was about to go on stage and give the audience the dubious benefit of my artistic talents, when I received an emergency call.

I arrived at the cabin within seconds, and found that the patient was Ben. Ben Lyons died that night. I remember all the details of the struggle and our endeavours, but mainly I remember my feelings, my terrific sadness, my sense of loss and responsibility, as I pulled the white sheet up over his head and drew a line on the life which had contributed so much to my childhood memories and so much to family life in the post-war years of Britain.

These encounters, of course, had an impact because of their strong association with the memories of my youth and all the ensuing years. However, a man's name need not be long-established in order to lay claim to the annals of the legendary.

The likes of Christopher Columbus or Captain Cooke, in the solitude of their little ships detached from the entire civilized world, must have been incredible characters, but I'm sure that, although modern exploration is based far more upon back-up and teamwork, the names of the few at the sharp end will go down in history. It is beyond the wildest aspirations of most of us to travel beyond the boundaries of our planet and visit places where, literally, only our dreams and stories can take us. Space travel lies beyond our own possibilities and, consequently, those who have achieved it become heroes, and those who were amongst the first become legend. It is fascinating to consider that by leaving our planet and viewing it in its entirety from afar would give the beholder a perspective of our domain, an insight into our place in the universe – in life, even. Thus I'm sure that there is a tendency not only to respect and admire our astronauts, but to be somewhat in awe of their experience, the possibility of their greater knowledge. What then can one say about Scott Carpenter or Alan Shepherd, both of whom I have known when they sailed with us on separate occasions on the *QE2*.

I became acquainted with Scott Carpenter and spent time chatting over a few beers in my cabin with him and his wife about his experiences not only as an astronaut but, incredibly, also as an aquanaut – he had achieved the record for the longest period at the greatest depths under the ocean aboard the ocean floor research vessel, *Sea-Lab*.

It is obviously extremely difficult for the layman to discuss space travel because, being outside our sphere of experience, we are unable to contribute to the discussion or to draw our own conclusions. Consequently, we have to content ourselves with questions and answers. In the early days, the astronauts must have been absolutely fed up with answering inane questions from the average man who, unable to grasp or associate with any of the concepts of life in space, could only relate to the problems of his own world and ask, 'How do you take a pee in a space suit?' Every now and then, however, a revealing comment is made, an insight given – an opportunity to experience directly through the eyes of the man involved, as when I was chatting on one occasion with Alan Shepherd, during a cocktail party in my quarters. He commented, 'I'm a very hard man, very hard. In fact, amongst all the people that I work with, I'm considered to be one big S.O.B., and they're probably right. That's how I am, and I've become more so as the years go on.

'But, the first time I ever launched into space, and I was able to look back and see the earth as a planet, when I looked through the window . . . I choked up, I have to admit it, I really choked right up!'

I don't know about the rest of you, but I felt that in these days when computers and machinery influence our every move, it was great to learn that the people who travel into space to explore the universe on our behalf are indeed human beings and not emotionless human machines.

There is one other person who stands out amongst the more fascinating personalities I have met and known. This man was present at, and participated in, one of the most significant milestones in the history of the world – the dropping of the first atomic bomb to be used in the destruction of mankind. I shared every evening meal

104

with this man, who sat at my table for a week. He was a big man, with a bigger personality; a strong, healthy character who was an extrovert, confident, self-assured man, well-balanced, pleasant and most convivial, and enjoyed life to its fullest. He is a member of my own profession, now living in Texas. He had been the navigator on the *Enola Gay* on that fateful day when it flew over Japan, and with a single blow, helped divert the entire course of the war and, thankfully, bring it to a halt, paradoxically saving the lives of many more than it killed, but at the same time, creating one of the blackest days in the history of mankind. I found it quite amazing to be sharing the company of a man who had been so close to the centre of this momentous occasion in history.

All these various characters have certainly made a tremendous contribution to the enjoyment of my position of doctor of the *QE2*, and have unquestionably added to the great social life on board.

IV
SPECIAL PATIENTS

Arnold

There are, as we all know, many ordinary people who stand out in the crowd for reasons other than being famous. Naturally there have been certain patients during my career whom I can recall instantly, and it is equally so with certain patients I have encountered on board ship. Similarly, I have very strong memories of particular characters who didn't come directly under our medical wing, but who were nonetheless part of the ship's history.

There are four particular patients whose stories I'm sure you will find interesting.

My first story is about a patient who was an old friend of mine, Arnold.

Late morning on the bridge of the *QE2*. The ship was in mid-Atlantic heading towards New York. It was a grey day with an overcast sky, but the seas were calm and we were ploughing steadily, comfortably ahead.

I had been standing and listening while our captain had been chatting via a pre-arranged radio link-up with the captain of a Concorde jet, whistling through the air many miles above us, also on its way across the North Atlantic. As on every other morning, we'd heard the *boom!* of its passage, like a gun shot, as it streaked by on its supersonic journey at twice the speed of sound. It was intriguing to reflect on the vivid contrast between the three and a half hours' trip of the Concorde, and the five-day ocean voyage of *QE2* – which, at a steady 29 knots, is in itself no mean feat in seafaring terms. The very best, the cream of the aviation and shipping worlds, two totally different entities were, for a short period, companions in their travels, linked by the invisible connection of the radio waves.

Having passed the time of day and exchanged a series of technical data, we had then been suitably impressed by the lunchtime fare of the Concorde passengers, which we felt was adequately matched by the prospects of the contents of our own five-course luncheon menu, to be enjoyed at our more leisurely pace. A few jokes passed between the respective captains before Concorde moved out of range, concluding a first in communications history.

I strolled down from the bridge and out for a few windswept minutes, onto the boat deck.

'Morning, captain,' a cheery voice called to me. To some passengers, anyone in uniform and wearing gold stripes is 'captain', during the early stages of the voyage. Eventually, as they settle in and become 'seafarers', they learn to recognize the distinguishing colours between the gold stripes – red for medical, white for hotel department, green for radio officers. Black, or no intervening colour, represents the deck department – the true sailors, who drive, navigate and administer the ship aspect of this floating hotel. Finally, purple is for the engineers, the unsung heroes, toiling unseen and unheard throughout the ship, in every corner, but principally down below, in the bowels, amongst the thunder of pistons, the scream of machinery and the stifling heat of the engine rooms. Here, amongst the engineers, is where the colour coding began.

It is well known, certainly amongst seafarers, that during the unimaginable tragedy that was the *Titanic*, throughout the turmoil and panic, every engineer on board remained at his post, despite the terrifying knowledge of their probable fate. They fought to repair damage and maintain the ship in a seaworthy condition, at least until help might arrive. This was not to be, and all those brave men of the engine room, together with many other valiant souls, were lost with the ship. Many years later, in recognition of this noble and selfless gesture of the *Titanic*'s engineers, the British monarch, King George V, ordained that the royal colour of purple be worn by marine engineers, as a salute to the bravery of their lost comrades, and as a sign of mourning. Thus, the tradition was born. In the ensuing years, other officers took different colours as their departmental insignia. Red, of course, was a natural choice for medicine.

Having passed along the blustery deck, I made my way back inside to pick up a few things from the shops around the double-room balcony. Here the *QE2* passengers can shop from some of the greatest store names in the western world, choosing their purchases from Harrods, Dior, Louis Féraud, Dunhill, Garards and Louis Vuitton. Exotic jewellery and clothes from the cream of the fashion houses are beautifully displayed throughout undoubtedly the most impressive shopping arcade afloat.

I went down the great spiral staircase linking the two levels of the enormous balconied double rooms, the largest entertainment area afloat, and off to meet a couple of great pals, Clive Brandy and his wife, singing star Iris Williams, in the Piano Bar, where we'd arranged to meet up with and enjoy an hour with Sammy Cahn, who had offered to play the piano and sing some of the many all-time-greats which he'd composed over his numerous years as a songwriter. It was a fabulous opportunity to spend some time with, and listen to the 'Master'.

En route, I passed the flower shop, one of the *QE2*'s many 'extras'. This was the only 29-knot floating flower shop in the world, where every day of the year the romantically inclined could buy a bouquet of fresh flowers to add an extra pleasure to his wife's dream cruise; or others, a dozen red roses for a new-found love. I always enjoy stopping here to savour the perfume of the fresh flowers, and smell the damp, fresh greenery – an unexpected pleasure in the middle of the ocean. Chatting with one of the pretty flower girls surrounded by her blooms, I was interrupted by an elderly couple who had stopped to say hello. They were a particularly pleasant man and wife, who lived in Canada and whom I had known over the years. I shall call them Arnold and Mary Grant.

They had both travelled with us on several previous voyages, when we had become good friends, and it was a pleasure to see them again. Arnold was eighty-four years old, and despite a walking stick, was active and lively, and sharp as a tack.

'We were in Toronto recently,' said Arnold, 'and we met some people at a friend's house. When we told them we were coming on the *QE2*, they said that their ex-doctor, who used to live in Toronto, was on the *QE2* – Dr Nigel Roberts! We said that we knew you, and that we'd pass on their regards.'

We chatted about my old pals for a while and laughed over a few jokes; then, for the umpteen-thousandth time in my life, I said, 'It's a small world, isn't it?'

'Maybe so,' replied Arnold with a wink, then added, with the wisdom of his years, 'but I wouldn't like to paint it!'

'Now!' exclaimed Arnold, 'guess what's special about this cruise?'

'I could suggest a hundred things,' I replied, 'but obviously it concerns the two of you, and if I remember rightly, you celebrated your wedding anniversary when you were on board around this time last year.'

'Well done,' said Arnold, 'you're right; but it's even more special than that. Not only is it our anniversary, but it's our Diamond Anniversary!'

'Sixty years married!' added Mary, with beaming enthusiasm.

'Well, well,' I said. 'Diamond indeed, and here's me not even on my way to a waste-paper anniversary yet! When's the big day?'

'Tomorrow,' said Arnold, with the happiest of smiles I'd seen in a long time. 'You'll join us, of course?'

'You try and keep me away!' I replied.

'Our children and grandchildren arranged this trip as an anniversary present,' Arnold added.

'We had a fabulous party last weekend, when the whole family got together. You wouldn't believe how many were there . . . it really was a wonderful time,' said Mary.

'Then we needed a couple of days' rest to recover, before we joined the ship!' Arnold chuckled.

I shook hands warmly with Arnold and had a hug and a kiss with Mary, and offered my sincere congratulations. I asked them both if they'd join Clive and Iris and myself for a drink, but they'd arranged to meet other friends. We made a date for drinks before dinner that evening, and provisional arrangements for the anniversary celebration the next day, and went our separate ways.

Having enjoyed a very pleasant hour in the Piano Bar, followed by a light lunch in the officers' mess, I was sitting in the Wardroom discussing a couple of the morning's problems with David O'Connel, the other doctor on this occasion, when my bleep went off. 'Please contact the hospital.' I phoned the hospital.

'We've just brought a gentleman down by wheelchair from the restaurant. He collapsed as he was leaving the table,' Sister informed me.

'I'll be right there,' I replied. 'What's his name?'

'Mr Arnold Grant.'

I arrived at the hospital to find Arnold already in a bed on the ward, pale and gasping behind his oxygen mask, the bright gleam gone from his eye. He saw me, and smiled weakly.

'I'm sure we didn't arrange to meet again quite so soon,' he tried to quip in an uncharacteristically small voice. How life revolves and changes in what appears to be the blink of an eye!

I took his hand. 'Don't worry, Arnold,' I said quietly, 'we'll soon have you sorted out.'

He looked up at me sadly, with a greater knowledge than I. Mary sat quietly in the corner, looking anxiously on.

Arnold had had a coronary, not severe, and, at that stage, without complications. Examination and investigations were all carried out, an intravenous line inserted, cardiac monitor attached, treatments commenced, and he was relatively comfortable. I went out to where

Mary was now waiting, to let her know what had happened, what we had done and, principally, what could happen. She listened and absorbed it all.

'Dr Roberts,' she said eventually, 'I hope that you won't mind my saying this to you.'

'Please ask or say whatever you feel, Mary,' I replied.

'As you know,' she continued, 'Arnold is eighty-four. He's had one or two ups and downs with his health, some of them quite serious. He had surgery for bladder tumours three years ago and it's possible that he may have some early secondaries which could cause him problems despite his chemotherapy.' She nodded slowly to herself. 'I suppose, overall, he's what medical people might call a poor risk.'

She placed her hand gently on mine. 'I know that eighty-four is a great age. If he died, you'd be right in saying that he was lucky to have enjoyed such a good life. No doubt we should all be content if we get that far, particularly if we've been fortunate enough to share sixty years with someone we love.' She paused . . . 'Married for sixty years, sixty years!' she reflected. 'He is *all* my life! Even though I realize that we've had more than our fair share of time together, it won't be any easier to lose him. I won't miss him any less. Society and medicine may see him as an old man who has had his time, and can accept his death, but I shall find it very difficult . . . it will hurt me as much, if not more, than if we were still only twenty-one together.'

She paused again, and raised her head; her eyes were glistening with tears.

'All I am trying to say, Dr Roberts, is . . . Please do whatever is possible . . . please do what you can, don't write him off.'

I looked into her tremendously sad and frightened eyes, at the plea that lay deep within them, eyes which such a short while ago had been filled with excitement and happiness when we had met earlier.

'I promise you, Mary,' I replied gently, reassuringly, 'there could never be any question of that. In addition to all the medical considerations, I also consider Arnold to be a very close friend. We'll pull out all the stops, you have my word,' I replied, then added, in an attempt to lighten the situation, 'Plus, we've also got to make tomorrow's celebration!'

Arnold was a terrific man and a terrific patient. The nurses all fell in love with him. He lay uncomplaining and grateful, as we buzzed around him throughout the day. And he improved! By the following morning, his colour was better, his pain controlled, and his breathing easy. Some of the sparkle had returned to his eyes and he was attempting to be his previous chirpy self.

The ward had become an explosion of colour. A profusion of anniversary cards and flowers reflected the love and esteem in which the many friends and family held this delightful couple. The radio room was inundated with telexes of congratulations and good wishes from so many people, as yet unaware of Arnold's present circumstances. The ship's flower shop poured forth bouquets and arrangements from many people on board who wished to say, 'Well done!' and at the same time, 'Keep going, we're all here with you, praying for you.' The hospital became a Mecca of well-wishers and concerned friends who were, of course, not allowed to visit our very unstable patient.

Arnold, however, was well aware of what was going on outside his protected, controlled environment. In the early hours, I sat by his bedside, observing, assessing, deliberating. Arnold, in turn, watched me, assessing my responses – a very tired, but shrewd and wise old man.

'Not too much chance of a wing-ding celebration tonight,' he said to me, with a weak smile. 'You know, Nigel,' he went on, 'I've always lived for the moment, and much more so now. Despite my condition, I'm just honestly pleased to be here today, to have managed to have reached this point, to see the wonderful influence that we've apparently had on people, through our lives. My only sadness is for Mary.'

Mary sat silently, supporting him with her devoted presence, as she had obviously done throughout their sixty years together.

'Happy anniversary, my darling Arnold,' she said quietly, leaning forward and kissing him gently and lovingly on the cheek. An additional shine came to his eyes. Despite the dreadfully mistimed developments, he was obviously very happy, very content.

'Happy anniversary to you both,' I said. 'From all of us. You know that we're all rooting for you.'

'Thank you, Nigel,' Arnold replied genuinely, 'I'm doing the best I can, honest!'

As the morning progressed, his condition became even more stable. This was one of the best anniversary presents! Everyone was delighted.

Julia, the nursing sister, was as usual checking readings, straightening the bed, readjusting his pillows.

'I must say that life has its compensations,' said Arnold to Julia, as she fussed around him.

'What makes you say that?' she asked.

'Well, if I have to be ill, it's most pleasant to have beautiful young ladies like yourself to take care of me,' he replied, winking at his wife.

'You just behave yourself and concentrate on getting better,' said Julia, smiling, 'that's the important thing.'

'Ah, a few years ago,' replied Arnold, winking at his wife again, 'the most important things in life were young women . . . and old port!'

'I'll have you know that I'm not such a youngster, anyhow,' joked Julia, 'I happen to have been qualified for a respectable number of years!'

Arnold paused and considered.

'Young lady,' he said, 'back at home, I have shoes that are older than you!'

As the day progressed, the ward continued to fill with flowers. Mary brought down more anniversary cards to help cheer Arnold up: cards from their children, grandchildren and even great-grandchildren; cards from friends, cards from well-wishers on the ship – they increased by the hour. There were so many people, so many friends that they had made, so many hopes, all wishing him well, all urging him on. Arnold lay surrounded by electronic machinery, tubes and pipes, all enveloped in a burst of colour, of flowers and cards. The day progressed well.

That evening, during dinner, the maitre d' approached the table and whispered discreetly, 'Excuse me, doctor, but you're wanted in the hospital.'

I took leave of my dinner companions and went directly downstairs, where, as I had expected, Arnold was having problems. He was grey and perspiring heavily. His oxygen mask had been reapplied. He looked at me helplessly, apologetically. Mary hovered over him, her smile of relief from a few hours earlier gone. She anxiously clasped his hand, trying to comfort him.

The monitor showed an extension of the coronary and he had developed an arrhythmia – an irregularity of the heartbeat. New medications were required, and the treatment was changed accordingly.

Through the night we sat and watched, adjusting treatment and then readjusting, making a point here and there, but we weren't winning.

Arnold was so appreciative of all the effort. 'Thank you, Sister,' he would whisper, 'you're so good.'

As dawn approached, his life was ebbing. In the dimmed light of the ward, we moved around the bed like shadows. His eyes half opened.

115

'Doctor,' he called, hardly audible through the mask, his voice almost lost in the quiet hiss of the oxygen, the soft whoosh of the water along the side of the ship, and the pulsating background hum. I went to his side. He pushed away his mask and took my hand, pulling me towards him.

'Doctor . . .' he said again, 'Nigel . . .' He coughed, fought to catch his breath. 'Looks like the last voyage, doesn't it?'

I didn't reply.

'We've had some laughs, eh? . . . I can't complain,' he gasped. 'There's only one thing important now.'

'What's that, Arnold?' I asked sadly, knowing his meaning.

'My wife,' he said. 'Take care of her, make sure she's all right, Nigel. She is a very wonderful lady.'

'You have my word,' I promised for the second time in twenty-four hours.

He smiled. Mary sat nearby. I reapplied his oxygen mask, checked his readings, adjusted the monitor, and walked from the ward. I looked back to see Arnold and Mary, in a small pool of light, holding hands; no tears; together, as they had been for sixty years, surrounded by messages of hope and love from all their family and friends.

As the sun rose, Arnold died.

Out there, on the vast ocean, where all of us were such a mere speck in this enormous expanse, eighty-four years had quietly come to a close.

The Professor

Cardiac problems are understandably not uncommon on board ships, principally, as I've said, because of the higher age group amongst the passengers. Some months after Arnold had travelled with us, we were presented with another type of cardiac problem, which, thankfully, we don't have to deal with very frequently.

Again on the *QE2*, we were sailing through the deep waters of the Indian Ocean, on our way from Mombasa to the Red Sea. Outside, the sun was blistering the paint. The ocean was flat and blue. The passengers were cooking in the heat, tanning even deeper, relaxing after their days of activity, and their safaris into the great outdoors of Kenya. Many of them had been to Tsavo game reserve under the distant peaks of Mount Kilimanjaro. Morning surgery was drawing to a close.

Sister called in the final patient, a tall, tanned, relatively healthy-looking English man in his mid-sixties. He was accompanied by his wife, a well dressed, attractive woman. He smiled, shook hands, and introduced himself and his wife. He told me that he was a Professor of Medicine at one of the London hospitals; he was now retired and taking life at a more comfortable pace.

'I'm sorry if I'm going to spoil your day,' he stated with a half smile, the initial introduction over, 'but I'm afraid I have a problem.' He went on to give details of his past medical history and explained that he had a cardiac condition which remained well controlled with treatment, but which, unfortunately, occasionally gave him trouble.

In the past he'd experienced a number of episodes of abnormal heart rhythm which, having failed to respond to certain physical manoeuvres which can be used to correct it, and also to the various forms of drug therapy which are available, eventually required 'cardioversion'. This is a technique whereby a very brief, high voltage electrical current is applied through the heart, via two paddles placed on the chest. This involves the use of electrical equipment which consists of a combination of an oscilloscope – or cardiac monitor – connected by various circuits to a capacitator, which would automatically discharge the electrical current at a precise moment during the pattern of muscle contractions of the heart. The oscilloscope and capacitator are synchronized to deliver the electrical charge – or shock – at this exact, optimum moment of the heart's cycle. If this timing is incorrect, there is a risk that, instead of correcting the rhythm, it may be converted to an even more dangerous, and possibly fatal rhythm, called ventricular fibrillation, or possibly directly to cardiac arrest. By an electrical depolarization of the heart muscle fibres, which needn't be enlarged upon, the heart's rhythm is hopefully corrected and reverts to normal. The abnormal heart rhythm was in itself not lethal, but if left uncorrected would progress to a more sinister rhythm and, ultimately, death.

The problem now was that during the course of the morning, the professor had developed another acute attack. He very calmly continued his dissertation. The casual observer could never have detected that, beneath this remarkably cool exterior, was a man who, unless his condition could be corrected within the ensuing hours, was shortly going to die. His wife, supporting him with her company, was equally aware of her husband's plight.

'I'm presently taking these medications,' he continued, placing a short list on my desk. 'Also,' he added, 'I've been through all of the usual physical manoeuvres to try and revert the rhythm, and so far no luck. I'm very sorry to have to do this to you,' he said, 'but I'm now in your hands.'

I considered the situation.

He spoke again, 'I take it that if medications don't work again this time, you don't have cardioversion equipment on board?' He was referring to the equipment described above.

'I'm afraid you're right,' I confirmed flatly. 'However,' I continued quickly, before the revelation had time to cause even further cardiac stress, 'We do of course have cardiographs, cardiac monitors and defibrillators.' I was referring to a separate capacitator which could administer the shock. 'If we can find a way to synchronize them, we have the equivalent of a cardioversion set. Let's see what the ship's technical folk can come up with,' I said. 'Meanwhile, let's get you to the hospital and see if we can't revert this rhythm with drugs.'

Down in the hospital, the professor was admitted to the ward, and connected to a monitor. Various attempts were then made to revert

118

the rhythm with intravenous medications. There was no response at all. As a result, the situation now, of course, became more grave.

I explained each intended move to the professor and he merely nodded agreement and said, 'Please go ahead, I'm confident that you know what you're doing.' As a professor of medicine, lying there with full knowledge of his condition, his responses and his prognosis, not to turn a hair, must have been extremely difficult, to say the least. No less so for his wife who was totally *au fait* with the situation and the dangers.

'I'm sorry, professor, but it doesn't look as though we're going to get any results,' I eventually had to inform him, with growing apprehension. He exchanged a long look with his wife. No words passed, but they had relayed volumes!

'Let me see what the electricians and radio experts have come up with,' I said, and left them together.

Next door, wires and circuit diagrams covered the room. 'What're the chances, Brian?' I asked.

He looked up slowly and shook his head. My stomach developed a knot. 'We just haven't got the necessary parts,' he said simply.

'Thanks for trying,' I replied.

I returned next door. Four eyes fixed on me.

'Professor . . .' I hesitated. 'No luck, I'm afraid,' I said candidly.

This man and his wife were far too well informed, far too intelligent, for me to hedge the subject, and no doubt they were both increasingly scared.

'Professor,' I said, 'I have to be frank with you. As you know, even if we had the equipment, this would probably be the first cardioversion ever carried out at sea. This isn't what you might describe as my speciality.'

They both nodded, understanding my meaning.

'We have to face the situation. We haven't managed to revert your condition, and we all know that if it continues. . . .' I left the sentence unfinished. I paused; no comment.

'In the circumstances, I'm going to have to attempt cardioversion with the equipment that we have available.'

Still no comment. The monitor in the background, flicking away, showed no change.

'I intend to observe the cardiac monitor, and to administer the shock manually with the defibrillator, and attempt to synchronize the two . . . visually.'

Thankfully, the risk of killing a patient by this procedure isn't enormous, but I would have to try telling myself this as I depressed the defibrillator trigger, and released a massive, jolting shock to a man who, seconds before, would be – to all outward appearances – normal, and chatting with me as now.

The professor didn't require long explanations, he knew what was entailed, the risks, and also, surely, what I was thinking! He considered for only the briefest of moments.

'You must do what you must do, Dr Roberts,' he said, and added, 'You have my complete trust.'

His wife stood by, silently watching, listening.

The professor had told me earlier that his daughter was also a doctor, a specialist in cardiology. I explained to the professor that, before proceeding any further, I would like to speak by phone with their daughter, to advise her of the situation, and allow her to comment.

'I hate to worry her, but of course, go ahead,' was the reply.

A phone call was put through to a home far away across the world in England, within minutes, or even seconds, by satellite communication. The professor's daughter listened intently to what had developed, what had been tried and what was intended. When all was said, I asked if there were any suggestions.

'You appear to have gone through the list,' she replied.

'You're well aware of his present prognosis?' I asked, and added, 'in the circumstances, we can only be winners. What do you feel?'

'Do what you must do,' replied the daughter, in almost exactly her father's words, 'and Dr Roberts . . .'

'Yes?'

'Good luck . . . and God Bless.'

I returned to our patient, paused pensively for a moment.

'OK,' I said, 'let's go to it.'

The professor was transferred to the operating theatre and the monitor reconnected. As it was considered that the high voltage of the defibrillator might also pass along the leads of the monitor at the moment of shock and damage the oscilloscope, a spare monitor was rigged up alongside the first and left unconnected. Emergency drugs and instruments were all set out, the staff hustling around now that we were on the move. Intravenous Valium was drawn up – the patient would have to be sedated, put to sleep, during the procedure. Now that he was settled, I listened again to his chest. *Lubdub, lubdub, lubdub, lubdub, lubdub.* . . . The professor's heart rattled along at twice its normal rate. I checked round – second monitor plugged in, defibrillator charged, all set to go.

I went outside briefly to the waiting room to speak with the professor's wife. She sat erect, quietly reading a magazine, all outwardly composed and calm, with no indication that inside there must have been turmoil; that inside, she was probably screaming, gritting her teeth, and sending out a silent prayer.

'Are you all right?' I enquired.

'Yes, thank you for caring,' she replied.

'We're about to go ahead, only a short time now,' I said.

'Thank you.'

I turned.

'Dr Roberts . . .' she called lightly.

I turned back. She looked at me, about to speak, but didn't.

'He'll be fine,' I promised, inwardly hoping against hope that I was right.

Inside the theatre, the professor lay still, lost in thought. I listened again to the roaring within his chest, *lubdub, lubdub, lubdub, lubdub, lubdub*. . . . His heart was pounding away at over 150 beats a minute. At the normal rate, the heart contracts at around 70 beats per minute, the whole cycle of closure and opening of the four chambers being completed in less than a second. Each phase within the cycle is reflected by a spike or a dip on the graph. At a rate of over 150 beats per minute, there were two and a half of these complete cycles shown on the graph every second! The button must be pressed at a particular *instant*, in *one* of these cycles, a particular spike in one of the patterns. *Lubdub, lubdub, lubdub, lubdub, lubdub*. The monitor appeared to be going at 1000 beats a minute. It was all very well to do this in the comfort and security of a cardiac unit in a teaching hospital. . . . It was not the greatest comfort, either, to know that the shock may possibly work even if not precisely in phase.

'Right, professor, I'm going to put you to sleep for a minute. All ready?'

He smiled a thin smile. He was well aware that, as the Valium surged into his vein, these could well be his final moments of consciousness.

'Dr Roberts,' he said.

'Yes?'

'I have complete confidence in you . . . complete faith.'

He knew very well how much I needed and appreciated these words . . . his support. He smiled again. The plunger of the syringe went slowly down.

Around the room, the staff stood watching – not a movement, not a sound. The professor's eyes closed, his breathing deepened. He drifted into deep sedation. *Lubdub, lubdub, lubdub, lubdub, lubdub, lubdub.* Just as fast, his heart raced along. I watched the monitor.

'Paddles, please,' I asked.

The electrodes of the defibrillator, holding all that enormous charge, were cautiously handed to me. Sister squirted two large patches of conducting jelly onto his chest with a noisy squelch.

Lubdub, lubdub, lubdub, lubdub. I placed the paddles on the chest, rubbing to make good contact. Ready. I watched the monitor, mesmerized. *Lubdub, lubdub, lubdub,* went his heart. *Lub-dub, lub-dub, lub-dub, lub-dub,* went the thump in my own chest.

'Stand clear of the table,' I said unnecessarily to a room full of people already well clear. There was not the slightest sound in the room. Everyone was watching the monitor, watching the button, holding their breath.

Lubdub, lubdub, lubdub, lubdub. The principal upstroke was coming and going so fast, so *fast*! Spike squiggle, spike squiggle, spike squiggle – the patterns were drawn on the screen. Finger on the button, I held my breath . . . Spike, spike, spike, spike, spike. The room was absolutely electric: every eye concentrated, not a breath was taken.

I tried to pick up the rhythm – spike, spike, spike, spike, spike, *watch-for-the-peak, watch-for-the-peak, watch-for-the-peak.* Everyone was still holding their breath, my heart was *pounding*, as I hoped against hope that I wasn't about to kill the man who, seconds ago, had given me his trust. . . .

BANG! I plunged down on the button. The body beneath the paddles leaped into the air with a shudder, back arched, arms and legs rigid, head and neck forced back, for a fraction of a second . . . and then relaxed, to fall limp. With a *zziiip,* the monitor blew.

'Attach the reserve monitor,' I instructed.

I stood back, holding the paddles stationary. A hand moved immediately, removed the plug, and reinserted it directly into the reserve monitor. The atmosphere was like the contained expansion of a dynamite explosion; still not a breath taken. The screen remained blank. *Come on, come on.* The screen flickered, then went blank, flickered again . . . and came to life. *Lub-dub, lub-dub, lub-dub, lub-dub.* . . . A common gasp burst from everyone's lungs, the entire room almost jumped! *Lub-dub, lub-dub, lub-dub.* What a beautiful sight!

'Wey! . . Heeey!' shouted someone, not able to contain the impulse.

After watching the monitor with elation for a while longer, I carefully replaced the paddles.

I called to the patient, 'Andrew . . . Andrew . . . *Andrew.*'

His eyes opened, he stared, unseeing, for a moment, blinked, focused. An enormous smile creased his face.

'All done?' he asked.

You could say that again!

Sometimes, unfortunately, as with poor Arnold, you can't help but lose. Losing always causes a great sadness, a sense of emptiness; but when you win. . . !

Jenny

The morning's work had been pleasant and uneventful. The patients had presented an undramatic cross-section of minor ailments, some of which would have been treatable by the patients themselves if they had been at home, but in present circumstances were interfering with the enjoyment of their dream holiday.

Billie, the nursing sister, who was to be the other half of our team during the crossing, had smiled, charmed and caringly led both the patients and myself through the events of the morning. Tall, trim, eye-catching, with a sparkling personality, Billie gave the patients the warmth and consideration which made them realize that they had become her personal problems. This quality, always so necessary in nursing, is of greater importance when patients are so detached, so far away from their homes, their families and friends, from the doctors they know, and who know them.

Our nursing sisters had been selected for their wide knowledge, their efficiency, their ability to organize, to cope and control. They were the cream of the nursing profession, but as more than one journalist had observed, the fact that they were very easy on the eye was an added bonus.

'How's the waiting room, Billie?' I asked.

'One more lady left, and then coffee, and I'll nip along and check Mrs Patterson who you saw first thing this morning, and make sure that she's settling well.'

A good day so far. That's how I like the first morning, nice and gentle so you get a chance to catch your breath after the last cruise, before you get snowed under with the new batch of problems. And so it had been, skipping lightly along with no worries.

The contagious sparkle of a young child's laughter came from the waiting room, the babbling-brook sound of uninhibited, carefree happiness.

'Another customer, Billie?'

'No, the last lady, Mrs Carlson, has her family with her.'

'Right, well let's have them in.'

'Mrs Carlson, would you like to come in? Yes, there's room for you all.'

I imagine that, as we mature and the experiences of life are absorbed and retained, all mankind must develop certain indescribable senses, the ability to perceive, to recognize a situation or atmosphere, although it hasn't been directly communicated to us. Within the medical profession, there is an increased exposure to the various human emotions of fear, apprehension, pain, sorrow, happiness, relief, mourning. There is also a need to establish a contact, a relationship of understanding and trust, within a very short time from having met a new patient. All these factors enhance the ability of unspoken communication, part of our sixth sense.

A young, impish boy skipped into the room with mischief and laughter in his eyes, but quiet and well behaved. Mrs Carlson followed him in. The lightness, the gaiety, the simplicity of the morning changed abruptly. A beautiful young woman, a mother, had entered, carrying in her arms a baby, held closely to her, protectively, with care, love and pride. She was dressed simply, inexpensively, was neat and clean. She entered with an attempted air of informality, a pretty smile on her small, flushed face . . . and tragedy deep in her eyes.

Suddenly the little room, close and quiet, with only the hum of the air-conditioning and the gentle vibration of the engines far below, was quieter, sadder. There was a short pause, while she stood politely waiting, whilst sister and myself simultaneously tried to read the situation. Billie stepped forward, touched her arm; it registered, there was a response, an understanding.

'Here's a seat, Mrs Carlson, and you can make yourself comfortable here, Mr Carlson,' directed Billie to the husband, who had followed his wife into the room. The child stood awkwardly; his parents seemed concerned by his presence. It was necessary to put him at ease first.

'What's your name, young man?'

'Peter.'

'Well, come and say hello, Peter.'

'Hello, doctor,' he said simply, with a big smile on his impish face.

'So, how old are you then, Peter. I bet you're pretty grown up.'

'Three, and a bit!'

'Shall we get nurse to find you a car or a train? Yes? OK, let's get

125

you on a stool over there, shall we, and you can play quietly, while I talk to your mummy.'

Mrs Carlson sat quietly, smiling, almost cooing, looking on at her lovely little boy, and holding her treasure.

'You OK, Mrs Carlson?'

'Yes thanks.'

'And you, Mr Carlson?'

'Fine, thank you.'

'Would one of you like to tell me the problem?'

Mr Carlson spoke. 'Let me give you the background, doctor . . . it's my wife who has the problem.'

'Yes, I gathered that.'

Mr Carlson was a stocky, athletic, mid-sized man. He had a good, honest face, with character, a full head of dark black hair, and sharp eyes. He was a strong-looking man, but seemed gentle, soothing. His hand touched his wife's chair, her hair, he found her hand and held it. Their eyes met. He swallowed, gave a nervous cough, cleared his throat.

'We have a letter from Jenny's doctor back in Virginia, with her medical details, but perhaps I can give you the full history.' He spoke with a soft Welsh accent; South Wales, I'd say, rugby player, a prop, probably.

'No rush at all, Mr Carlson. Your lad's happy over there, and the baby's sleeping. I'm in no hurry.' He smiled, and the tension eased.

'Well, we both come from near Cardiff, see. Moved to America six years ago. There wasn't any work for me in Cardiff. We'd just got married, and out of the blue I was made redundant – great timing, eh? Both our families still live in South Wales. Well, we'd saved some cash before we married, and a mate of mine, who lived in Virginia, had started a bit of business for himself, and he wanted me to join him. Jenny was twenty-one and I was twenty-three. Well, it was a hard decision you know, we're both from a small village, and our families have always been very close. We grew up together, I've known Jenny as long as I can remember. Thought she was a horrible little brat when she was a young 'un, until about sixteen, then we found we liked each other, you know.'

Jenny smiled, a happy smile, the sadness disappeared for a while. He smiled back, clenched his teeth and set his jaw. He squeezed her hand again.

'Nobody in the family ever left the area before; well, maybe to mid-Wales, but never far away from the family, see. Anyway, everyone says we should try it, despite not wanting us to go. We got the business going, only small, you know, car repair. No fortunes, but it's given us a nice little home.'

Jenny nodded, her eyes distant, reflecting, thinking no doubt of the home which they had created together.

'We've been happy there, very happy, except. . . .' He faltered, his brow furrowed, the words were gone.

Jenny took over: 'When the business got going and we settled in, we decided it was time to start a family. Well, we did . . . and there he is.' She beamed, radiating love towards her child in the corner, playing happily, unaware, and unheeding of the conversation. 'God has been good to me, hasn't he, doctor?' she sighed, 'God has been good to me.'

She paused and reflected.

'The trouble was, it wasn't a good pregnancy for me. I'm still not sure of the medical names you know, and I can't grasp the full details, but . . .' she took a long deep breath, 'but, the baby inside me, and the swelling, and the water, you know, and . . . whatever.' She paused, faltered, obviously distressed. 'Well, apparently it put some strain on my heart, it couldn't cope, and somehow the pregnancy damaged my heart, and although it wasn't too bad, it was permanent. Well, we were both all right, Peter and me, after a while, but the obstetrician said that was it, no more children, got to play it safe. There could be more problems, and worse, next time.'

She held her baby close, tightly, ran her fingers over her face, held the tiny hands. She looked quietly down at her as she slept. The picture was dramatically painted, the full story told by this scene across the desk.

She continued. 'After a couple of years I felt fine, see? The doctors used to examine me regularly, and told me how my heart was, not good, but not really bad either, see? We both loved Peter so much, he gave us so much happiness, and he brought us even closer together.'

She paused again, reflecting once more, reconsidering all those decisions and discussions which they must both have had, over and over.

'We hadn't any other family in America. Everyone was at home, and we hadn't seen them since leaving. We were our own family, and we really, really wanted another baby, see? If it could be even half as beautiful as our Peter, and that would be it then, no more after that! But we'd be a unit then, wouldn't we? We both come from large families, and the idea of a single child was really hard to accept.' She was pouring out all their reasonings, their pros and cons, reliving and reconvincing, for my benefit, but mainly for their own. I didn't interrupt. Billie sat in the corner with Peter, listening from a distance.

'Colin didn't want me to take the risk, although it didn't seem much of a risk then, because I was doing fine, wasn't I? Or so we thought . . I thought. You know, doctor, you don't seem to allow yourself to accept what is painful or distasteful if it doesn't fit your life, even when you know that the specialists must know better, you know what I mean, doctor? And they didn't insist, they only advised . . . yes, strongly advised, I admit. This wonderful little addition to our lives is everything we dreamed of. She's healthy, she's beautiful, and she's a little girl! Don't you think that's wonderful?'

'I was wrong!' Mr Carlson suddenly interrupted emotionally.

'No, darling, we've been over and over this, we made our decisions together, out of love,' she replied, gently. 'You can guess of course, doctor, that there had to be a price to pay . . . well, there was!'

The tragedy was back in her eyes, her smile faded, she held her baby closer, if that could be possible. Her husband's head hung down, his shoulders sagged, his strong athletic frame now looked frail. He gave a short sharp intake of breath, nearly a sob. Peter looked around abruptly, puzzlement suddenly in his eyes. His father coughed quickly to cover his emotion, braced himself, placed a loving arm around his wife's shoulder. Peter, his world appearing normal, went back to his toys. We were all quiet. The ship's noises carried on, accompanied by creaks and vibration rattles, and Peter's chuckling as he played with an action man.

'How bad is the damage now, Mrs Carlson?' I asked, softly.

They both paused, neither wanting to put the answer into words.

'It's very bad, doctor . . . There's been a lot of damage. My heart is just being kept going with drugs and I could . . . something might happen, at any time . . . any time.'

Silence.

'I must get home, doctor, I must get home!' Mrs Carlson blurted out desperately.

'We have to get back to the family,' Mr Carlson added.

Mrs Carlson spoke again, urgently now. 'I *must* see them all, my Mam, my Dad, everyone. They're all waiting, they all know, my sisters and brothers. They must see us. We haven't seen them since we left. There's nephews and nieces that we've never seen, and they haven't seen our two, either. I have to get home, I have to!' Her sentences were rushing out in a torrent now, explaining, pleading, to someone higher than all of us. 'We haven't got the money really, but we sold the car. I must see them, my Mam, my Dad, they're waiting . . . Oh, dear!'

There was panic in her voice. Her quiet composure was breaking. The control, which she had maintained so well, was in danger. It was also reflected in her husband's eyes as a desperate concern for his wife. What they had been trying not to say, trying not to believe, was nearly in the open, there in his eyes, in his expression, his disbelief, his desperation. His beautiful wife . . . NO!

To be able to reach out, across the abyss, and touch such a patient as this is an art which cannot be taught. This isn't, and can never be, in the books. This capacity must come from the person within the doctor. It entails giving a part of yourself, after which you are invariably left with a vacuum, and weariness. The art of medicine is distinct from the science. Now is not the time for medicines, but for understanding, for tenderness, compassion and warmth. Both man and wife cried out for a reprieve, a reversal, or even a delay of sentence, but both knew that this could not be; although, on the surface, they chose to ignore it.

The consultation was, of course, on the instructions of Mrs Carlson's own doctors, to inform us on board of her condition, and the possibilities of what could develop. Her medical notes, investigation results and cardiographs gave all the details, and told the same tragic story. Underlined throughout the report was the fact that their basic fear, that the inevitable could literally occur any day, was very much a dramatic possibility!

There were five days to go, . . . to England, to Wales, to home.

Her history and records having been studied and absorbed, I examined her pale white, frail white, china white chest.

'There wasn't much money left over for clothes,' she half joked, as she pointed out a repair to her underskirt, the neat, trim handiwork performed with as much care as she had spent making her babies' clothes. 'Still, it would be silly to buy new clothes in the circumstances . . .' She stopped herself short, and glanced quickly, apologetically, at her husband.

Both her history and the medical records had prepared me for the tragic findings of the examination, but this could not diminish the great sadness of listening to the damaged heart of this lovely woman, this loving wife and mother. There was no need for change or adjustment of medications, her condition was exactly as described, and was being maintained as best as modern medicines could achieve.

All was complete, the visit over. We had made contact and learned all the facts. They were aware of us and our capabilities – where we were, who we were, how to reach us. Arrangements were made to keep a close eye on the situation throughout the voyage, and we rounded off the morning in a far different mood to the start; sadder, wiser, wearier.

As the day wore on, the weather and sea became unsettled. The ship started to dig into a typical, late-season North Atlantic crossing. By this stage most passengers had their sea legs, but the occasional land lubber was arriving in the hospital pale and perspiring, lining up for their miracle cure, jovially referred to, by our American friends, as 'a shot in the ass'. My thoughts, which hadn't been far from Mrs Carlson, became concern. If the weather was too rough, could she cope? If she became ill, it could upset her entire medical balance, which was precarious at best.

I went down to their cabin, on the lower decks, to check. I tapped lightly on the door to avoid possibly disturbing the baby. The door flew open, Mrs Carlson stood there with a worried expression, and for a brief moment I became alarmed.

'I called to check that you were OK,' I said with concern.

Her expression changed, she smiled, chuckled and then laughed, 'I'm fine, but look at this!' She stood back from the door. There on the bed lay Colin, looking more than a little sorry for himself.

'Fair weather sailor,' she said, and laughed again. She stepped across and stroked his hair and brow. 'Peter's having a great time in the nursery, and the baby's asleep. This is our present problem!'

I was more than relieved. Colin's problem was easily cured. I left them in their reversed roles of patient and nurse.

The following day was settled. Billie called in on our number-one patient and spent a happier half hour chatting together with her. We were one day nearer home, and they were both responding by the minute. Having checked her readings, they were found to be unaltered. Unknown to the Carlsons, we advised the cabin stewards and stewardesses that there was a problem. Although details couldn't, of course, be given, they realized the degree of concern, and life was made easier and more comfortable for the family.

That evening was the night of the captain's cocktail party. With a little coaxing, Jenny had been persuaded to make up, dress up, and go quietly to the party, entering through the back door to avoid line-ups. Peter and the baby were in the care of a children's nanny, and both were comfortable and settled. It was a pleasant opportunity for Colin and Jenny to relax and enjoy an evening together. I saw them sitting in the corner, watching the activity, enjoying the atmosphere.

'My word! What a romantic, good-looking couple we've got here!' I quipped.

Both smiled, holding hands. 'Will you join us?'

'You bet. This is one of the nicer moments of my job! You really do look good, both of you.' Again she was dressed simply, inexpensively, but very attractively, and there was an air about them both that looked and felt good. They were sharing a moment, and it showed, and that moment was happy.

Later in the evening, after dinner, I noticed them again sitting quietly, this time in the dark, just as close, still touching, and watching the show. She was laughing at the comedian. She caught her breath, coughed lightly and then suddenly developed a coughing spasm. I started forward. She settled . . . and was all right again. She clapped along with the singer, and tapped her feet to the dancers and music. I watched from where I sat, enthralled by the whole situation.

At the end of the show, they caught my eye. I crossed over and sat for a while, chatting as before about her children and family.

'I reckon that's the liveliest night I've had in a long time,' she said finally, and getting up slowly, she added, 'You'll excuse us if we leave. I'm afraid I'm rather tired.'

'Of course. Are you all right?'

'Yes, yes. Thank you.'

As they left, she turned and laid her hand on my arm. The lights were low, her eyes shaded but shining. She paused, looked into my eyes. She had a tremendous depth, another knowledge. 'Thank you,' she said, quietly, simply, and then they left.

The third morning at sea, the ship was mid-voyage and mid-Atlantic, a long, long way from land, and even further from anywhere of consequence. This is the period of maximum isolation. Of all the times when the ship is on its own, this is the Daddy. There is absolutely no back-up, and except in extreme exceptions, no support.

So, we were alone. Whatever occurred now would have to be handled by our own facilities and personnel.

Towards the end of the morning, Billie approached with a troubled look, an air of concern.

'I've just been with Mrs Carlson. I'm sure she's not doing so well today, but her husband says she's fine, not to worry and not to bother you. I think you should see her fairly soon.'

'No time like the present, Billie,' I replied. 'Let's go and see.'

Mrs Carlson was lying in bed, her breathing shallow and laboured, her face pale, with a dusky blue around her lips. Her eyes had lost their sparkle, and her hands lay limp and cool by her sides.

'How long has she been like this?' I asked her husband.

'There's no problem, she's OK, just tired, that's all,' he replied. 'Don't worry, doctor, she'll be fine, I know, you'll see.'

'How long, Jenny?' I repeated.

'About four hours . . . I woke up pretty breathless, doctor, and it's getting worse. I've started coughing bad, and my chest feels tight. It's hard to get my breath.'

Examination confirmed the impression that she was developing congestive heart failure, and was deteriorating.

'We're going to get you along to the hospital, Jenny, just to check things out and adjust your treatment; we can keep an eye on you better down there. Don't worry, we'll soon have you right,' I said, trying not to alarm her.

'Oh no, let me stay here with the children, don't take me away from Colin and the children, please don't separate us,' she pleaded.

'Jenny, we need to correct what's going on, otherwise you could be in trouble. I need to keep you under supervision in the hospital,' I had to inform her.

'Doctor, just a minute. You know, and I know. I don't have that much time left with my family. Don't separate us!'

'I understand, Jenny; but I must do the best we can for the moment. They can all visit you in hospital, and I'll get you back here as soon as I can.'

She was moved as quickly as possible.

'Where's mommy going?' Peter kept repeating. The baby cried and cried, Colin stood and sat, sat and walked, dazed, unsure, lost.

'We've got to get home,' he said. 'They're all waiting. She's got to get home, to her family, you know!'

In the hospital, the staff buzzed. Cardiographs were run, a monitor attached, blood taken, oxygen masks, needles, vials, syringes, medicines, more graphs, more checks, everyone working, watching, hoping. No response. We tried again – nothing.

After a short while, though, she began to feel better. Once the medicines had started to work, the results were rapid and effective. Glances were exchanged between the sisters, tentative smiles across the room. The atmosphere of controlled, rapid efficiency, slowed down, the anxieties eased. Her breathing improved, her colour returned, her whole appearance changed. This battle was being won!

132

Jenny steadily improved through the day: a weary smile returned, the dull limpid haze went from her eyes, the panic from her voice.

'Doctor, can I talk with you?'

'Of course.'

'I know that you were concerned that Colin hadn't contacted you this morning, but let me explain.'

'I'm sure I already know why.'

'Very likely you do. You know then, that despite his having to accept all that's happened, all that we've been told, he finds it almost impossible to realize that . . . he's going to . . . lose me.' She hesitated. 'I do too, sometimes . . . To lose him and my babies, oh God, it hurts so much! And to lose my mam and dad, and the family, and I haven't even got home yet. . . . Oh dear, doctor. Oh dear!' she blurted out. She paused a while, to collect herself.

'Well, I'm sure that subconsciously he has a block, it frightens him so much. He closes down and won't accept what's happening at times. This morning we were scared, so scared. . . . Oh God, it does frighten me so! Then he pretends, you see, but he doesn't know it. He thinks everything's all right, that there's no problem. He wishes it that way, you see. Don't blame him, doctor, it's so very hard for him!'

This very lovely lady, so unselfish, was offering reasons for her husband's reactions.

'I don't blame him in the least, not at all,' I assured her. 'Now, we must get you some rest.'

'Can I go to my cabin?' she asked.

'Soon, you're doing very well, let's not spoil it! Perhaps in the morning, all right?'

'Can I see the children?'

She held her baby in her arms, her eyes closed, head back on the pillow, her husband and sleepy son close around her. So many thoughts she must have had, so much sorrow. She hummed a gentle lullaby. She opened her eyes, and slowly looked up.

'Doctor.'

'Yes?'

'You'll get us home, won't you? They're waiting, you know, I've got to get there, I'm going to see them!'

'You bet!'

The next morning was bright and calm. The ship surged forward at a great pace, the current behind us. The bow-wave was hissing, frothing, dancing in the clear brisk morning air. We were making good time.

The mood in the hospital was light. All had remained well through the night. Two other patients, admitted the previous day, were also doing well.

Jenny sat in bed knitting.

'What's that going to be?' I asked.

'A coat for little Ann. Like it?' She held it up. The sparkle had returned, the determination.

'Look's more like a glove to me!'

'If you think that's small, what about these boots?'

'Boots? Thimbles more like,' I replied, happy with the lightness of the occasion. 'Let's see how you are, see if we can't get you out of here.'

'Doctor,' said Jenny, in a conspiratorial whisper. 'One and a half more days, eh?' She gave an excited giggle, like a school-girl, her worries gone for the moment. 'Then home!'

'Yep, we'll soon be in England.'

'You know, don't you, doctor, that if you don't let me back to my cabin, I'll sign myself out, and I'd rather not. You know what I'm saying?'

'Well, you're not good, but you're no worse than when you came on board, and you're as stable as we can hope to get . . . Family, here we come.'

She was settled into her cabin, with the stewardess buzzing around. Billie had set up a mini-hospital; her husband and children were in close reach.

The day passed uneventfully, Billie chatting socially and keeping a woman's eye on the family, helping with the feeding, and tidying odds and ends ready for packing the next day. We were nearing home and the excitement was obviously growing. The chatter was louder. There was more talk of Wales and old times and the reunion to come. I called in throughout the afternoon and evening, partially as a controller and dampener of the increasing activity. To everyone's relief, the evening and night passed uneventfully.

Daylight broke on an excited family; it was the last day of the journey. As the morning passed, we travelled south of England and headed towards Cherbourg. There would be a short call in France, mainly to disembark the European travellers, and then a quick trip across the Channel, and home!

I made a brief visit to Jenny, to see if all was well, and to make sure that nothing was going wrong while we had the facilities of the port at hand. There were no problems. To add to the excitement, a message had been delivered to the ship – Jenny's parents and her

134

brother would be meeting the ship in Southampton on arrival. They were overjoyed! Jenny fussed and laughed, and tears of happiness were close. What a strange experience it was, an incredible mixture of happiness and sadness.

The ship's brief visit to France had come and gone. We had a smooth ride out of the harbour and back into the gentle roll of the Channel. The paper work was being wound up, reference letters written. Patients were advised, loose ends tied up.

Another transatlantic voyage was coming to an end, with all its problems and challenges.

Two hours out of Cherbourg, I was sitting in my cabin writing when the telephone rang. Breathlessly, a steward's voice started to speak: 'Mrs Carlson. . . .' I dropped the phone and ran; the urgency in the voice was message enough.

'No! *No!*' I was gasping, '*No!*' Not even fate could be that callous, that unfeeling, that cruel!

The cabin door was partly open. I rushed in, stopped abruptly, and was overwhelmed, shocked to a standstill by the atmosphere. Billie arrived almost abreast of me, and also stood breathless, staring.

Mr Carlson sat on the floor, his back propped between the corner of the bed and the dresser, one leg bent up to his chest, his other out straight. Jenny, stretched full length across the floor, nestled in his lap, her head fallen to one side, resting, peaceful, uncaring. No more fear, no more excitement, no more tears. . . . Dead. Cruelly, wrongly undeservedly *dead*, her life all gone, her hopes all gone.

I knelt over her. Her dress was pulled back. She wore again her underskirt with the sewing which had embarrassed her, and which now meant so little. Her shoes were missing, her frail, pale chest was bare and still. She held in her hand the unfinished baby's coat; a trail of wool passed over her still body and under the bed. Her other arm was stretched out, her hand caught against the baby's cot. Her beautiful baby, to whom she had given not only life and love, but the sacrifice of her own life.

Colin sat unseeing, caressing her lifeless cheek.

'She'll be all right, she'll be all right, don't worry. I've tried to give her her tablets but she won't swallow them. I keep asking her why she won't, but she won't listen, she won't take her medicine. But I'm sure she'll be all right, don't worry.'

The scene was devastating.

In the room next door, Peter was playing, oblivious to his mother's plight. He had unknowingly become a motherless child, and his

135

innocent chuckling laughter rang through the wall, while his mother lay, sprawled awkwardly across the floor. Billie leaned down and took up the baby. She held her on her shoulder. She held her tight, very tight. She looked down at the beautiful mother, whose joys, sorrows and hope she had shared, and turned and walked past me to the door. She paused; she was silent, tried to speak, but didn't. Great tears welled up in her eyes, spilling, and rolling down her cheeks, onto the baby. I was swallowing hard. Rarely had a patient meant so much to me, or a moment been so emotionally charged.

I stood at the porthole, striving for control. There in the distance were the dancing, twinkling lights of England, and Wales beyond, and home.

I recalled what she had said to me on our first meeting, as she lovingly held and surveyed her beautiful family.

'God has been good to me, hasn't he, doctor? God has been good to me.'

I tried to breathe deeply again. I swallowed hard, but it was no use.

Fiona

Sitting comfortably in the surgeon's lounge of a fully equipped city hospital, secure in the knowledge that you're surrounded by the most up-to-date facilities available in the surgical world, that you're within easy reach of the best back-up support units that can be assembled, and that you have a full complement of highly trained staff to work alongside and around you, is a very reassuring environment in which all surgeons should ideally be able to work. Unfortunately, this is by no means always the case. Even allowing for the less fortunate areas of the world, or the more remote regions, there are still many areas within the so-called advanced countries where the medical facilities or expertise leave much to be desired. Understandably you are much less likely to be able to expect these standards on board a ship out at sea. Not for the average ship's doctor even the basic comfort of being a specialist in the subject in the first instance; it is merely one of his many roles.

Having examined a patient and decided to operate, the ship's surgeon cannot enjoy the luxury of phoning the laboratory for a technician to visit the ward and carry out all the necessary investigations, which include blood grouping, cross-matching and delivery of the required number of units of blood for transfusion. Nor is he able to casually advise the operating theatre sister to prepare for a surgical case in half an hour's time, nor even to contact the nursing staff to prepare the patient, or phone the anaesthetist to organize the anaesthetic. Even if these facilities were all less than perfect, it would be great to have them on board and available if necessary.

As I've previously discussed, surgery at sea on a large ship such as *QE2* affords the luxury of two doctors to share the task, but on a smaller ship, carrying only one doctor – you're everything.

Given less than an average degree of good luck, should the lone doctor on a smaller ship be faced with a surgical emergency, the chances are that there'll be at least one doctor amongst the passengers who will step forward and volunteer to share the load. Principally, he would be able to handle the anaesthetic, whilst the ship's surgeon got on with the surgery – or vice-versa if the volunteer should be a surgical specialist. However, what if the odd occasion should present itself when there are no other doctors on board at all, and the ship's surgeon is out there on his own?

Back in my early days at sea, sailing again in the Pacific Ocean out from California, we were on a long sunshine cruise down to New Zealand and Australia, via Hawaii and the South Pacific Islands. Being one of the smaller vessels, there was only one doctor assigned to the ship, but on this trip we had two nursing sisters. There were around eight hundred passengers on board and fortunately we hadn't been excessively busy, which allowed time to enjoy the beautiful weather to which the Pacific Ocean was treating us.

The sea was calm and smooth, sparkling brilliantly in the dazzling sun which was sitting almost directly overhead, beating down on the wooden decking and the passengers sitting and lying around the pool. The decks were cooled by a gentle flow of air as the ship surged onwards. At moments like these, detached from the intensity of modern living, away from the frustrations and pressures of the city-dweller, and the anxieties and drama of world affairs, life takes on a relaxed, almost glowing contentedness. It is pure escapism.

I stood at the rail, way out at the head of the ship. The wind dashed against me, roaring in my ears, catching my breath – invigorating. I gazed out over the vast emptiness of the ocean, wondering how many hundreds, perhaps thousands of miles there were between our minute presence and land in every direction. Which continent or countries lay to east and west? How far away was land directly ahead. It's a strange sensation to be so remote, contained in a unit so completely independent, with all the comforts of modern life, alone, unseen, unheard by the entire world.

Down below me, the bow was slicing through the calm waters. The sharp cutting edge of the ship cleaved the still, deep blue, sending a clear flowing rush of water back along the curving steel on either side to curl over and smash into a rolling, sparkling, noisy froth of vivid white, which whipped off down the side of the ship, spreading out and out, off to distant, unknown horizons. And there, just a few yards out from the bow, the calm surface suddenly broke into a multitude of splashes as a cascade of flying fish dashed out over the water in their escape from the onrushing giant. With 'wings' outstretched they took off across the mirrored sea in arrow-straight

138

flight over its surface, only to splash back again into its enveloping safety in the distance. Another two, a few more, and then an entire shoal burst from just below the surface in unison.

I stood for ages gazing, meditating, dwelling on the depths beneath us: all the mountains and crevices, the millions of never-to-be-seen corners of the world, the shadows and life passing below, plankton and whales, debris and monsters.

Suddenly, I saw a grey shadow below the surface, streaking, streaking, keeping dead ahead of us, hardly shifting, as though locked to the bow. The form swerved, rose, and came clean and sharp from the water, like a missile, in a long curving arc of silver grey. With the smallest of splashes, pointed nose first, it zoomed back into the water and onwards again . . . a dolphin. One of the most spectacular sights on the ocean you might ever be lucky enough to witness. As I watched, others appeared all around, a whole school: blurred grey shadows sizzling through the water, exploding out intermittently, leaping high into the air, turning, spinning, falling. Now they were playing with us, as though overjoyed to see a long lost friend. There, in the surge of water cascading back from the bow, two were sporting – dipping and swerving in the rush almost without visible movement, matching the ship's speed of over 20 knots; on and on and on, gambolling, leaping, playing. Who can ever know why?

I can't recall how long I stayed. As on many previous occasions, time stood still. It was a superb show – one of nature's circuses.

Eventually I left the deck and wandered inside. Strolling down the corridor towards my cabin, I saw the duty sister approaching.

'Just coming to find you,' she called.

'Problems?' I asked.

'There's a Mr Chester, who called in at the hospital. His daughter isn't well and he'd like you to make a cabin visit.'

The spell was broken; the daydream of the dolphins' world receded into the distance.

I collected my bag and went to the cabin. Inside, Mr and Mrs Chester, a young American couple, were patiently waiting. Tucked up in bed was their daughter.

'Hello young lady, what's your name?' I asked.

'Fiona,' she replied, quietly.

'And how old are you, Fiona?'

'Eight,' she whispered. One word answers, no more.

Sitting on the edge of the bed, I brushed the hair from her eyes and asked, 'So tell me, Fiona, what's a pretty little girl like you doing in bed when it's a lovely day outside?'

139

'My tummy hurts!' she complained, in a little voice, and with a genuine expression of pain. I chatted for a while with Fiona and her parents who, at this stage, weren't overly concerned but, being sensible and caring, thought it wise to get an opinion. Fiona was apparently a very lively little girl. On the previous day she had been as bright as a button, but this morning she had woken up a little out of sorts.

'She didn't want to eat breakfast,' Mr Chester told me, 'she felt a bit nauseated, but she hasn't vomited.'

'Later she said she developed a tummy-ache,' his wife continued.

'Did she eat anything unusual for dinner last night?' I asked.

Mrs Chester considered a moment. 'No, nothing unusual, she had some crab cocktail,' she said.

I examined Fiona. There was very little to find. Her temperature was normal, her abdomen soft, no tenderness, and the remainder of her basic signs were OK. I discussed the situation with her parents, and advised them of the various possibilities. These included a mild gastritis or possibly an early gastro-enteritis. At this point it would have been unfair to worry them unnecessarily with the possibility of other, more serious diagnoses at the back of my mind.

'What I'd like to do,' I explained, 'is treat her conservatively for the moment. I always prefer to play it safe with children, so just to be ahead of any developments, I'd like to take her along to the hospital, where we can keep an eye on her for a few hours this afternoon. Of course you can both come along as well.'

Ten minutes later, Fiona was settled in the hospital under the watchful eyes of the nursing sisters.

Having settled our patient, there was time for a little light-hearted entertainment. During the afternoon the ship was due to pass from the Northern into the Southern Hemisphere, thus crossing the equator and giving cause for the time-honoured ship-board ritual of the 'crossing-the-line' ceremony.

'While Fiona's resting, why don't you catch the ceremony,' I said to the Chesters. 'It's good fun if you've never seen it before. It only takes half an hour and it will be a good distraction for you both.'

'You go ahead,' Mrs Chester directed her husband. 'I'll be happier sitting here.'

Later, looking down from an upper deck, I watched Mr Chester laughing in the sunshine. King Neptune, wielding a trident and dressed in traditional gaudy regalia, his seaweed tresses topped with a crown, held court accompanied by his entourage, which included his 'wife' and a trio of lovely dance girls, each with a shimmering mermaid's tail. The traditional 'village-drunk' fell around the deck hovering precariously over the pool as he teetered back and forth, and was being beaten over the head by the enormous sorbo rubber truncheon of the equally traditional large, flat-footed 'bobby'. The crowds fell around laughing at their antics.

Now the offenders, or victims, were paraded. Anyone crossing the line for the first time should theoretically be put through 'Neptune's Baptism'. However, due to large numbers and the fragility of the older passengers, this isn't considered a very advisable or practical ploy! Therefore, a handful of volunteer passengers are given an 'extra special' dousing to compensate. The offenders who have entered Neptune's domain and never crossed into the other half of his realm before are presented, prosecuted and sentenced. The sentence is to be lain upon a table, covered with a sheet, lathered, shaved, and have their innards removed! They are then hurled into the pool for the baptism.

For the 'surgical' part of the ceremony, the ship's doctor and nurse traditionally join the team. Dressed in operating gear and wielding enormous, frightening, bogus wooden instruments, the surgical team prepare the patients by slopping huge dollops of creamy foam all over them. They are then 'shaved' with a three-foot cut-throat razor. With a tremendous flurry and fanfare, the surgeon and nurse dive beneath the sheet and, amidst a heaving leaping commotion, proceed to withdraw strings of sausages, old kippers, lumps of cow's liver, tomato ketchup, and anything else revolting enough to turn the onlookers' stomachs. Having been stripped of their 'vital organs', the victims are then tipped from the table into the pool, and the team is all ready for the next!

Today, as I unfortunately had a patient down below under observation, someone had stepped in to take my place at the last minute, and here I stood as a spectator. The audience loved the slapstick, and cheered and applauded.

'Take out his kidneys!'

'Out with his liver!' they shouted.

Amidst flying offal and squelching cream, the surgical procedures drew to a close, and pandemonium broke loose! As you can imagine, none of the participants – including Neptune in all his finery – were missed out in the orgy of cream pie-throwing and ducking. The audience was delighted.

Meanwhile, six decks below, away from the boisterous laughter, the sparkle and cheers of Neptune's court, in a silent, darkened ward a sad little girl lay quietly, her condition . . . worse!

I had slipped away from the festivities after a short stay, and stood again beside Fiona's bed. An hour after her admission, she now had an elevated temperature, had vomited, and her abdominal pains persisted. More particularly, on examination of her abdomen she appeared to have some early tenderness in the right iliac fossa – the location of her appendix. In addition to the discomfort in Fiona's abdomen, it was of no help whatsoever that the new developments were causing a somewhat similar reaction in my own.

We were now at our maximum distance from land: medically, our period of greatest vulnerability. Here we were, in the centre of an expanse of ocean so vast that the mind finds it difficult to grasp, faced with the possibility of an acute surgical emergency. Hopefully I was wrong! I took Mr and Mrs Chester to my office, and calmly acquainted them with the facts. They sat quietly, and absorbed every word.

Even in the ten years since this incident, the advent of modern medicines and therapy has resulted in a tremendous development, in that an appendicitis which is detected as early as Fiona's, can, in many cases, be treated medically with intravenous agents, so avoiding the necessity for emergency surgery. On board ships, we frequently find that emergency surgical problems present in the very early stages, and are consequently diagnosed sooner, giving a far better chance of response to non-surgical procedures. As you may well guess, at the time of Fiona's problem these more recent forms of therapy were not established. However, other medical approaches could be tried, and the sooner they were started the better.

The basic rule at sea is: don't operate unless it is absolutely necessary, especially so far from back-up facilities and with only one doctor. I explained the situation to the Chesters. It was still very early to diagnose Fiona's condition; it was by no means certain that she was developing an appendicitis. In our circumstances, out here at sea, however, it would be very foolish not to assume the worst and wait until the signs were more positive. By this time, the likelihood of a response to medical treatment would almost certainly be lost. There were indeed some risks to the conservative treatment, but these had to be weighed in conjunction with the overall picture. The Chesters considered the facts, they considered their beautiful little girl, and accepted my recommendations.

Fiona was a remarkable child. In her discomfort she listened patiently as I sat on the edge of her bed, holding her hand, and explaining what we were going to do. I know, and have treated, many adults who would not have been so brave. A naso-gastric tube was inserted

142

into her nose, and she was urged to swallow by the nursing sister, as, with great gulps, the tube passed down to her stomach.

'That's it, Fiona, it's there,' I assured her, comforting her.

'Ppheeeww!' she gasped after a small gagging episode, and beads of perspiration broke on her pale brow. She took a deep breath, leaned back, and smiled weakly.

'I'm sorry, Fiona, but we have to get on with the next step now,' I apologized to her.

'That's all right, doctor.'

I was deeply touched by the calmness, understanding and co-operation of so young a child.

'You'll feel a needle prick, and a little pain in your arm, but it won't last long,' I promised.

She gritted her teeth and looked away towards Sister, who was holding her other hand, and wiping her moist forehead. The intravenous catheter slipped in as easy as a wink. She hadn't moved a fraction or made the smallest whimper. Before connecting the infusion, I withdrew a sample of blood and handed it to Sister to place in a specimen bottle for grouping and cross-matching, and a blood count. The infusion was connected, and her treatment was under way.

'All over!' I said, and was given another half smile. 'Now, you just get comfortable and rest for a while,' I told her. 'Let's see if we can make you better!'

'I'd certainly like that!' she replied, with a little sigh. The lights were dimmed, and with her nose peeping above the sheets, she closed her eyes.

Up on deck, two young boys were re-enacting the afternoon's surgical pantomime. With a technique as slick and easy as pie, they pulled out make believe kidneys, liver, intestines, . . . and possibly an appendix! Life surely is a cabaret! I paused and considered, and dearly wished that it were that easy.

Now the preparations commenced. If the conservative treatment didn't succeed, if the child progressed on to a full-blown appendicitis, we had to be prepared to act. A meeting was held with the two nursing sisters, and plans were drawn up. The first priority was to locate another doctor on the ship to act as anaesthetist, if it should become necessary. I phoned the bureau.

'Would you be good enough to scan through the passenger list and let me have the names and cabin numbers of any doctors that we have on board?' I asked, briefly giving the reason.

'Certainly, I'll come back to you as soon as I can,' came the reply.

'Right, Kay, you can get out the blood donor list, I'll group

Fiona's blood and see who we'll need as volunteers. I shall want two units, one to be on the safe side, as there won't be anyone who can take more once we're under way. It won't be used unless we have to, and I doubt very much if we'll need even one. Carol, I'd like you to check the surgical equipment, and get the boys along here to clean and sterilize the operating theatre under your supervision. I'm going to get a white cell count and check Fiona's blood group from the specimen we got just now, then I shall want to check the anaesthetic equipment and make sure everything's working OK. Mrs Chester will be at Fiona's bedside. Kay, you'll keep the observations and I'll check her periodically. All clear?'

They nodded.

'Right, let's go, before we get caught up with evening clinic.'

As accurate as I could make it, Fiona's white blood count, which reflected the extent of any inflammatory process which was progressing in her abdomen, was elevated to a level somewhat below a convincing diagnostic conclusion. Even so, it was elevated, and was another step towards the inevitable diagnosis. The next job was to determine her blood group. As I completed the test, the phone rang.

'Bureau here. We have six doctors' names for you, Dr Roberts. Shall I read them out?'

'Yes please,' I said with relief.

Six doctors. Good! That meant that there was a better chance of finding an anaesthetist amongst them, or alternatively a surgeon, in which case I'd give the anaesthetic. I wrote down the names and cabin numbers. Better check out the gas machine before I contact them, I thought. A quick trial run confirmed that the valves were OK, the meters working, the tubes and bags not leaking, the cylinders full. That was another item ticked off. Thank goodness we don't have to go through this very many times a year, I thought.

'Kay, I'm off to have a chat with these doctors,' I called. 'Fiona's blood group is on her card on the desk; can you contact the donors? Tell them that we don't want the blood yet – hopefully we won't want it at all – but can they be on stand-by just in case. And tell them no alcohol this evening. Check that they've no medical problems at present and look through their records, make sure there are no contra-indications since they were last donors.'

'Consider it done,' Kay called back, and I left the hospital with my list of doctors.

'Right,' I thought, 'start at the top of the ship and work down.' I knocked at the first cabin. When the door opened, my face must have dropped noticeably. I didn't speak. 'Can I help you?' asked the man. 'Are you all right?' Before me stood a gentleman wearing a clergical collar!

'Good start,' I thought, as I made my way to the next cabin. Knock knock.

'Hello, can I help you?' a bright young man enquired as he opened the door.

'Are you Dr Morris?'

'Yes, I am.'

'Are you a Doctor of Medicine?' I asked.

'No, my doctorate is in mathematics.'

My heart sank. I chatted briefly and left.

At the third cabin I knocked, and knocked again. There was no reply. The cabin steward was approaching along the corridor. 'Dr Allen went out on deck with his wife ten minutes ago,' he told me.

'When he returns, could you ask him to get in touch with me in the hospital?' I asked.

'Certainly, doctor.'

The fourth doctor was a doctor of nuclear physics. I couldn't believe it! Never mind an anaesthetist or a surgeon, there didn't seem to be *any* form of medical doctor, nor even a dentist who might be prepared to help. My heart was beginning to race. The next one has to be, I reassured myself, but no . . . a Doctor of Philosophy! Now I was beginning to worry. I almost ran to the last cabin on the list. I knocked again desperately. No reply. I went down the corridor to the cabin steward's pantry, where he was sitting reading.

'Hello, Peter. Dr Thomas, cabin 269,' I said, 'do you know if he's around?'

'Didn't get on, doctor! He and his wife were supposed to have joined the ship in Hawaii, but they never showed up.' I stood, staring straight through him.

I headed back towards Dr Allen's cabin. Perhaps he'd returned. I knocked on his door very hard.

'Not back yet,' called the steward, 'I've been watching for them.'

'Would you know if he's a Doctor of Medicine?' I asked, dreading the answer.

'Yes, he is, but he's retired now,' came the reply.

'Thank goodness! Well give him my message, won't you,' I told him, with relief. 'As soon as he returns,' I stressed.

I returned to the hospital with a much lighter step. Maybe not an anaesthetist or a surgeon, I thought, but a doctor at least.

Back at the hospital, the smell of antiseptic nearly bowled me over.

'The boys are doing a good job on the theatre,' reported Kay. 'The emergency abdominal pack is in date and all the other equipment has been checked out.'

'Good,' I said. Another tick on the list.

'Two blood donors are on stand-by,' said Carol. 'There were plenty of volunteers on the list in her blood group.'

'I wish I could say the same about my list,' I replied. 'How are things next door?'

'Not too good, I'm afraid,' Carol replied. 'I'll get her charts for you.'

I walked through to the ward. Mother and father sat alongside their pale, fragile-looking daughter. Fiona's temperature was rising, she was perspiring lightly and appeared a little more toxic. When I examined her abdomen I caught my breath, accepting the inevitable. There was no doubt about the diagnosis now, and more importantly, her condition didn't appear to be responding to conservative treatment.

'How are you feeling, Fiona?' I asked.

'Not very good,' she replied, pouting, her bright eyes now dark, and for the first time, a tear appearing.

'Sister will sit with you for a little while,' I told her, 'I'm going to have a chat with mummy and daddy, OK?'

Next door, I spoke as calmly and undramatically as possible, in order to avoid alarm. 'I'm afraid it doesn't look as though the medical treatment is going to work,' I said frankly, 'but we can give it a little longer yet. We may still get a response, keep your fingers crossed.'

'What if she doesn't respond?' asked Mr Chester.

'Well, if necessary, we'll operate,' I replied confidently. 'As I've explained to you, we don't operate unless it's really necessary, but if it goes that way, then we have all the facilities that we'll need. This won't be the first appendicectomy performed at sea by a long way,' I smiled reassuringly, 'and, as you know, an appendicectomy is a nice simple operation.' Under the desk I crossed my fingers and touched wood as I said this. An appendicectomy, as well as being one of the easiest operations in the book, is also notorious for being one of the most difficult and dangerous if there are complications. I went on to explain what preparations had been made, and also that I was expecting another doctor to arrive at any moment to discuss the anaesthetics. Two very anxious people returned to their child.

Kay entered the office. 'I've managed to treat one or two minor problems myself and I've asked the non-urgent cases to come back tomorrow,' she explained, 'but there are a few patients who need to see you.'

Thank goodness there were no serious problems and we got through without much delay. A coronary or fracture now would have been all we needed to add to our present problems. As I sat writing up the notes, Kay came in again. 'There's a doctor . . .' She paused. 'Dr Allen has arrived,' she said. She stood back, looking at me. What was wrong? 'Come this way, Dr Allen, Mrs Allen,' called Kay. They entered, Kay still watching me, and now I realized why. Dr Allen was led in by his wife. He was carrying a stick, a white stick. I was speechless!

New plans had to be made. First a tannoy around the ship – perhaps a doctor was travelling under a different title. We waited, and waited. No-one!

'Carol, my dear, it would appear that, should we operate, you will be our newly appointed anaesthetist!' I told her, in a vain attempt to make light of the problem. She looked at me aghast! 'I'm only kidding, honestly!' I added quickly, realizing that I had nearly scared the pants off her, 'but you *will* have to be second-in-command. First you'd better get hold of the blood donors,' I said, to give her something to distract her.

In light of the new developments, I had now decided that we would allow an extra period of time to determine whether the medical approach was a failure. Meanwhile, it was about time that the captain was brought up to date. He listened to all the facts, figures, pros and cons.

'Good luck, Nigel!' he said. 'I don't envy your decision. Anything we can do to help?'

'Yes, I'll need someone intelligent as a spare pair of hands,' I said. 'Preferably someone who won't faint!'

'Perhaps the second officer would care to brush up on his emergency medicine, he's going to a cargo ship shortly,' said the captain.

'Good idea,' I replied.

I went once again to the bedside. Fiona lay beneath the sheets, her small body hardly making a mound. She was perspiring more freely. Her breathing was deeper, more rapid, her temperature and pulse rate slowly increasing. Her abdomen was more tender. My own mouth was dry, and I could feel my own heart pounding. I stood watching. Fiona's eyes opened, slowly. She watched me, watching her, grimaced, and closed her eyes.

I went next door. Two units of blood lay on the desk. The donors sat up on their beds at the end of the ward, drinking sweet tea.

'Thanks, fellows,' I said. 'You know how much we appreciate it, especially one young lady next door!'

'Any time, doctor, any time.'

'Carol, let's have a word,' I called, and led her into the operating theatre.

'As you know, if there isn't a response to the conservative treatment very soon, we're going to have to operate, despite not having a second doctor,' I said flatly. 'Now I don't want you to get yourself worked up, you can only do what you can do,' I said gently. 'I shall give the anaesthetic, and when I've got Fiona well anaesthetized and under control, I want you to take over the anaesthetics.'

'Oh dear,' said Carol, simply.

'I'll be keeping a close eye on you,' I reassured her. 'It will be quite simple to just maintain the anaesthetic. I'm going to show you the whole routine and then I'll go over everything again until you're happy, OK?'

'OK!' she replied, with a tremor in her voice.

We went through it, and through it, and through it again.

'Happy?' I asked.

She flashed a tentative smile. 'Right with you!' she said.

I fussed around with final preparations, rechecking the anaesthetic trolley and equipment, drawing up emergency drugs into syringes, labelling them, then drawing up the pre-med drugs, and more labels. Finally, more lab work; the two units of blood had to be cross-matched. All done. Now I just had to sit and watch.

I sat on the ward in the semi-light, for a while. I examined Fiona's abdomen again. No better. I fidgeted for a while longer, re-examined her. Was she more toxic? Were the bowel sounds less?

The day had turned to evening as all our preparations had moved steadily on. A child's life was under consideration. She lay there, totally unaware. What a decision, and no-one to share the load. If I were to operate too early, and the child died, then there would always be the question, was the operation really necessary? On the other hand, if I hesitated too long, went in too late, and the patient then died, there would inevitably be the accusation that I should have moved earlier. Decisions, decisions. The timing had to be right. Who lays the blame? Who makes the accusations? Your colleagues? No! Yourself, only yourself.

The decision was made.

'Mr Chester!'

'Yes?'

'Can I have another talk with you both?'

148

Outside I broke the news. 'I'm afraid that we've now come to the point where we have no choice,' I told them quietly. 'Fiona's condition is deteriorating steadily. The drugs aren't having any effect,' I said, knowing the devastating effect my words were having on them both. 'If her appendicitis continues unchecked, she'll very probably perforate the appendix and develop peritonitis.'

'That's very serious, isn't it, doctor?' asked Mr Chester, not really wanting to hear the answer. 'What could happen?'

'Mr Chester, if Fiona's condition progresses unchecked, there is a strong possibility that she could, . . . die.' I replied, trying to soften the words, but how do you soften the word death?

Now I had to relate that I had even more bad news. 'I'm afraid that we have no anaesthetist,' I told them cautiously. 'I shall have to be both anaesthetist *and* surgeon.'

They both looked at me wide eyed, uncomprehending, and slowly the information sank in.

'I've very carefully weighed all the considerations and likelihoods, and I've decided that even in the circumstances, we should operate now.'

'Can't we wait until we get to port?' Mrs Chester asked, half pleading.

'That's three days away,' I replied, 'it would probably be too late if it were only twenty-four hours.' The facts all had to be stated and I explained them all. I had to have their support, but of course, most of all, I had to have their permission to operate. It was necessary for me to communicate what I truly felt, and the considerations I had made. They sat silent for a short time and then talked briefly. Mr Chester finally addressed me.

'We're completely behind you, Dr Roberts, we know the decision isn't taken lightly. I'm sorry that we've hesitated, but she's our only child. We love her so very much.'

My heart, already pounding, reached out to them both.

The most difficult step – the decision to act – was over. Now to get on with it.

The lights were now full on in the ward. We had gently disturbed Fiona and, apologizing, I gave her a pre-anaesthetic injection. She was looking decidedly unwell. The second officer arrived looking none too sure of himself or the world, and a little pale. After every sentence he kept swallowing hard. I changed into theatre clothes and proceeded to scrub up, but not fully, as, first, the anaesthetic had to be given.

We wheeled Fiona's bed to the door and lifted her gently across to the table. The atmosphere in the theatre was becoming decidedly tense. Fiona, drowsy from her injection, lay half asleep. The Chesters had been taken to either their cabin or a quiet corner by a member of the cruise staff who was to try to keep them occupied.

I had decided, in the circumstances, to keep the anaesthetic as simple as possible. Without the least struggle or discomfort, Fiona was asleep and passing gently into deeper anaesthesia. Her breathing was regular and deep, her colour good.

'All right, Carol,' I said, 'I want her just like that. If she needs to be deeper, I'll tell you so, and you'll turn the knob in this direction until the valve points where I say, and vice versa, just like we've practised, all right?'

'All right,' she answered. Only her eyes peered out at me above her mask.

I turned to the sink and finished scrubbing up, keeping one eye fixed firmly over my shoulder. In the corner, trying to disappear into the wall, was squeezed the second officer, looking more than a little scared and terribly out of place in his ill-fitting spare gear, which we had found for him. Kay helped me on with gown and gloves. I was ready.

Outside the ship the waves slipped by, the flying fish flew, the dolphins whistled through the water, and way, way beyond, so far away, so many thousands of miles, the world went on, completely unaware of us. Even here, on the ship, the people upstairs eating, showering, drinking, dancing, laughing, seemed equally far away. Almost every one of them was totally unaware of the activity, the drama which was proceeding only yards away from them, beyond the bulkheads.

I stepped to the table. Kay handed me forceps and a dish of antiseptic. I splashed antiseptic all over Fiona's small, small abdomen. There was not an ounce of extra fat, thank goodness, something in our favour at least. The operation would be the easier for that. The drapes were applied and attached, and the instrument tray on its trolley was swung over the lower end of the table. I checked the anaesthetic machine visually; all was well. Colour – good. Breathing – good.

I took the scalpel; I sensed the second officer cringe. I looked at Carol. She nodded. I looked at Kay and winked reassuringly.

'Here we go!'

I cut the skin, and the second officer said, 'Uh!'

'Don't you dare fall over in here!' I warned, 'there isn't enough room.' He straightened up.

There had been not the least flinch from Fiona at the initial incision. The anaesthetic was working well. I cut down through the muscle layers and finally through the inner lining of the abdomen, the peritoneum. I held my breath and probed. What would I find? I inserted my fingers gingerly into the wound, eased the intestines to one side and felt around gently. I increased the traction on the wound margins and Kay held the retractors firm, her eyes darting from my eyes to the wound and back, trying to read my thoughts. I stretched the peritoneal edges further, reached in deeper with my fingers, swept behind the soft, bulging viscera. Around the back I touched a firmer structure and eased it gently, gently.

'Well, how about that?!' I exclaimed. The fates, indeed, were kind. As my probing fingers eased back, up popped the appendix! It wasn't adherent to any other organ, or inaccessible in some remote corner of the abdomen. It was inflamed, ugly and smelly, but not perforated. Was I glad to see it! I nearly cheered.

'Retractor. Clamps. Scalpel. Scissors. Needle. Ties.' Everything moved along well. The appendix was out – still intact, no leaks – and into the dish together with its clamps, with a clatter. Stump inverted, purse string tied, a quick check around inside – no problems.

'Ready to come out.' The atmosphere was full of elation. Behind the masks I could sense the smiles. 'Cat-gut suture, please.' The peritoneum was coming together nicely; the patient was relaxed, no tension.

BANG! Suddenly, under the drapes, a leg rose sharply and booted the instrument trolley. The instruments flew in every direction, clattering noisily on the floor. Fiona arched her back. 'What the . . . ?' Her leg kicked out again . . . the child was waking up! She shifted sideways, shoving against me. Kay, with her years of theatre training, spread her arms, leaned forward, and pinned the little body to the table. Carol's eyes were twice their size, the whites like headlamps. Caught with needle and tweezers grasped in both hands and the cat-gut running to the half closed peritoneum, I looked frantically at the anaesthetic trolley. The flow meter reading was *down*!

Fiona arched again. I cast the tweezers aside, and held my free hand across the wound. Carol looked terrified. Frozen. In the far corner, the second officer, in alarm and horror, grasped at the wall as though to save himself from falling, not sure what on earth to do. Eventually gathering himself, he dived amongst the fallen instruments, grasping and grabbing, and gathering them up.

'Carol!' I said. No response. 'Carol,' I repeated, very quietly, very calmly. Still no response. 'Carol, don't worry about the movement, all right? . . . ALL RIGHT?'

She nodded slowly, blankly.

'Turn to the machine,' I instructed. She turned. 'That's right. Now, nice and easy, turn the knob on your left clockwise. Easy . . . easy!' A robot response, still terrified. 'Good. Now, turn the knob next to it anti-clockwise . . . good . . . a bit more . . . more . . . that's it!'

Suddenly, the table heaved again. Another kick, and more instruments flew off the tray and scattered with a crash on the floor. Everyone in the room was covered in perspiration.

'OK . . . OK, now turn the top dial up a notch.' She was still pale, zombie-like, but was doing everything quickly and correctly, her strict training coming into play.

Fiona jerked again. The wound margin tugged at the cat-gut length attached to the needle which I still held tightly gripped in the needle holder. I managed to keep hold of it, and with my other hand wrestled to maintain pressure across the wound. The child settled a little, her breathing deepened.

'Another notch on the top dial, Carol,' I continued, still quietly, slowly. 'Good . . . Good.'

Wait . . . wait . . . The struggling was less, now much less. No more kicking. Steady, deep respirations, good colour, no more movement. Back to sanity!

With added urgency I closed the peritoneum, and then the muscle layers. Time seemed to be standing still. Everything seemed so slow . . . slow . . . and finally, the skin sutures were done.

Leaving Kay to apply the dressings, I joined Carol at the top. 'Well done, Carol! You did great! You really did.' Carol's colour was returning, her eyes no longer popping. She looked as though she could do with an opportunity to fall over.

'I'll take over here, go and have a sit down for a minute,' I told her.

'I'm OK, thanks,' she replied. 'Will she be all right?'

'She'll be fine,' I promised, optimistically. I tailed off the anaesthetic, removed the mask and tubes, and now gently shook Fiona. 'Open your eyes for me, Fiona, open up!' I instructed. No response. 'Fiona, can you hear me?' No response. 'Fiona! . . . FIONA!' The eyelids flickered, opened. Fiona looked out on the world, closed them again, and drifted off into comfortable sleep. I heaved a giant sigh, and suddenly felt weary . . . very weary. What a long, long day, and it wasn't finished yet.

Fiona, still asleep, was returned to her bed, and made comfortable. Her infusion was adjusted and her signs checked. Then I sat down – nearly dropped down. After a short rest, I sent for the Chesters, and gave them back their child.

Mrs Chester's tears flowed freely. She kissed her little girl's cheek, and sat, touching her tiny hand, with the catheter and bandages attached, just watching.

'We're not out of the woods yet, though!' I warned.

Eventually I told them, 'Go and get some sleep. Sister and I shall be here with her all night, so don't worry, go and rest.' Reluctantly, they finally left.

I sat silently in the semi-dark, listening to all the ship's noises around, suddenly aware of them once again, and observed our patient, our charge. After a couple of hours, I went into the light next door to complete yet another task, to write up the notes on all the events of the day, the details of the anaesthetic and operation, and left sister to watch the patient. I wrote and wrote . . .

'Wake up! Wake up!' a voice was calling. I lifted my head. I had fallen asleep there at the desk, amongst the notes and charts, out like a light. Sunshine was streaking in through the porthole.

'Come on, quick!' said Sister. 'Quick!' she urged.

'Why? What's the matter?' I asked, suddenly fully awake.

'Our patient's complaining,' she replied.

I dashed next door, adrenalin gushing. I moved quickly to her bed, where she was half sitting up, eyes open.

'Fiona, what's the trouble?' I gabbled out.

She paused, screwed up her face at me, and said slowly, very deliberately, 'I'M HUNGRY!'

There is never sweeter music to the ears of the surgeon following an abdominal operation! I sat down and smiled, a very contented smile.

We had both had a successful day's surgery, Neptune and I!

V
FUNNY BONES:
THE LIGHTER SIDE

Health and Humour

Eccentric passengers may well be a nuisance, but they can certainly bring some very amusing moments to everyday life on board ship. In much the same way, even within the more limited environs of the medical department, there's a heavy sprinkling of lighter moments to balance the drama. Our patients as well as our passengers can produce some very impromptu moments of hilarity which are really welcome, as a damn good laugh is often the best form of medicine for the doctor himself.

Most of these spontaneous moments occur within the surgery or hospital, and are usually all the funnier for their interruption of the normal flow of a serious morning's work. Top of the list in this respect is an incident which occurred a few years ago on the *Cunard Princess*, one of our cruise ships sailing amongst the spectacular glaciers of Alaska. The story involved our Chinese Medical Petty Officer, Mr Lee, known to all as 'Lee', a young man from Hong Kong.

We were having a very busy morning. The waiting room had been packed and we had all been dashing to get crew members back to work and passengers off on their day-tours ashore. Lee had taken charge of the waiting room while Chrissie, the nursing sister, pushed on with dressings, treatments and dispensing. He took the names of the patients, and wrote out record cards for them. A large lady sat with her husband in the corner.

'Do you wish to see the doctor?' Lee asked the gentleman.

'No, I'm not the patient, I'm fine,' replied the husband, 'but we'd like an appointment for my wife, she isn't too well.' Mrs Burns, we'll call her.

The morning surgery continued. I had seen a couple more patients, written up their notes and had sent them through to Sister. 'Next please, Lee,' I called. Lee went into the waiting room.

'Mrs Burns,' he read from the next card, 'this way, please,' and showed her in. 'Would you like to come in as well, sir,' he called to the gentleman sitting with her. They were both shown in by Lee, who seated the lady in front of me, and the man next to her.

Mrs Burns was a well-built American lady. She was tall, broad, stocky, and had a very ample, 'operatic' chest. In contrast, the gentleman was small, lean and wiry, with what sounded, from his few words, like an Irish accent. The lady had a purposeful presence, whereas the man had an uneasy, agitated appearance. They didn't seem a very likely couple at all.

'Now Mrs Burns, what's the problem?'

'I've got a head cold, and I've developed a bit of bronchitis,' she replied, and went on to describe her cough, wheezing and chest symptoms. Her replies were, I thought, rather hesitant, as though she were unsure of them. She had to be coaxed to give her details. When I asked her about her past medical history she was even more reluctant, but eventually she told me of previous chest infections and also mentioned some past gynaecological and urinary tract problems. It was hard work getting the story out of her; for whatever reason, she really didn't want to discuss personal details, but this isn't unusual when a patient is first confronted with a new doctor.

'Right,' I said, 'let's have a look and listen what's going on.' Mrs Burns stood up. I examined her throat, ears and sinuses and said, 'OK, now can you take off your blouse so that I can listen to your chest?' This she did slowly, very deliberately, and stood in her bra. As I've said, she was a woman of broad back and very ample bust. I turned her away to face the far wall and unclipped her bra. Everything eased out!

'Breathe in and out deeply through your mouth,' I instructed, and listened to the back of her chest. The room was very quiet, no sound from the chaperon, who sat quietly watching the whole proceedings.

'Right. Can you turn around and let me listen to your front, Mrs Burns,' I said.

'Just a second!' she interjected. 'Just *hold on* a second!'

'Why? What's the problem?' I asked, surprised

'This is all very well,' she replied brusquely. 'So far, I've gone along with you . . . the personal questions and the examination,' she continued, 'but I am *not* showing off my bust to *him*!' she said adamantly, pointing at her partner. Oh dear! I thought, I was right, they are an odd couple, obviously don't get on well together at all. Probably undress in the dark!

'Why? What's the problem?' I asked again, not really wanting to get involved in a marital conflict.

She was spluttering and wheezing. 'Who . . . Who . . .' she stuttered, '*who the hell is this guy anyhow?*'

'*What?*' I exclaimed, astounded. 'Your husband of course!'

'What do you mean, my husband?' she exploded. 'My husband left half an hour ago, I've never seen this man before in my life!'

I couldn't believe what was going on. 'Who are *you*?' I demanded of the man.

'I'm James O'Connor,' he yelped, as he leaped to his feet like a scalded cat!

'What the heck are you doing *here*?' I squawked.

'*You* brought me in,' he said.

'No I didn't,' I replied.

'Yes you did. Yes you did!' he blurted out defensively. 'Your man showed me in.'

I was lost for words. 'Why on *earth* didn't you say something?' I finally got out.

'I thought it was the way you did things on board ship,' he said.

'You've got to be *joking*,' I exclaimed, totally flabbergasted. 'Didn't it strike you as being strange?'

'Well, come to think of it, I did think it was a bit peculiar!' he said, in his strong Irish brogue. I didn't know whether to laugh, or what. Mrs Burns still stood wide-eyed, clasping her bosom like an affronted maiden.

'Did you think that you'd have to go through the same routine?' I asked incredulously.

'Well, I was beginning to wonder about that,' he said.

I was holding on to my sides. I was desperately trying to stop myself bursting out laughing.

'Mrs Burns, what can I tell you? I'm so sorry, I can't apologize enough. I just don't know what to say because, believe me, this doesn't happen too often.'

There followed what seemed to be an endless, electrically charged pause, while Mrs Burns looked contemplatively from me to our Irish intruder, and back. 'No harm done!' she said eventually, suddenly bursting out into laughter at poor Mr O'Connor, with his hands clasped and looking like some bewildered Leprechaun. We all roared uncontrollably with laughter.

After the affair was all over and we eventually returned to normal, I sat and chatted to our Chinaman, Mr Lee. He apologized profusely for all the embarrassment which he'd caused.

'How on earth did you let that happen, Lee?' I asked him.

'I don't know,' he replied, 'I didn't realize that her husband had got up and left, and that someone sat down in his place.' Then, with absolute sincerity, with a totally deadpan face, and without any intention or awareness whatsoever of his cliché, he said apologetically, 'They all look the same to me.'

No-one could ever write fiction as funny as these natural episodes of humour, which are all the more hilarious for their spontaneity; however, just occasionally, I wonder whether the passengers aren't in fact playing their own games for a few laughs. One of these incidents springs to mind, when I had to stop and think, 'This man has to be kidding. He's pulling my leg.'

Again, I was working on the *Cunard Princess* at the time. The hospital area was comparatively small, and the X-ray room was close by the consulting room. A lady came to visit me, having tripped over whilst ashore that day and injured her ankle. The injury was fairly severe and I had decided to X-ray the area. I called in our medical PO, Mr Lee, who, amongst other roles, we had trained as a radiographer. Lee took the patient next door in a wheelchair to arrange for the X-ray. As he was fairly new to the job, I told him that when he was ready to shoot, he was to give me a call and I'd check the settings and ankle position. In the meantime, the nursing sister escorted the next patient in from the waiting room to see me.

This gentleman was bright and chatty, and commenced by telling me what a great ship we had, how much he was enjoying his cruise and that he was having lots of laughs. He went on to tell me that his fun was being spoiled by a cold which he had picked up at home, and which was now giving him a few chest symptoms. Could we clear it up for him? I took a few more details and was about to ask him to remove his coat and shirt so that I could examine him, when Lee gave a light tap on the door to let me know that he was ready.

'Excuse me a moment,' I said to my patient, 'I'm just going to nip next door to take an X-ray. I'll only be half a minute.' With that, I left him in the consulting room and went around to the injured ankle. Having quickly sorted the X-rays out, I left Lee to get on with the developing, and went back to the chest complaint.

I had left the door of the consulting room ajar. As I walked in, the patient was in the middle of the room standing rigidly erect, hands on his hips, shoulders thrown way back, holding his breath, chest puffed out and fully dressed with coat, shirt and tie on. He was facing directly towards the opposite wall. He turned 90 degrees to face the other wall, took another deep breath, and resumed his posture.

'Oh, you're back, doctor,' he said, suddenly noticing me over his shoulder, and releasing his breath with a gasp.

160

'Yes, it doesn't take long,' I replied, wondering if I'd caught him in the midst of some home-brewed exercise routine.

'This ship really is unbelievable,' he enthused, 'your facilities are fantastic. We haven't even got facilities like this back at home! Do you know, doctor, I never even *knew* that you could take an X-ray through the wall, just like that!' I was wondering what the heck he was talking about. 'That quick, that easy!' he said, 'and I didn't even need to take my clothes off! I hope the results are good. Marvellous . . . marvellous!'

Well, would you think he was kidding? When I explained the situation, he laughed and said that of course he knew all along, and was just having a lark, but I'd seen his performance, and I wasn't at all convinced!

There was another occasion back on the *QE2* , however, when I doubted very much if the patient was joking. To this day, I am amazed that so many people unquestioningly follow what they must feel are absurd instructions, which they only *think* they've heard.

During morning clinic one day, an enormous lady came to see me – and I mean enormous – not in height, just around the middle. She could barely make her way through the doorway. She waddled across the room, puffing like a set of bellows and spread herself over what, until that moment, had seemed like a perfectly normal sized chair. In a surprisingly squeaky little voice, she explained her problems at some length.

Having obtained all the details, I needed to examine her. I looked from her to the couch, and back to her again, trying to assess the relative sizes. She was short, the couch was high. She was wide, and the couch was narrow. I decided that it would make more sense to get her onto a bed in the ward. 'Would you like to go along with Sister?' I said to her. 'She'll show you to a ward. I'd like you to undress, if you would, and then I can examine you.' That's not a confusing statement is it?

Sister led her off through the waiting room, showed her into the ward, and left her to strip off. Meanwhile, I was seeing the next patient, a quick case which only took a couple of minutes. I washed my hands, and when I turned around my eyes must have nearly popped. The fat lady, having completely stripped off *all* her clothes, had returned for her examination. She sat there, like a babe, but what a babe! A white mountain, flowing in all directions, perched like a landed walrus on the buckling chair. And she had waddled through the full waiting room . . . ! Sister, who had been busy in the treatment room, was almost frantic. The patient, in contrast, was cool as a cucumber . . . a very large cucumber.

I suppose the answer is never to take anything for granted. Always be specific. But then, you could miss out on a few laughs.

The practice of medicine at sea isn't limited to the confines of the ship's hospital, and in addition to conventional cabin visits or emergencies which may occur in literally any corner of the ship, a patient may approach the doctor at any time, out on deck, in the corridor, during a show, in the nightclub or, most commonly of all, at a cocktail party. Naturally, then, you can also expect to encounter the lighter side of medicine outside the hospital at any time.

On one such occasion, I was enjoying a drink at a cocktail party with one of our entertainers, a very talented, and very funny man – Alan Stewart. For whatever reason, we were discussing this very subject of cocktail party consultations. Alan was being very sceptical and wouldn't accept that people might be forward enough, or indeed what he considered to be rude enough, to intrude into the private conversation of a doctor whom they'd never met before, and present him with a medical problem – unless, of course, it was an emergency situation.

As we chatted, a large brusque lady approached and rudely stepped between us, shouldering Alan out of the way.

'You're the doctor, aren't you?' she enquired, almost challenging.

'Yes, I'm Dr Roberts. What can I do for you?'

Totally excluding Alan, she went on, 'I've had wind for several months now,' she declared in a broad Yorkshire accent. 'My doctor's given me different tablets for it. It's got better, but when I eat vegetables, or if I've been out drinking the night before . . .'

Alan stood smiling. He knew this was a set-up, I wasn't fooling him! Gradually, he registered the look on my face as this lady poured out bizarre details, informing the world at large, and myself in particular, of her plight. Slowly he realized that it wasn't a set-up at all. I allowed the woman to ramble on; she was illustrating my earlier conversation admirably: '. . . and the dog won't stay in the house, and my husband's lawyer says . . .' the lady went burbling on.

After a while, I began to notice several heads in the room turned towards our group, smiling and occasionally pointing. The lady's voice wasn't that loud, and they surely couldn't hear her from over there. The intruding patient stopped abruptly, and looked down.

'What the 'eck?!' she exclaimed.

I turned to see what the problem was. Alan Stewart stood slightly

A force to be contended with. Sunshine Primary School's cricket first team, 1951. Mr Thorburn, headmaster, left; Mr Barns, games master, right; myself centre front (wicket keeper).

Another great team. My first 'permanent' merchant ship, *Pacific Princess*, on the day of her official name change from the *Sea Venture* to *Pacific Princess* when P&O took control of her. Myself far left, front row.

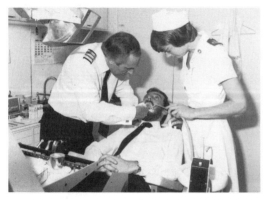

Ship's doctor and sometime dentist, helped by Senior Nursing Sister, Angela Eddleston.

The two-bedded female passenger ward, with Senior Nursing Sister, Michell Gunter.

Another year, another team (left to right) Myself, Senior Nursing Sister Angela Eddleston, Medical Orderly Tommy Thomson, Nursing Sister Julie Hunt, Medical Petty Officer Brian Killick, Nursing Sister Wendy Lister and Dr Eric Donald.

Setting up an X-ray in the *QE2's* well equipped X-ray department.

During *QE2's* inaugural transit of the Suez Canal in 1980, two sets of immigration officials set up desks outside the doctor's surgery. Here are the Israelis and Egyptians. Having befriended both parties I then played mediator and coaxed them to pose for what could possibly be an historic photograph.

'Crossing the line' ceremony, world cruise in 1988. Entertainments Director, Bob Doherty, in the 'surgeon's' costume, dumps one of Neptune's victims into the pool as the mermaids look on.

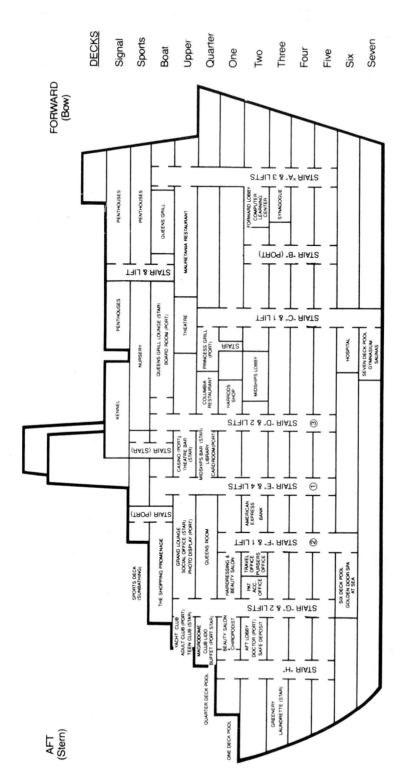

Plan of *QE2*'s interior, designed to help passengers find their way around. (*Cunard Lines*)

Inside QE2...

The Grand Lounge. formerly the Double Room. *(Cunard Lines)*

The Queen's Grill. *(Cunard Lines)*

The Control Room. *(Cunard Lines)*

The Princess Grill. *(Cunard Lines)*

Even the serious business of life-boat drill can become a light-hearted diversion on a cruise ship. 1st Officer, Roy Heath (now Staff Captain), with passengers on the *Cunard Princess*.

Cunard Countess Medical Officer's cabin. The doctor's quarters can be very comfortable, even on the smaller ships.

Medical Officer's cabin on the *Cunard Princess*.

Probably the world's most magnificent harbour. The *QE2* approaches the
Sydney Opera House and Harbour Bridge during the 1981 world cruise. The
proportions of the ship can be seen in comparison to the surrounding
structures.

A typically terrific send off for the *QE2*. The ship leaving Sydney harbour on
her world cruise, 1981.

Actor Robert Young picks up a few tips for his *Marcus Welby M.D.* TV role during his press interview on our visit to New Zealand, following Fiona's surgical crisis.

A serious note. On the bridge of the *Pacific Princess*, with one of the finest Masters ever to sail, the late Captain John Crichton (left), discussing details of a medical Mayday in Alaskan waters. Purser, Dick Bull, is on the right.

behind my left shoulder. As the conversation had proceeded, Alan had quietly undone the belt and zip on his trousers. He was now standing, apparently listening intently to the lady's woes, with dinner-jacket and bow-tie smartly in place, with his trousers down around his ankles, shirt tails and underwear flapping!

'It's quite all right, madam, do carry on,' he said. 'I'm next in line,' he continued, with an absolutely deadpan face. 'When you've finished your consultation, I just want to show the doctor this little problem I have here.'

As you can imagine, the woman was dumbfounded, but Alan's impromptu sketch just hit my funny bone, and I couldn't stop laughing. The lady turned on her heel and stalked away with her alimentary problems, presumably to go in search of a more responsive ear.

Unfortunately, not all cocktail party consultations are that funny!

Not all impromptu or intrusive consultations present themselves at cocktail parties; they can happen at any hour of the day, irrespective of time or circumstances. Some, of course, can be dealt with simply and quickly, and in a way, that's part of the job. Others, however, may be concocted merely as a means of approach, and there are yet others which warrant a non-medical solution to both treat *and* discourage the patient! This may occasionally provide some spontaneous humour to compensate for the intrusion, as on the following occasion.

Every cruise has its characters, amusing or otherwise, and on one particular Mexican cruise we carried three such characters, who were unforgettable: three ladies travelling together, all fair, forty, and fat. Enormous, in fact. They were extroverted, contagiously happy-go-lucky people, and their combined presence in any room made it full in more than one sense. At the outset of the cruise, these ladies announced themselves as the Rrhoea sisters, being individually named Dia, Gono, and Pyo! Their activities – including the 'Rrhoea Trio' attempts at singing – kept everyone entertained.

Late one evening, I was comfortably settled in a quiet corner of the nightclub, taking a drink with a young lady, when we were approached by one wandering colossus, who parked herself down at the table and announced loudly and abruptly, without preamble, 'I've got diarrhoea!'

'In that case, it's just as well that you're not Gono or Pyo,' I replied, quite wittily I thought, for that hour of the night. However, without acknowledgement or pause, she continued.

'I've had it for three days, and I thought it was time I got rid of it!'

163

Three days, and I was getting pestered at 1 a.m.! She then went into a very vivid description of the problem, much to my concern and the obvious embarrassment of my companion, whose ardour was cooling rapidly. Despite my suggestions, and my initially polite, but finally abrupt interjections, she continued undaunted, with a full and colourful account!

Eventually, having no luck in postponing this tirade, I announced,

' 'Well, there's only one way to cure a three-day diarrhoea at this time of night and in the present circumstances; that's the champagne treatment.'

She paused, puzzled, and her dissertation ceased while I called a waiter and informed him, 'This lady would like a bottle of champagne, please. Bring her a bottle of the best you've got, and she'll sign the bill.'

The waiter departed, and the Rrhoea sister exclaimed, 'I didn't realize that champagne was good for diarrhoea.'

'No, my dear,' I replied, 'you've got it wrong. The champagne is for us. The *cork* is for you!'

The joke was in fact well appreciated. She insisted on paying for the champagne, and we all shared it with a laugh. On the following night when I arrived in the same lounge, a reception committee of all three sisters approached me. I was presented with a huge necklace of corks with a card attached, which read. 'Mobile dispensary, for dealing with late night problems!'

Intrusive consultations are by no means limited to face-to-face meetings. As with many other professions in this modern world, the telephone, in addition to being a boon to communication, can be a pain. On board ship, being so readily accessible, means that the phone is occasionally more likely to ring for minor problems than if you lived two miles away from your patient in a shore-side practice.

On the *QE2*, we have a night sister who is the front line of the department after hours. She filters all our night calls, and takes care of the minor problems. The duty doctor is only called if there is a patient that the night sister is unable to handle. All our nursing staff being very highly qualified means that when the phone goes off at night and the duty doctor is dragged from the depths of sleep, there is always a very good reason. Consequently, the adrenalin is pumping from the first ring, and I'm ready to start running to the emergency. However, on our cruise ships we have no night sister. The doctor, the nurse and the Medical Petty Officer share the night duty roster, and any night calls are referred through from the ship's night steward directly to whoever is on call.

I recall one occasion when, having spent the earlier half of the night in the hospital dealing with emergencies, I had tumbled back into bed and eventually drifted into a deep sleep. At 4.30 a.m. the phone gratingly jangled me out of the arms of morphus, and I snatched up the receiver.

'Doctor?'

'Yes.'

'I'm Mr Smith, cabin 1234.'

'Yes?'

'I'm with my girlfriend.' There was no great urgency at all in his voice.

'Yes?'

'Well we've been sort of . . . well, messing around together, you know.'

'I'd appreciate it if you could get to the point, Mr Smith. Are you calling me to brag, or have you got a problem?'

'Yes, I've got a problem.'

'So?'

'I've got crabs!'

'Congratulations!'

'I've never had them before.'

'Mr Smith, do you really consider this to be an emergency?' I asked, thinking of the heart patient who might need to call me back at any time, and bearing in mind a full day's work was due to start in three hours.

'No, of course it's not an emergency,' he replied, 'but what should I do?'

I paused. 'At 4.30 in the morning, Mr Smith, I suggest that you scratch!'

Thankfully, not all patients are so inconsiderate, but you'd be surprised how many times I've been woken in the middle of the night by a call declaring, 'Doctor, I can't sleep!' In complete exasperation, I'm often driven to reply, 'My dear lady, does it make you feel any better, now that you know that we're both awake?'

Being so easily available can also sometimes put you into some potentially sticky situations. Every now and again, the ship's doctor – or any doctor for that matter – becomes, unwittingly, the target for some hungry female's amorous intentions. In seeking a means of approach, they may occasionally use a very misguided and particularly annoying ploy – the unnecessary night call. Let me emphasize to any recklessly aspiring ladies that when a doctor is working, and particularly when he's dashing from his bed to a so-called emergency, it is most definitely a very inappropriate time to be giving him a 'come-on'.

The emergency call usually occurs at around midnight to 1 a.m. after an evening's drinking and a few confidence boosters for the so-called patient. After years of interrelating with patients, the ploy is easily recognizable. As the cabin door opens, you can sense the situation immediately: seeing the patient confirms all. The lights are low, usually soft wall-lights. The patient is half-sitting on well-placed pillows in a carefully arranged bed, with just a suggestion of the covers being pulled down. The air is heavy with perfume. The patient tries to look sultry, and in fact looks fit and well: full make-up, every hair in place. A scanty nightdress, of course, sets the scene. Profuse apologies flow for the inconvenience, the 'patient' recognizes that 'of course there are so many greater problems than little old me, but I'm so worried!' There follows the dying swan act with the revelation of . . . a chest problem, that naturally requires an examination.

There is only one way to play this game: absolutely formal, straight down the line. Too attentive, and you could be considered to be responding. Too offended, and you could reaffirm that there is indeed no truer saying than 'hell hath no fury like a woman scorned!' As far as I'm concerned, these encounters stop right there. The briefest of very formal consultations, maybe two aspirins, and home, to my *own* bed!

Wise words, from years of experience. However, it would be a clever man indeed who could anticipate and avoid all life's pitfalls without at some stage getting his fingers burned. One of the more memorable incidents of my sea-going career is a hard one to believe, but, I assure you, completely true and – only in retrospect – one of the funniest.

It was 30th December, and I was on board the world's most famous floating social centre, as we sailed south into the exotic territories of the Caribbean. In fact, it had passed midnight and was into the early hours of the last day of the year. The cruise was two days old and during the course of the evening I had met a particularly attractive young lady at the captain's 'Welcome Aboard' cocktail party. Having wined, dined and danced, we were now sitting quietly in a corner of the nightclub, where the music was low and the lights were lower. The ocean was calm, and a bright half-moon sparkled on the gentle waves out beyond the windows of the nightclub. My partner was beautiful, intelligent, dreamy and relaxed. Everything in the world was rosy.

From the far side of the room there was a crash as a glass went flying from a table. A figure could be seen elbowing and shoving its way through the seated couples, knocking chairs and drinks, creating a path lined with agitated passengers and growing hubbub. The intruder gazed around and then ploughed on through the small group of couples on the dance-floor who were groping each other in the seductive lighting and slow music in the thinly disguised pretence of dancing. Tripping over the lip of the dance-floor, and arriving on his knees at my table in a final shattering of the carefully nurtured atmosphere of romance, the night steward burst upon us.

'Doctor, quick,' gasping for breath, 'there's a lady in her cabin, she's *gorn!*'

'What do you mean, gorn?'

'Gorn! Dead! She's dead!'

The romantic atmosphere was now also certainly 'gorn'. My partner had drawn back, alarmed, wide-eyed and a little pale.

'OK, George, OK . . . just one thing first. If you find someone dead, it's not likely that you'll improve their condition by trying to destroy half the room. Right? OK, let's go.'

From romance to running, and all in less than ten seconds. Down the empty corridors we went, just the hum of the air-conditioning and the ever present background sounds of the ship working all around, and the thud of our footsteps on deep carpet.

'I got a call for a nightcap from this cabin, see, about half an hour ago, doc; I was busy, and by the time I got there she was gorn!'

Having grabbed my emergency bag from inside the hospital, we were soon at the cabin. I banged open the door and burst into the room. It was empty – or so it appeared. Just one wall-light was glowing and the cabin was fairly dark. George was pushing at my shoulder, directing me towards the corner and pointing, 'There, there, doc, look!'

The bed was situated against the far wall, and here on the adjacent wall at a 90-degree angle was the dressing table. Protruding from the space between the bed and dressing table was a jumble of arms and legs, one slipper missing, and pointing in the most unco-ordinated, apparently disconnected and awkward directions. The limbs were spindly and long, like sticks with appendages at each end. I flicked on the bedside light and kneeled down. If you can imagine a rag doll tossed carelessly into a corner by a bored child, then you have the picture of this extremely frail old lady jammed between the bed and dresser. It took very little time to confirm the instinctive impression that this dear old lady, having enjoyed one of her last Christmases on earth and now far from home, way out on the ocean on this last day of the year, was indeed dead . . . dead *drunk*.

'George, you found us a real Lulu here!'

George coughed and spluttered, 'Well I'll be damned, she aint gorn at all!'

'You might as well get back to the night pantry, George, they'll all be screaming for their Horlicks. I can manage here. Thanks for your trouble.'

' George departed, mumbling, 'Cor blimey! Cor blimey!'

Alone with our reveller, I extricated her from the corner and she unfolded over the floor. I looked down at her in amazement. The vision, who later proved to be seventy-nine years old, was a sight to behold. Presumably as a consequence of an unbalanced alcoholic diet of plenty of booze and minimal food, there was little if any meat on her fragile bones. I'd say that she'd have been lucky to weigh over six stone. Amazingly, she wore the flimsiest of see-through nylon négligés. She had long, long, dyed, platinum-blonde hair down to the middle of her back and the largest butterfly false eyelashes I think I've ever seen. She was heavily made-up with red rouged cheeks and dark red lipstick painted on a rose-bud mouth. She was some dame!

Lifting her from the floor required as little effort as picking up a child. I placed her down on the bed and she flopped like a dishcloth. Her breathing was deep, and she was far away in her alcoholic dream-world. I opened up my medical bag and took out my stethoscope. Turning back to our lady, I gently lifted up her nightdress to expose her chest for examination. Except for the nightdress, she was naked.

As the négligé came up under her chin and exposed her body, there was an abrupt transformation. If anyone has ever seen a Dracula film and can remember the usual close-up of the 'dead' vampire's eyes as the sun goes down over the horizon, you'll be able to visualize the ensuing scene. As the air hit the nipples, the eyes clicked open, bloodshot and staring! Gradually they rotated, slowly, until they found and locked onto my face. I was mesmerized, immobilized!

At this stage, I was leaning over the low bed, all dolled up in full dress-uniform complete with bow-tie etc., holding up the corners of her nightdress, stethoscope dangling. Like a praying mantis going for its first meal after a month of fasting, the spindly old arms shot up from her side and grabbed me around the neck. If I had been expecting the move, I doubt whether I could have dodged fast enough, but in the circumstances I was totally surprised and stood no chance at all. One energetic yank and in my unstable position, leaning down over the bed, my balance was gone! I went nose down, straight into her memory of mammary tissue! She had me in a hold with my nose flattened up against her breastbone, instruments flying.

From above my head, out of the rose-bud lips, came a growing gurgle which finally burst out into a full, screeching, screaming voice:

'I LOVE YOU! OOOH! OOOOOH! I LOVE YOU! I LOVE YOU! I LOVE YOU! OH! OOH! OOOOOH!'

I was flabbergasted. From doctor to prey in the blink of an eye! I became frantic. Christ, if anyone hears this wailing and walks through the door now!

I am aware that there are those cynics amongst us who don't believe me when I say that, despite my clammering to extricate myself, I was hampered by the fact that I was genuinely afraid to break the old girl in half – her arms were like matchsticks. We kicked and rolled around, with me trying to yelp through a flattened nose and mouth, and the wailing continued. 'I LOVE YOU! . . . OOOOOH . . . I LOVE YOU!'

Suddenly, thankfully, she ran out of steam. Her moans tailed off and her arms dropped to her side, leaving me gasping. I pushed myself up from on top of her, and reached up to hold down her arms in order to protect myself from a repeat onslaught. Perhaps I wasn't imaginative enough, but I'm sure that few people would have expected a change in tactics from this little old bag of bones. Who could know that in her alcoholic state, she might be able to simulate a young Russian gymnast? With one knee still resting on the bed as I lifted myself up, I was caught in mid-manoeuvre. Her back arched, and her legs came up in a lightning move. Keeping a careful eye on her ams, her legs were far from my mind, but suddenly, not far from my neck! In a jiffy, I was firmly transfixed in a leg-lock.

In full mess dress, and having recently left a very enjoyable situation in the nightclub, I now found myself in the most incredible of positions imaginable. The first situation – nose down into her wrinkled breasts was amazing enough, but that had nothing on this new position. I couldn't even breathe, not that I even *wanted* to! And the screaming was off again, 'I LOVE YOU! GOD . . . OH GOD! OOOOOH . . . I LOVE YOU!' On and on and on.

The bed erupted. If bones get broken now, to hell with it! I'm getting out of this! I was thrashing around like a trapped rabbit with its head in a snare, legs sticking off the end of the bed, kicking up and down. We were leaping around as though in death throes, and the screaming went on. We bounced off the bed and ended up on the floor.

Now there was banging on the wall from the next door cabin. Oh God, this could really make great listening in court!

As I started to go blue, an amazing silence hit the cabin. As though a switch had been turned off or she'd been hit on the head with a club – preferably a very large one – she stopped everything abruptly and went limp, out cold.

I groped my way up off the floor and collected myself and my senses. Did that really happen? She was off again into the depths of alcoholic stupor. I picked her up and put her back into bed, very carefully, and checked her over. She was all right, in fact better, I'm sure, than I was. She was tucked in and settled for the night. Over the next few hours, I called back at the cabin to check her condition – from a distance of course – and she remained well.

The following morning, hardly as bright as usual, I set off to check the cabin calls from the previous night. I arrived at our lady's cabin and paused outside the door. Straighten up, deep breath, knock and enter.

Sitting up in bed, with the morning sun in the porthole behind her head, like a halo, was a lady who would fit everyone's description of their favourite old aunt. Wearing a flannelette nightdress with a lace collar, no make-up, no eyelashes, and hair up on top of her head in a bun, wearing wire-rimmed, half granny-specs, and reading a book, was a complete vision of respectability and innocence.

'Hello, doctor, what on earth brings you here?' The scene was so totally different that I almost felt I'd come to the wrong cabin.

I hesitated, coughed a little. 'Well . . . well, my dear, I'm afraid that last night . . . well, you weren't entirely . . . um, the night steward found it necessary to call me,' I eventually blurted out.

'Oh dear, oh dear! What on earth happened?'

'Well . . . er . . . never mind the details. I've just come to check that all's back to normal.'

'My goodness, yes, I'm fine. Oh dear, oh dear! Please give my apologies to the steward, and I'm so sorry, doctor, if I caused you any trouble.'

'No, no, of course not,' I said, nearly choking on my words.

'I'm really sorry, I'm so sorry. I hope it wasn't too serious, or too much bother!' She went on and on with her apologies. 'What on earth could have happened? What could the matter be? I'm so sorry.'

Finally, I quietened her down and managed to give her a quick examination without further interruption. During the examination, she just lay quietly and looked on shyly without further comment, apparently deep in thought.

Having made sure that all was OK, I packed my bag and headed for the door, stating, 'As long as you're well now, there's no harm done. Let me know if there are any worries. Goodbye.'

In those days, back in 1975, it was my habit to wear long sideboards, or as they're called in America, sideburns. As I reached the cabin door, our lady called out, 'Oh, by the way, doctor . . .'

'Yes, my dear?' I paused half-way through the door, my hand on the door knob.

She put down her book. Absolutely straight-faced, she gazed directly into my eyes. A pause.

'If you didn't have those sideburns,' she said, innocently, quietly, holding my gaze, *'I'd love you even more*!!'

Eccentrics

If you decided to sail on *QE2* for no reason whatsoever other than simply 'people-watching', then you most certainly wouldn't be disappointed. The enormous variety of characters and their activities is fascinating. I must admit, however, that actually dealing with some of these people is an entirely different kettle of fish. I can only admire the patience, and indeed tolerance, of the front-line staff – particularly the bureau personnel who sometimes may have to take the full onslaught of an angry mob, and calmly tolerate dreadful abuse when things go wrong. These are the exceptions of course, and under normal circumstances the bureau square is a very tranquil centre.

Although dealing with an assortment of inane questions on a full time basis definitely wouldn't be my cup of tea, I always find it an amusing pastime to spend ten minutes in the vicinity of the front desk, just listening in to some of the conversations and questions. Whatever ship you may go on, I can guarantee that the staff will always tell you that there is one question, above all others, which is asked time and again and never ceases to amuse and amaze us all. 'What time is the midnight buffet?'

Close on the heels of that classic is another prize-winner: 'Do the crew sleep on board?' I promise you, that question is posed an unbelievable number of times. How about this one – again one of the top ten: 'Excuse me, officer,' calls the passenger standing at the foot of a staircase. 'Do these stairs go up?' Without being silly or sarcastic, it's sometimes hard to answer!

On another occasion:

'Excuse me, young lady.'

'Yes, madam?'

'Could you tell me, is the water in the swimming pool fresh water or sea water?'

'It's sea water, madam.'

'There, I told you so, Edith,' she says to her companion, 'that's why it moves so much!'

You'd be very surprised, I'm sure, to learn of the lack of geographical knowledge of some of our 'worldly' travellers outside their own shores. Venezuela, for example, being included on a cruise itinerary around the Caribbean islands, appears to confuse no end of people. Apart from their inability to grasp the correct name of the country – referring to it as Venezulu – many holiday-makers seem to consider this stop on their voyage as another island. 'What currency do the Vene-Zulus use on this island?' they sometimes enquire.

One particular tour manager had a possibly too dry sense of humour. I was standing near the tour office desk one day, prior to our arrival in Venezuela, when a brusque lady enquired, in a grating voice: 'Young man, is there an organized tour around this island that I can take?'

The manager caught my eye and gave me a conspiratorial wink. 'Yes, madam,' he replied. 'It calls at Caracas, and then goes on to Rio de Janeiro, Montevideo, Buenos Aires, Santiago, Lima, Bogota, and back to Caracas.'

'Oh hell!' stated the lady abruptly, 'I can't take that . . . I've got to get back for lunch!'

I can't imagine why these apparently absurd questions should recur so frequently. Perhaps on holiday the brain goes into second gear. Maybe people just want an excuse to talk to someone, or perhaps ships are such new and confusing environments that some passengers just wander around in a constant state of bewilderment. The answer, probably, is that in a relaxed atmosphere people just don't have to stay sharp or face problems. That's all behind them in the office or the boardroom. It's a pleasant change to switch off and have someone else to do the thinking for you, and what does it matter anyway? So it becomes a habit to speak before thinking. If this were not so, how else could one of my table companions ask, 'Doctor, is your wife married?'

Sometimes the new environment and new terminology is just too confusing altogether, and therefore I suppose it's understandable when some little old lady enquires: 'Have I got it right, young man? Is there a port side to the ship, and a starboard side?'

'Yes, that's right, my dear.'

'Well, how come you only have port-holes?'

When it comes to brain-teasing situations, probably the most confusing of all new experiences for any passenger – and crew – is the crossing of the date-line. People who may be sharp enough to own and run an entire industry, or to lecture classrooms of students back on dry land, often get bogged down with the simple problem of mid-Pacific time zones. It is most amusing to listen to people jostling figures around, trying to work out how on earth you can either lose a day or gain an extra day, depending on which direction you cross the line. There is one occasion I recall, when this confusing problem gave rise to an amusing scene.

The *QE2* was travelling on one of its annual world cruises. This year's itinerary was 'The Great Pacific and Orient Cruise'. We would set sail from Los Angeles across the enormous expanse of the Pacific Ocean to fabulous Tahiti. Each night, as we moved further west, the ship's clocks were wound back an hour, and the passengers were all advised to do likewise with their own watches. Having left Tahiti on Sunday, we were to spend two full days at sea en route to the unspoilt beauty of the small South Pacific island of Tonga, during which time we would be crossing the date-line. This meant that we would have to finally compensate for all the accumulated hours we'd gained, and move the time forward a full twenty-four hours, thus losing a day. Instead of arriving in Tonga on Wednesday, we'd be arriving on Thursday.

On Sunday night the passengers were advised to set their watches back one hour, and again on Monday night to adjust to local time. Some travellers are not entirely sure why even this simple adjustment should be necessary, but will usually just accept the situation. So far no real confusion. On Tuesday night, it wasn't so easy!

The passengers were advised over the public address system that 'Clocks will be set back by one hour tonight as usual. However, they will also be set forward twenty-four hours – one day ahead. Tomorrow morning, as on previous days, when you get up the time will be 7 a.m. not 8 a.m. However, it will not be February 8th, but the 9th, and finally, it will not be Wednesday, but Thursday. In summary, when we arrive in Tonga tomorrow morning, it will not be 9 a.m. Wednesday, February 8th, but 8 a.m. Thursday, February 9th. Is that clear?' *Clear!* Well, I smile just thinking about the individual passenger's reactions. No wonder they were bewildered! Most people just said, 'OK, I'll take your word for it,' and adjusted their watches accordingly. Some, however, wrestled and wrestled with this new teaser to make sense of it, but never succeeded. One gentleman in particular was unable to make head or tail of the problem. He was convinced that something was wrong.

Eventually the ship approached Tonga, and everyone was up on the decks in the lovely early morning air watching our approach, together with our confused friend, who despite his misgivings, had been persuaded to set his Day-Date Rolex at 8 a.m., Thursday 9th. Having dropped anchor off the coast near Vavau, we were greeted by a host of beautiful local grass-skirted girls in their dug-out canoes. There was cheering and shouting. Everyone waved to the excited people below, who danced around and waved back with equal enthusiasm. Our friend had made his way to the front of the crowds on deck and was standing against the ship's rail. As often happens in the hubbub of noisy occasions, there was an unexpected break in the cacophony – a short spell of relative silence. Our bewildered friend, who had still refused to give up his quest for a solution, grasped the opportunity of the moment . . . he'd finally get his answer!

He leaned way out over the railings, took a deep breath, and at the top of his voice, he yelled down to the crowds of Tongans below, 'WHAT THE HELL DID YOU PEOPLE DO WITH WEDNESDAY?'

He was never convinced!

In addition to the usual fascinating variety of characters which we normally carry on the ship, any world cruise on *QE2* produces a collection all of its own. On shorter cruises or transatlantic voyages, these characters often don't have sufficient time to emerge from the woodwork. Alternatively, they may be in evidence from the outset, but there just isn't sufficient opportunity to meet them.

Of course, long periods away from the home environment and family security may well be the precipitating circumstances for minor psychological and psychiatric upsets. On the other hand, some of the more elderly passengers may well turn the corner just by virtue of being yet another three months older. There are various forms in which senile dementia may manifest itself: it appears mainly in innocent and acceptable traits, but occasionally in an antisocial or alarming manner. It is not at all unusual for the staff and other passengers to accept some of these lesser problems as part of everyday life on board, and humour the people concerned. Thus, it is often easier to play along with some of the senile fantasies, as long as they're harmless. . . .

On my way to the hospital each day from my cabin, I usually take the same route. On one world cruise I used to pass a dear old lady each morning standing outside her cabin door with an umbrella. On the second or third day I enquired, 'Is it raining out on deck?'

'No idea,' she replied, 'I haven't been out, and I don't intend to.'

'Oh, where are you off to then?'

'Just waiting for the bus.'

'Which bus is that, then?' I asked.

'The one that takes me to breakfast,' she told me in a manner that suggested that I shouldn't be so uninformed.

'What if it doesn't turn up?' I continued with interest.

'I suppose I shall have to walk again,' she said.

'But of course, naturally,' I replied.

Better make a few enquiries and keep an eye on this one, I thought. The cabin staff reassured me that she was fine, and over the ensuing days there was no deterioration in her state. Eventually, it was just as easy to play along.

'Bus late this morning?' I'd call as I went past each day.

'Shouldn't be long now,' she'd call back.

Looking back now, perhaps she thought that it was *me* who was the oddball.

There have been many other occasions of course, when I haven't been so quick to catch on. On one particular cruise, for instance, an elderly lady who was slightly incapacitated and who had some difficulty getting around, became unwell. It wasn't a serious illness, but as it was difficult for her to come along to the hospital to see me, I used to visit her in her cabin and chat with her for a while during each visit. She told me at one point that her daughter was a little worried that she wasn't improving. I told her to reassure her daughter that there wasn't a lot to worry about.

On the next visit we chatted again, and she told me that her daughter was still concerned and didn't like her appearance. 'OK,' I said, 'tell her I'll have a chat when I call tomorrow.'

The following day her daughter wasn't there, but was still apparently worried. 'Well, ask her to call me in the hospital, or be here when I visit you tomorrow,' I instructed.

'Fine, I'll do that,' she replied.

Several days later, the lady was much improved but I still hadn't managed to see her daughter to put her mind at rest. After a further few days, out in the middle of the Indian Ocean, the old lady said again that she would appreciate it if I would speak with her daughter. I explained that, despite all the messages, she hadn't been to see me and I still hadn't met her. 'I'll call back this evening and have a talk with her,' I said. 'What time will she be here?'

'I'm not sure,' was the reply.

'Why's that?' I asked.

'I haven't seen today's schedule.'

'What schedule's that?'

'The airline schedule, of course. I don't know the arrival time of today's plane.'

'Oh! I see. She flies onto the ship each day, does she?'

'But of course, how else do you imagine she could get here, doctor? Swim?'

I felt quite stupid, to say the least. I've no idea why I hadn't caught on sooner.

There are other characters who just defy explanation. In polite terms, they fall into the category of eccentrics. This title is often only accepted due to the fact that they have sufficient money for their so-called eccentricities to be tolerated, otherwise they'd no doubt be under care, and considered by one and all as oddballs.

What would you make of a man who arrived on board ship on the first day of a world cruise, booked for the entire ninety day passage, wearing a soft woollen shirt, no tie, a suit and sandals and one suitcase? Nothing extraordinary you might say. You're right. At a squeeze, you may be able to travel for ninety days with only one suitcase, especially if there's sunshine all the way, and you don't intend to take in too many formal occasions. But if I tell you that what he stands up in is every bit of clothing that he has, and that inside the suitcase are – wait for it – cans of pears! Don't ask for the explanation. We never got one. And why pears? Of course, the cruise was well on its way before people became aware of our fellow passenger's increasingly antisocial aroma and appearance. By this time he had proved himself to be quite convivial. The social staff eventually coaxed him to wash and clean his garments and subsequently encouraged him to acquire some extra clothing from the ship's shop. Thus equipped, he re-emerged, but I must say everyone kept a very, *very* close eye on him.

There are those passengers also, who teeter on the borderline of eccentricity, just stable enough not quite to go over, as with the very pleasant lady who travelled with us on several world cruises and wore a different hat on *every* day of the cruise, from small box hats to enormous picture hats. It won't take you long to work out that on a hundred-day cruise, a hundred hats in a hundred hat boxes takes up one hell of a load of room. So, our lady always booked two cabins around the world, one for herself, and yes, one for her hats!

Then there was 'Kissing Annie', an elderly fire-ball who insisted on kissing every man on the ship that she met, wherever they were, whenever they met, every day of the cruise. If a man was nowhere in sight, she practised a simple alternative: if it moves, kiss it!

177

There are countless examples of these characters on the *QE2*, just as there are all around us, in everyday life. On board ship, however, life seems to be distilled into a greater concentration, and of course living in such constant close proximity, you're more aware of any unusual happenings or people. In order not to totally convince you that ships are full of these oddballs, I shall refrain from the temptation of relating too many of these stories at length; however, there is one beauty that I must pass on before we leave this particular subject.

Another year, another world cruise. The cruise was not many days old when a report filtered in of an odd incident. A passenger had been sitting quietly at the back of the Queen's Room lounge, watching a show, when he suddenly felt a sharp whack on the back of his head: not a heavy blow, but sharp enough to sting, and make him jump. He had leaped up and spun around. There was nobody behind him, just a lady some yards away, walking quietly and slowly out of the room. He didn't know what to make of it, and sat back down to watch the show.

A couple of days later, an elderly couple were sitting on a couch at the end of the theatre bar dance area. They were chatting and enjoying an after-dinner drink. Whack! 'Oh!' yelped the old lady, 'what was that?'

'What was what?' replied her startled husband.

'Something hit the back of my head!'

The old gentleman peered over the rear of the couch, wondering what on earth his wife was talking about. Nobody was there, only a little lady walking quietly towards the exit.

The following afternoon, a young man was sitting in the back row of the cinema balcony. He had had a good lunch and was gently dozing off to sleep as the film went on. Whack! He was brought rapidly out of his dream world by a sharp smack on the head! Still half dozy, he peered back into the dark. Nobody was there, except perhaps the tail end of a woman going out through the swinging doors.

The incidents continued. No-one actually complained or officially reported them, because they weren't severe enough, but they were naturally mentioned to others, including the staff, who were now keeping an eye open.

Whack!

'Did you see that?' a surprised bar-keeper exclaimed to an officer.

'See what?'

'That lady over there, just going out of the room. She smacked that old fellow on the back of the head with a belt as she went by – for no reason at all.'

The officer dashed out, but too late, the culprit had slipped away into the lift.

Over the following few days, more sightings were made of a little woman walking into the bar, belt out, passing behind a couple sitting in the corner . . . Whack! After another couple of incidents, the 'terrorist' was identified at last. Fortunately, nobody had been really hurt, just shocked, and maybe a little alarmed.

The lady was taken to one side and lectured very severely. She listened intently, and with some remorse. That, supposedly, had resolved that problem.

An hour later, at the back of the Club Lido, Whack! In the Columbia restaurant, lunchtime, sipping a spoonful of soup. Whack! A Bingo session in the Double Down Room. 'House!' Whack! She was certainly making her presence felt.

At a conference the following morning, the lady's behaviour was discussed. It was my strong opinion that our belt-wielding friend should be provided with an air ticket, given a refund, and asked to leave the ship before she really flipped and became a psychiatric case, with all the complications of restriction and committing her to a psychiatric medical facility in some remote corner of the world. However, it was decided to give her a further chance and one of the senior members of the hotel staff was designated to supervise her activities and advise her that she'd have to leave the ship if there were any further adverse reports. To the surprise of all concerned, and myself particularly, it worked. The belt disappeared and there were no further sore heads or surprised people.

Some weeks later, the ship called into Cannes in the Mediterranean on an inaugural visit, and lavish preparations had been made to entertain the local dignitaries and press to a lunchtime reception on board. During the reception, the ship would be officially welcomed to the port and there was to be an exchange of speeches and gifts. The guests arrived in droves, very elegantly turned out, and all thrilled to be invited aboard this great and famous ship. The press surged on board, cameras flashing, notepads at the ready, eager to report their impressions and keen to find a new angle on this renowned and well reported visitor to their port.

Executive chef, John Bainbridge, and his staff had been busy – or should I say even busier! There was tray after tray of delicious food, superbly presented as always, laid out in the Q4 Club at the aft end of the ship. There would be drinks to start with, followed no doubt by more drinks, then speeches, presentations, and finally this mouth-watering buffet. The captain, senior officers and cruise staff were all in attendance as hosts, and the reception was proceeding excellently. Who should wander into the room but our head-bashing friend of a few weeks earlier.

She called to a waiter, 'I'll have a gin and tonic.'

Bob Haines, the cruise director, ever on the alert, became aware of her presence in the room. He made his way over to her and explained courteously, 'Excuse me, madam, this is a private function and only for invited guests. I wonder if I can offer you a drink and make you comfortable in another lounge?' The lady turned quietly away. Walking to the buffet, she took a plate and casually helped herself to various items of food from the display.

'I'm sorry, madam,' said Bob, 'but I'm afraid that the food and drinks are for our invited guests from ashore. The restaurants are open now if you want lunch, and there's also a buffet lunch on deck.' The lady turned away towards another tray of food.

Bob caught up with her and continued politely and persuasively, 'Perhaps we can arrange for a tray of food to be brought out for you, to the lounge next door. Your drinks are on the house,' he added, 'it will be our pleasure.'

The lady paused, responding at last. She turned to Bob, smiled thinly, and looking him impassively in the eye, she said quietly, 'F . . . off, you S.O.B. bastard!'

'I beg your pardon?' Bob spluttered.

'Beg my A . . .! you *. . .!! . . .**! *. . .!!! ** . . .! she exploded in a torrent of foul language that would have made a truck driver blush. The assembled guests blinked, and carried on. Surely they hadn't heard what they thought they'd heard?

'*Madam*!' said Bob indignantly, drumming himself up to confront her. 'This is entirely uncalled for, totally out of place.'

'Oh yes?' she replied loudly, 'Well how about this . . . ?' Whereupon she lifted a plate of potato salad from close at hand, and slapped it, smack in the middle of his chest.

'MADAM!' Bob exploded, 'this is disgraceful! Remember where you are!'

'Oh yeah! Well you remember this!' SMACK! A plate of vegetable salad bounced off the top of his head. Bob stood his ground, mayonnaise running under his collar. Whoosh! He dodged, and a meringue flew past his ear.

'Can't eat the food, eh?' yelled our one-woman demolition team, suddenly getting into full swing. ZAP! A salmon mousse found its

180

target, and was followed very rapidly by a dish of dessert. Bob, weaving and ducking like a prize fighter, was nonetheless no match. WHAACK! The dessert arrived. Bull's-eye! Bob stood transfixed! Erect, aloof, and totally dumbfounded, he peered out disbelievingly through a Key-lime pie, his livid red colour making stark contrast to the delicate, pastel-green of the lime filling. Our distinguished cruise director was beginning to look more like the buffet than the buffet!

The area erupted, and was instantly transformed into a set from a Chaplin movie. The only fortunate aspect of the proceedings was that the guests were all gathered at the far end of the room by the bar, away from the action. They looked on boggle-eyed at the incredible impromptu cabaret which was being played under their noses.

'Use the other lounge, eh? You f***ing **. . . . ***,' she shouted at Bob, as she went down the table, scattering the various trays of delicacies with a spectacular flourish. The visitors watched in alarm. The wonderful display of food which they'd been hungrily admiring was disappearing at a rate of knots. The hotel officer in charge of catering, witnessing the destruction of his magnificent presentation, dashed forward. He was a tall, dark, extremely smart young man, who was particularly polite and formal, and stood poker straight.

'Stop that immediately!' he commanded, with a voice heavy with indignation and authority.

She stopped abruptly, paused, looked up at him standing before her, his smartness and presence commanding her attention. She considered this new situation momentarily, then SWISH went her foot, hard up between his legs!

'Woohhh! . . . Aaaahhh!' gasped the officer, as he went cross-eyed, and caught a bowl of fruit salad in the ear to add to his discomfort.

'You **. . . . .**. .*!' she yelled, and crowned him with a shrimp delight.

He reached out weakly to ward off his assailant, but she held the position of command. Grasping his waving hand, she yanked back his thumb in an attempt, apparently, to dislodge it from his person. Kneeling in pain, his free hand protecting his assaulted crotch, his eyes now performed a double-double-cross, under the stress of the new onslaught. His mouth opened wider in the onset of a howling yelp, and was immediately filled with duck pâté, complete with decorative feathers.

Reinforcements arrived. Someone had called the security department and the hospital. Among the first to arrive was Tommy, our chain-smoking Northern-Irish medical attendant, wheezing like a church organ. With the eye of an old campaigner, he sized up the battleground. With the dance floor as a run-up to gather what speed he could muster, he dashed, tripped, and went into a flying rugby tackle on the assailant's legs. He crashed to the floor with his glasses flying. He had hold of a leg, and clung to it for dear life, despite the crème caramel now stuck on his head.

'You **. . .!! . . .**!! **. . .!!' the assailant screamed, as, with the strength of hysteria, she took off across the floor with Tommy bumping along on the end of her leg, like an extra boot, while she continued to howl abuse at him.

The battle was almost done. With her quickstep hampered by her newly acquired appendage the whirlwind was soon overpowered beneath a scrum of figures. With a flurry of arms and legs and a tirade of abuse towards the amazed guests, she departed the battlefield in the direction of the hospital.

Needless to say, the unfortunate lady was very unwell, and required considerable care and attention. Following appropriate treatment on board, she was eventually discharged from the ship into medical care ashore, before being returned safely to her home country.

One can only wonder what on earth our distinguished visitors thought of the show!

VI
DRAMAS AT SEA

Man Overboard

Just the thought of being lost at sea is enough to give me the shivers! However, this is an extremely uncommon and almost impossible accidental occurrence. Even so, every now and then, adults do go over the side, but usually by design.

The ship's rail is a relatively high structure. Getting up, onto, and over it is nearly as difficult as getting over a five-bar gate – not a simple manoeuvre at all – and I doubt whether you've heard of many people accidentally falling over a five-bar gate! Of course, there's always the chance of getting pushed, but that's for Agatha Christie novels. This is for sure: if you go over, there's not much chance of coming back to lecture on the subject.

Unquestionably, every man-overboard incident is a compelling drama, but let me present two stories which you may find of particular interest. The first is a total and still unsolved mystery.

Several years ago, during one of *QE2*'s world cruises, amongst our passengers there was a titled lady from one of the mid-European countries. As befitted her status, she was exceedingly elegant and sophisticated; her presentation was delightful, her manner gentle. Her clothes were exquisite, with an endless flow of beautiful gowns from the world's great fashion houses, and she was tastefully adorned with the most glamorous of jewellery. In short, she represented everything that the *QE2*'s image portrayed. She was travelling alone, and had booked passage from America to New Zealand.

During her stay on board ship she made an assortment of new friends, all of whom were enchanted with her company. She was very noticeable around the ship and, as the voyage progressed, she became one of the more easily recognized world cruise characters, by passengers and crew alike, but although she became a delightful companion to her new-found friends, she remained slightly reserved.

185

Certain details of her life and background, and no doubt her inner thoughts, were never discussed. However, it was determined that she was a widow, her husband having died many years previously in unrevealed circumstances. She was apparently almost alone in the world, had no close relatives, and few close friends. On a day-to-day basis, life, to all intents and purposes, appeared mainly rosy, but one could intuitively feel that, beneath her happy and pleasant exterior, there was a deeper, perhaps sadder, aspect of her life.

As the ship neared New Zealand, our lady made enquiries at the bureau regarding an extension of her cruise, and arrangements were made for her to continue with the ship until Singapore. Presumably she was enjoying the *QE2* and her new associates – or perhaps, on reflection, the appeal of returning home wasn't sufficiently attractive, at least, for the time being.

The cruise continued. Little more of her character and background was revealed, except that it was apparent that she was a very wealthy woman – the various arrays of precious jewellery were eye catching. Before we reached Singapore she made a further decision, and again rebooked with the bureau to continue her journey on to Japan.

The days continued, nothing untoward occurred. The cruise remained most enjoyable, and her company remained equally pleasant. As we all do at times, she naturally spent occasional periods sitting quietly alone, gazing dreamily out over an endless ocean. Who knows what she may have pondered? Who indeed knows what any of us are thinking?

Before our arrival in Japan, she made yet another visit to the bureau. This time, she extended her cruise to Hawaii: six days of sailing across that enormous stretch of North Pacific Ocean to the beautiful island of Oahu, which has all the splendour and romance of the tropical Hawaiian islands. The cruise continued, everyone was having a great time; new faces to befriend who had joined the cruise along the way.

Six long days at sea. This is the time that I enjoy most on a ship, when we are not dashing in and out of harbour. The ship settles into a routine, the backlog of work is sorted out and there's time to meet new people, enjoy each other's company and the full benefit of the family atmosphere of the ship. True cruisers will know exactly what I mean.

Our elegant lady continued to take part in all the activities and was, as ever, charming company. As Hawaii approached, she didn't revisit the bureau; she had apparently finally decided that Oahu was to be her ultimate destination on this cruise. The days at sea went well; the lady, as usual, was in evidence on every evening, including the evening before arrival in Hawaii.

On her last night before disembarking, she was more elegant than ever, glittering with both personality and diamonds, and was, as always, dressed beautifully. The following morning, the ship made its graceful entrance into Oahu, past the memorable site of Diamond Head mountain and the city of Honolulu spread out along the shores beside it. I had gone to the bridge and had watched Captain Bob Arnott bring this 'Leviathan' alongside the dock which was thronged with excited people, thrilled to see the *QE2*, this remarkable ship, visiting their port.

As the ship was tied up and the gangways went down, the captain was approached by one of his deck officers. The cabin steward had reported that our lady hadn't slept in her bed last night. This, under normal circumstances on a ship, wouldn't be a cause for comment, but as she was due to disembark this morning, he had naturally expected to find her there with her bags packed and ready to go. Her bags indeed were not packed. Some of her clothes were in cases, but the packing was far from complete. The steward had checked with the restaurant; she hadn't taken breakfast. He phoned around the various rooms – no luck. Eventually he reported the situation to his head of department, who in turn had advised the captain. Announcements were made over the PA system. Known friends were contacted – still no luck. The captain was again advised of the developments. He, in turn, instigated a full search of the ship.

No lady, no letter, no notes, no clue. She had disappeared! She was last seen leaving the casino late in the evening; nothing more. The weather had been calm, the ship had been steady, the decks were dry. Her activities had revealed nothing, her conversations had been quite normal. So what had happened? How? Why?

There was no question whatsoever of taking the ship back out of harbour, for several reasons. If she had been in the water for any length of time, the cold temperature left no possible chance of survival. The time of the possible incident was completely unknown. A multitude of manoeuvres were carried out as the ship approached Hawaii during the night. The sea wasn't rough, but certainly wasn't flat. The winds and current around the islands are infinitely variable. The captain's decision was, unfortunately, very simple to make. In addition to these factors, the ship was already tied alongside and in these circumstances it would be the role of the coastguard to initiate a search. Between them they considered it a non-starter.

Rumours abounded. Everyone was shocked. Friends analysed past conversations, looking for hints, discussed the company she may have kept, worked and worked at the teaser – not an inkling. Her safety deposit box was opened. It contained money, valuables and jewellery of an estimated worth of $2,000,000! The sleuths were amazed and stumped, but they still sought a solution.

The ship had been party to a further drama on that same day of arrival in Hawaii. An Australian passenger had been apprehended by the authorities as he walked off the ship with a large case full of opals. He was charged later in the day with smuggling. Had he met our lady? Had he befriended her? Was there a connection? Two dramas! Everyone was determined to connect them.

Alternatively, as the ship was docked before the search was carried out, had she perhaps slipped quietly ashore, unnoticed, into Oahu? If so, for what reason?

The solution which I preferred was the most romantic of all, and emerged some months later. There was an unconfirmed report, which reached the ship, that the lady's husband had been a fighter pilot during World War II, and had flown extensively over the Pacific waters. Tragically, he was shot down and killed; his body was never recovered. It appears that his plane crashed into the ocean and sank into the depths. The location? More or less a point on the North Pacific ocean which *QE2* had passed at around midnight on the night prior to our arrival in Hawaii.

If that's not true, I don't wish to know!

The second story involved two people whom I knew very well.

Most ships, during their years of sailing, will acquire admirers, faithful supporters who, although they don't work on board, travel frequently and become well known and familiar faces. Eventually they become close friends and, ultimately, part of the family.

The best example of this was a certain American lady who had travelled so frequently with the ship that she managed to achieve more times at sea on board *QE2* in one particular year than I did. Over the years she had a love affair with ships, and particularly the *QE2*. Her name was Lulu Edwards. Lulu's shore-side interests revolved around the Reynolds Tobacco Company – or vice versa. To regular travellers on the *QE2*, Lulu was as well known as the senior officers – in some cases, perhaps more so.

Amongst our other well known passengers was a married couple who, over the years, had travelled frequently on all our ships, and who – partly because of their shore-side connections with Cunard, but mainly because of their particularly pleasant company – were long established family. I shall call them Edwin and Rose. Edwin and Rose were a great couple, very vivacious, outgoing people, who always contributed more to an occasion than they received. They knew the *QE2* from end to end, including the personnel and many of the repeat passengers, and they were welcome faces in all of the officers' and crew's social areas on board.

As the years progressed, Rose unfortunately developed an increasingly incapacitating illness. Although still a regular passenger, she was unable to enjoy her cruises as before, and eventually her disability created some degree of discomfort and distress. The quality of her life, and consequently – as they were such a devoted couple – Edwin's life, also, was diminished, but to what extent nobody really knew, as they weren't of a nature to impose their problems on friends. They continued to joke and smile through their tribulations.

Every year, *QE2* takes a Christmas cruise, which is always very active and great fun for the passengers. A couple of years ago, Edwin and Rose were on board to join the revelry of one of these Christmas jaunts. As always, they were glad to be aboard, and were welcomed by all. As the cruise progressed, it was apparent to all that Rose's health had deteriorated, and her incapacity increased. To friends who were close to them both, Edwin showed an increased concern, and was obviously more deeply distressed. However, in true form they involved themselves in all the goings-on around the ship; they were present at all the parties and, as always, added to the fun.

Christmas Day arrived. The ship was at sea sailing around the beautiful waters of the Caribbean. The choice of parties and functions to attend on board ship on Christmas Day is staggering. Bear in mind that the *QE2* is 'home' for over a thousand people! Edwin and Rose were invited to many of the staff gatherings and were in evidence at a fair cross-section. They contributed to the celebrations, laughing along with the crowd, never complaining or showing any worries. Lunchtime came and went, then more celebrations; the parties and activities progressed into the afternoon. Edwin and Rose were still there, joining in.

As the day continued, the activities slowed and the happy crowds went off in various directions to rest up in preparation for the next round of activities during the evening and night. Edwin and Rose departed. They reappeared in the early evening for even more cocktail parties and then went in to enjoy their Christmas dinner in the company of their friends. After dinner, they took their leave to move on to other celebrations.

The following morning a note was found in our friends' cabin, addressed to the security officer who had been a close pal over the years. As a result, the ship was searched from end to end, and from end to end again. It couldn't be true! . . . but it was. They were gone!

Edwin and Rose had walked happily away from the parties and festivities, away from their friends who they'd known for so many years, walked to the upper decks of the ship, carefully helped each other over the ship's rail, stood in the cool night breeze, looking out over the calm Caribbean seas, took in the fragrance of the night air and distant islands. Life had given them many pleasures, they had shared wonderful days together, days when the most precious of all life's commodities, good health, had been their gift. The sadness which Edwin now felt and shared with his lovely wife, as her illness caused her more despair, must have been overwhelming. Hand in hand they stood, perhaps pausing, reflecting, never closer, perhaps never more in love. Holding tight they stepped from our world, and dropped rapidly, quietly, down into the deep waters surging below.

They were never found.

Burial at Sea

Although some of my friends at home find it difficult to believe, it is my experience that in any prolonged discussion about ships, the subject of death and how it is dealt with at sea will inevitably arise. As strange a subject as it may seem, there are many interesting aspects.

If you consider the types of passengers on a ship from the point of view of character and age, it's fairly apparent that there will be a tendency for more elderly and more mature people to travel. Consequently, the average age on board will be higher than in an equivalent holiday community ashore. It is very natural to assume then, that with an older than average cross-section of the community on board, there will be a high incidence of deaths. Surprisingly, this is not the case. This may be for a combination of reasons.

Firstly, the standard of medicine which is achieved on all the better ships these days is of a very high level. Secondly, probably as a result of the immediate availability of the medical facilities and the possibility of closer attention, supervision and follow-up care, excellent results are achieved. Thirdly, it would be very difficult, and most unusual, for anyone on board ship who was unwell not to be detected early and referred for medical care promptly. A fourth factor is that most, if not all, passengers who may recently have been ill, and particularly the elderly, will have been cleared by their own doctors before leaving home. Thus the elderly people who are restricted to staying at home are, ironically, the ones more likely to become unwell. The chronically ill passengers who travel with us are usually referred directly to the medical department by their own doctor, and therefore come immediately under our medical supervision.

There is a more gloomy aspect. It would be great to be the masters of our own destinies, but unfortunately this isn't so: we are certainly unable to choose the times of our illnesses. Occasionally there are those amongst us who, depending upon your view point, are either unlucky or lucky enough to die during the height of an enjoyable holiday. In most instances, if a death occurs on board ship the majority of the passengers will never be aware of it. The 'town's' internal system is set in operation, and the incident is dealt with very quietly and discreetly.

It never ceases to surprise me how rumour and general conversation can distort facts. Without fail, if a death occurs on a long voyage, someone will have time to pass on snippets of misinformation. Invariably, within a few days there'll be distorted figures of 'several deaths', maybe 'suspicious circumstances', a 'passenger lost overboard', and so on. The death of one passenger can often become five or six with the retelling over a week or two.

Consider the train of events.

'Did you know that a gentleman from our table died yesterday?' asks a passenger of his fellow voyagers.

'Oh really? Well, someone else has died too, a man who played bridge with us,' comes the reply.

'Well, well. The ship must be going through a bad patch because the man in the cabin next door to me died as well, yesterday,' adds another.

If only they stopped to work it out. They are often speaking about the same man! And so the numbers grow.

Despite the inevitable rumours which result from lack of specific information, it is still considered best overall to restrict the information, mainly for the sake of the spouse. There are occasions, as you may well imagine, when it is even more necessary to be discreet – when the partner *isn't* the spouse!

If a death should occur, then understandably the next of kin are extremely distressed, and naturally become the top priority. The spouse and relatives having been considered, comforted, advised and taken care of, what of the body? Do we carry coffins? Do we have a morgue? Can the captain still perform a burial at sea?

The body having been taken to the hospital, it is the doctor's decision whether the cause of death was natural. He will decide whether there are any circumstances which need to be explained, and if the cause of death can be determined with reasonable certainty. If there is any significant doubt, then the body must be preserved and transported to the next port of call where it is subjected to a post-mortem examination; the authorities then take care of its disposal. Under very exceptional circumstances, an investigation may be carried out on board ship.

192

If the ship's doctor is satisfied that the death was from natural causes, then there is a choice of outcomes. To the surprise of some people, the captain of the ship is still empowered to carry out a burial at sea. As a passing point of interest, many passengers are even more surprised to discover that the captain is *not* empowered to carry out a marriage at sea – that is to say, one which would be official – and hasn't been able to do so for many years. Marriages are, in fact, carried out on board ships, but these are conducted by a memeber of the church, or if the ship is in port, under the auspices of a local official. Possibly some captain might oblige the occasional couple who wish to officially cement an on-board relationship. However, this marriage would – conveniently or otherwise – only be for the duration of the voyage. Burial at sea, on the other hand, is permanent!

So, if the doctor and the captain are satisfied that the circumstances are acceptable, who gets buried at sea? Alternatively, approaching the question from the other end, who doesn't get buried at sea? If the next of kin should decide – or the deceased person has previously stipulated – that the body must be returned home for burial or cremation, then again it is kept on board until the next port of call. Arrangements can then be made with local funeral directors for the journey home. In some instances the next of kin may decide to keep the body on board until arrival back in the home port. In these cases the body must be preserved for the remainder of its sea voyage. In days gone by this was achieved in various ways. One of Britain's greatest maritime heroes, Admiral Lord Nelson, was placed in a barrel of rum following his death at Trafalgar, and the body returned to England for his state funeral. In more recent times, bodies have been preserved in bath tubs filled with ice. In poorly equipped ships, the body has been kept in the meat locker or meat fridge. However, recently built ships of any acceptable standard do *not* store the bodies alongside the lamb chops! All vessels that I've ever sailed on have a morgue and generally, the builders are never pessimistic enough to cater for more than three bodies.

A couple of incidents come to mind, regarding ships' mortuaries.

The location of the mortuary varies from ship to ship, depending on many factors relating to design and space available. On one of the ships on which I served, the mortuary was down below in the same area as all the main freezer storage rooms, a cold, stark, isolated area surrounded by large, solid units. The low chugging noise of the engines was interrupted regularly by the heavy, sighing 'thuuuumpp' of the big sealed doors. The storekeeper in this area was a little old

Italian man, a very boisterous, noisy character, who, to put it mildly, was not at all amused by the fact that the mortuary was down a small, dark alley-way adjacent to his freezer compartments.

On one occasion we had prepared a body and placed it on one of the shelves in the fridge. After a few hours, during the late evening, I went down to check that the freezer was working correctly. The fridge was a large, walk-in affair and, not too sensibly, the light switch was on the wall inside – in the dark. I groped around blindly, pressing and pulling various buttons and levers on the wall until I found the right one and the lights came on. I checked around and made sure that the temperature was OK and everything was working.

All walk-in refrigerators have some form of safety device which can be used if the door should close and trap you inside. The safety device for this freezer was an alarm bell which, when activated by a push-button inside the fridge, sounded in the storekeeper's office and cabin. Unknown to me, as I fumbled in the dark, groping for the light switch, I had pressed this button.

The old Italian storekeeper, not aware that I had gone to check the fridge, but knowing that there was a dead body in there, was alerted by the alarm. When I had finished in the freezer, I pushed open the door and stepped out into the dark, quiet alley-way. At the end of the corridor, a set of clenched, white knuckles, together with the forehead, eyes and nose of a very pale face, peered round the corner of the wall. As I emerged, there was a loud sigh, then *thump!*, as our terrified storekeeper spread himself on the deck in a dead faint. It was the first time that I had ever seen him in a non-speaking role!

Part of the reason why I always check the mortuary after the first few hours relates back to an incident during my earlier days at sea.

On this particular ship we had a brand new refrigeration officer, a young engineer who was in charge of the maintainance and repair of the fridges and freezers.

An eighty-year-old gentleman, whom I had met earlier in the cruise, had socially confided in me that he was on his honeymoon, this being no less than his seventh bride! He was a wild old character, who in his own words had a load of money to 'blow' and was intent on having a fling with his young bride, who was forty years his junior. As has often been observed from a mathematical angle, eighty into forty won't 'go' too many times, and this problematical equation was resolved in the old man's case when he pegged out on the final hurdle, or 'jump', of his life's race course. His bride was amazingly cool about the incident; indeed, she was quite pleased that she had made his passage across the Styx a pleasurable trip.

A change of menu. Lunch ashore with friends during a *QE2* call at Madeira. Getting fresh with Bert Weedon's wife, Maggie, in company with the singer Iris Williams.

One of the attractions of the job! 'Nigel's Angels', friends and table companions on a *QE2* Bermuda cruise. (Left to right) Sophia, Debbie, Carol, Tammy.

'Off the hooks' and on the town. A night ashore in Manilla during *QE2'S* world cruise 1985. Spa manageress, Susie Mitzkat, myself, Nursing Sister, Tina Callow, social hostess, Margarita Jordan,

The Chairman of Trafalgar House, the parent company of Cunard Lines, Sir Nigel Broakes and Lady Broakes host a cocktail party in their penthouse suite for the ship's senior officers during the 1988 world cruise.

(Left to right) Dr David O'Connel, Staff Captain Keith Stanley, Mrs Joan Arnott, Captain Robert (Bob) Arnott and me.

Libby Morgan, Senior Nursing Sister on the *QE2* 1988 world cruise.

Myself with Billie Bailley, Senior Nursing Sister, in the operating theatre aboard *QE2*.

Two possible reasons why we see so many male patients! Our physiotherapist, Eve Tytherleigh, and Nursing Sister, Julia James.

On stage in the Lido night club. Impromptu after hours 'treatment' for the passengers, with 'Mr Guitar' Bert Weedon, Steve Clark of the Clark Brothers act, and friend and associate of many years, Dr Tony Bowen.

The officers' 'Ward Room Show'. Joe Loss and his orchestra in the background. At least he found my performance amusing!

Christmas Eve in the Double Room. *QE2* officers, crew members, entertainers and concessionaires get together for a lantern procession in their 'winter overcoats' and bring some traditonal Christmas cheer to the Caribbean, leading the passengers in carol singing.

The Captain's cocktail party with dentist, Keith Mason, Cunard Group Medical Director, Dr Peter Oliver, and Dr Alan Kirwin.

Dentist, Keith Mason. The *QE2* calls at France. Returning from the supermarket at Cherbourg with French pâté, cheese, wine and fresh bread for the traditional Medical Department departmental sailing party.

The doctor's cocktail party is held on every voyage, when friends such as Ernie Wise and Mrs Denise Murphy (no, not Mrs Thatcher!) can relax in the Principal Medical Officer's quarters.

A rare gathering of the medical staff at a crew changeover at Banbury on the *QE2* 1985 world cruise. Back row: Dentist Keith Mason, Nursing Sister Carol Hargreaves, Dr Alan Kirwin, NS Ellie Ellicot, myself, NS Libby Morgan, NS Sara Murray, NS Chrissie Owen, Dr David Holroyd, Medical Petty Officer Brian Killick. Front row: Medical Assistant Derrick Stickland, MA Ray Gorse, MA Malcolm Woodford, NS Julia James, physiotherapist Eve Tytherleigh, MPO Frank Henshaw.

Reception committees come in all shapes and sizes. This gathering is typical of many of the South Sea Island welcomes, including our 'date line' arrival in Tonga, but in fact these dug-outs are from the San Blas islands off Panama.

QE2 sails into New York past the World Trade Centre.

This was taken during the 1988 world cruise.

Having taken his smiling body to the hospital, I contacted the refrigeration officer, and in nautical terms, asked him to 'flash up' the mortuary. Being new to his job, he asked what temperature I required and as I wasn't aware of our new engineer's inexperience, I merely informed him that the body would be on board for about three days and that I'd appreciate it if he could set the temperature as usual. Presumably not wanting to admit his lack of knowledge, he said, 'OK.' The body was prepared, sent down, and placed in the morgue.

Sometime later in the day, I visited the cabin of the 'grieving' bride. She was coping quite well and had settled down, apparently deriving some minor consolation from the prospect of the insurance pay-out. During our discussions, she advised me that she had decided that she would like the wedding ring from her dead husband's finger and she would also be very grateful if I could arrange for him to be dressed in his wedding outfit, which was on board. Anything to oblige!

I went along to the morgue, with a couple of attendants, to collect the body and take it back to the hospital. Inside the freezer, I was caught abruptly by the intense cold, and on examining the temperature gauge found that the old Casanova was -30 °C! If you bear in mind that *deep* freeze is around -14 °C, you can imagine the condition of our recently departed reveller. If he had been dropped on the dockside he would have shattered! Trying to remove his rings certainly wasn't a clever idea: his fingers might have popped off like icicles! As for trying to get him into his wedding suit . . .!

Having located our refrigeration 'expert' and rendered my appraisal of his talents, I instructed him to 'get cooking' and defrost the body.

Meanwhile, back in the cabin, I had to find an explanation for not complying with his wife's wishes. With a flash of inspiration, I explained that the ship's mortuary was of a very modern design: our engineers had set a time-lock on the compartment in order to maintain a stable temperature, and this was set to release just prior to our arrival in Singapore.

The ice block melted, the rings were removed, and dressing the body was, to say the least, infinitely easier. Everyone ended up happy.

All's well that ends well. I'm sure the old boy would have been in hoots at the story.

In days gone by, with few exceptions, anyone who died on board ship, was buried at sea.

One of the long-standing traditions of the British Navy is that the ship's bosun was, and still is, responsible for the arrangements for the burial. This includes sewing the body, with some form of heavy weight tied to the leg, inside a canvas bag. You may be interested – or upset – to know that in the days of wooden galleons, the final stitch always passed through the nose of the deceased. This procedure was originally devised as a safety check to make sure that the man was really dead, which in fact was not as unnecessary as it may seem – he might possibly have been dead drunk, or maybe comatosed, and of course, following the height of battle, the severely injured might easily have been confused with the dead by inexperienced, non-medical personnel. A more interesting reason for the check, however, was that in the days of press-ganged crews, it wasn't uncommon for a man to feign death when the ship was near land. He would then be dumped over the side in his canvas bag. Inside the bag would be a knife, strapped to his side by his pals so that he could cut himself free and swim for shore, and freedom.

For his unsavoury morning's work, the bosun was traditionally paid with a bottle of rum and on busy trips he probably ran the risk of becoming an alcoholic!

Nowadays, the restrictions mentioned earlier apply to burial at sea. Having satisfied the requirements, the next of kin may then request or be given the choice for the burial to take place. You may be surprised to learn that modern satellite navigation is able to pinpoint not only the position of a ship on the ocean, but more specifically, almost the location of the bridge of a large liner. If the more sentimental of us wished to return to the burial place of a lost relative or friend with a wreath each year, you could do so very accurately. Being practical, burial at sea makes very good sense, particularly as it avoids the enormous expenses and hassle of flying the body home, not to mention the already high costs of a normal funeral – and emotionally it can be an extremely moving ceremony and occasion.

The ceremony is conducted by the captain in the presence of the next of kin, friends and a small party of senior personnel and interested, or involved, officers and crew. The party will include the bosun and the bosun's mates who handle the body and tipping devices. If a minister from the appropriate church or religion is present on board, he may also be in attendance, or conduct the ceremony.

The ceremony is usually conducted in what is referred to as a shell door space – an access opening in the side of the ship, usually near the waterline and preferably towards the stern. It is carried out on most occasions at the very first light of dawn, which has the added advantage of deterring the curious onlookers on the decks above, and preventing the odd-ball amateur photographers from getting their 'souvenir' shots of the body hitting the water! The body, enclosed in the canvas, is placed on a board, which is mounted up on trestles, and lies in the opening with feet pointing out to sea. A flag of the nation of citizenship is draped over the form, if available – if not, a Union Jack is used.

The setting is very dramatic in its simplicity: the semi-light of dawn, a chill in the air, the ship heaving and rolling over the grey ocean; the half-illuminated faces of the quiet, still figures around the body, in contrast to the hissing, lively surge of the sea along the ship's side; under the flag, with its tails dancing and fluttering in the breeze, the starkness of a small form, poised on the edge of an enormous, dark expanse, the endless stretch of curling water outside our cocoon, reaching out to the horizon.

'. . . we commit his body to the deep.'

The bosun and his assistant grasp the board and tilt it slowly. The body slips away from under the flag, and there is a distinctive quiet, low zzzziiiiiiiip as the coarse canvas runs over the edge of the board. A pause . . . then the indistinct 'splash' as the sea takes its charge. The sudden realization of finality. The sharp contrast between two adjacent moments – now here . . . now gone – underlining the division between life and death.

The ship moves on, the body and person abruptly separated from the community, left behind in the increasing distance, in the past. There, where the body lay moments before, is an empty space. The ship, your world, life . . . continues.

There are, inevitably, many stories relating to burial at sea; some amusing, some serious and many apparently irreverent. One well known and often related incident occurred on a passage to South Africa, on board the *Edinburgh Castle*.

Following the death of a passenger on board, the body was to be buried at sea. The bosun, as usual, made all the necessary arrangements, and as dawn approached, he and his assistant transported the body to the shell door, laid it on the trestle table, and draped it with the flag. Having completed the arrangements, it was then the bosun's duty to contact the various persons concerned and gather the funeral party together for the ceremony. His assistant – the bosun's mate – was a newcomer to the job. In his eagerness and curiosity, he decided to test the tilting action of the board on the trestles. With the unrestrained enthusiasm and strength of youth, he gave the board a vigorous shove. The board tilted abruptly, and, without complaint or comment, the co-operative body shot briskly out into the dark, and the bosun was left with a very essential participant missing from his funeral arrangements.

Having displayed his disapproval with a boot moving as briskly as the departed body towards his assistant's rear end, the bosun considered the situation. The ship was slowing, the funeral party was waiting to be gathered, and there was little time left. What a dilemma, at 6 a.m.!

His solution was simple. While he gathered the captain and funeral party and delayed the proceedings as much as possible, the mate was despatched to the vegetable locker to collect two bags of potatoes and lay them under the flag! In the darkness of the alcove and the early dawn light, it would be impossible to distinguish the shape, and certainly nobody would lift the flag. A mad dash ensued.

A short while later, the bosun very apprehensively led the party into the shell door space. To his great relief there, in the dim light, attended by the grave, quiet figure of the mate, lay the 'body' under the flag.

All stood round with heads bowed. The simple service proceeded. The words were spoken; the captain gave a small nod to the bosun. The board was tilted, and the form slid gently out from under the flag and disappeared over the side of the ship. The bosun heaved a sigh of relief, but amongst the small gathering, nobody was quite sure what they'd heard. With heads bowed and furtive glances from side to side, each tried to determine from the other faces whether anyone else might have heard the same thing. Nobody was sure, and nobody would mention it. Had they really heard *Splash!*, and then again . . . *Splash! Two* splashes?

In gentler and more considerate times, before the pressures of commercialism, high oil prices and, more particularly, tight time schedules, the ship would be stopped or slowed down during a burial service as a mark of respect to the deceased. However, these times are gone and it is not uncommon for the body to be launched over the side with the ship at full speed . . . whereupon it occasionally goes skipping over the waves like a flat stone, before sinking to its resting place.

A burial at sea, of course, doesn't necessarily require a body. It is often the custom for people who have been cremated to have the urn and ashes buried at sea, or their ashes scattered to the winds, over the ocean. The normal ceremony of scattering the ashes can be just as touching and dramatic as a burial at sea, but isn't always so. Sometimes the urn is merely dropped into the ocean by the captain, or whoever, at a specially designated spot. All very simple. However, events can sometimes take an unusual turn.

On one occasion the ashes of a former shipmate were brought on board, with the request for them to be 'buried' off the coast of South Africa. He had been a popular man and it was decided that, before launching the urn off into the blue yonder, a group of his old buddies would have a few drinks together to toast his memory. The wake became a happy and unsteady occasion; the drinks flowed freely. As it happened, nobody in the cabin had ever been involved with the burial of ashes at sea before. As spirits were downed and enthusiasm raised, some bright spark made the observation that if the urn was thrown into the ocean, it would float, and might end up on the west coast of Africa.

'No it won't!'

'Yes it will!'

'It'll sink.'

'It won't.'

The alcohol obviously did nothing to enhance the technical level of the discussion.

Nobody by that stage was sober enough to conclude that you should merely remove the lid and throw it in separately; instead, someone suggested a 'float test'.

'Fill the bath-tub!'

Sure enough, there amidst the staggering, hazy forms of the mourners, the urn bobbed up and down in the bath-tub.

'Fetch the carpenter!'

'What for?'

'Drill it.'

'What?'

'Drill holes in the urn – then it'll sink!'

The carpenter arrived. Holes were drilled, and back into the bath-tub went the urn for another 'float test'. Sure enough, down it went, and up came bubbles of air through the holes. Unfortunately, they were bubbles filled with the ashes of dear departed friend. . . . A boozy hand reached in, grasped the urn, and yanked it out. Water spouted from the holes as from a colander, accompanied by our departed friend's ashes. At this rate, he wouldn't be departing any further than the bathroom floor!

The urn was quickly dropped into a box and, at the head of the funeral procession, was transported rapidly to the ship's rail, leaving behind a trail to permanently mark the final passage of an old shipmate on his journey off the ship.

His remains remain at sea, but he would probably have been happier had he known that the remainder of his remains remained on board!

In relation to the ceremony of ash scattering, a windy day is not the greatest asset. A tale was told to me by one of Cunard's captains – he now holds the company's most senior position at sea – of an incident in which he was involved as a young deck officer. He was serving at that time under a captain who was a particularly formal man, not renowned for his sense of humour; a man whose presence and gaze conveyed paragraphs of words.

A retired employee of the company had died in recent weeks, and had been cremated. It had been his request that his ashes should be scattered at sea from the bridge wing of his old ship. The urn and his remains were subsequently flown out to the ship, which was sailing in the Caribbean. Arrangements were made for the ceremony.

The ship was cruising in warm waters, and the rig of the day was 'whites'. In respect for their departed shipmate, all the officers attending the ceremony were dressed formally, and were in starched, snow-white, tropical uniforms called 'number 10s', buttoned crisply and smartly to the neck.

The assembly having gathered, the captain, dressed in his Sunday best conducted the short service. He turned smartly to our story-teller, who had been given charge of the urn, and instructed him to go ahead with the dispersal of the ashes over the side of the bridge wing.

We all know what he *should* have done, but he didn't! Perhaps because of the formality of the occasion, or not having ever been involved in such a ceremony before, he unscrewed the cap of the urn and scattered the ashes, yes, *up*wind! A sudden, sharp gust, and they were gone – as quickly as that! He turned back from the side and confronted the captain . . . with horror. The captain, in his immaculate white suit, had been transformed to grey from head to toe.

The captain stood and glowered. Not a word, not an utterance. Glowering! Our deck officer was pinned to the rail by the gaze. What should he do, what could he say?

'I, I . . . I . . .' he stammered. He looked at the sight.

'Sir . . . uh, Sir,' he said, as the piercing eyes looked out from their grey surrounds. 'Don't, uh . . .' He rolled his eyes to heaven, for inspiration. 'Don't . . .'

Finally, he got it out.

'Captain, Sir . . . *Don't lick your lips!!*'

The tale that follows is probably the most outlandish one I know on this subject.

Some time ago, the departmental head of a ship which has long since gone was a particularly nasty, very unpopular character. He gave the members of his department a very hard time and was, without exception, disliked by all. It is a very sad reflection on the man's life that a severe illness and his eventual demise, whilst on leave, didn't arouse much sympathy or cause the shedding of at least one tear on board ship. As had been his wish, he was cremated.

One day, a short time later, an urn containing his ashes was brought on board ship for burial at sea. As fate would have it, the urn appeared on the desk of a lifelong enemy who had been harassed along with others for many years. This man – who is in fact a good friend of mine, and who related this story to me – was himself an infamous character, with a wild and wicked past and an equally devilish mind.

From the urn, he took a little heap of ashes. Placing a pinch of the ashes into every one of several envelopes, he then distributed the envelopes round all the members of the department who had previously worked under their now dead boss. Accompanying the ashes, was a note which stated, 'Try sniffing a pinch of these ashes, courtesy of your ex-boss. He got up everyone's nose all his life, so he should make great snuff!'

Mayday

When you're working on board *QE2*, although you're unable to see the outside world or breathe the fresh air for a major proportion of the day, you are nonetheless aware of the weather beyond the steel boundaries of your cocoon. From the medical department's point of view, the most obvious reflection of the state of the ocean is the incidence of seasickness, and on a sunshine cruise, the lobster faces, blisters and moans are the barometer of exterior weather conditions.

There are, of course, areas of the ocean where the weather is pretty well predictable, and the North Atlantic out of season is one of these areas. Having passed through the iceberg belt on a westbound crossing of the North Atlantic, a ship sailing on the more northerly but paradoxically shortest route known as the Great Arc approaches the vast area of relatively shallow waters off the coast of Newfoundland and Nova Scotia – the Grand Banks. Here, amazingly, in the middle of the ocean, you become aware of distant lights all around as the ship sails past oil rigs and fleets of small fishing boats. Due to the abrupt change in depth of water and the associated temperature difference, it is not at all unusual to find the ship suddenly blanketed over with thick, swirling sea fog, even during the summer months. The seas here are relatively calm, but the weather is often damp, misty, grey, eerie and depressing, as was the case during my next tale.

The *QE2* was on a westbound journey. The ship had left Southampton three days earlier, and having called in for a brief few hours in Cherbourg, France, she had then turned out into the endless heaving swell of the unfriendly North Atlantic towards Boston, Massachusetts. It was late autumn and no-one was expecting a suntan.

Early afternoon, on the fourth day at sea. I had shared lunchtime with two particularly good friends of mine, the first of whom was Staff Captain Keith Stanley who, despite his tender years, had already experienced what must have been his ultimate professional thrill, when he was appointed as the youngest ever captain of the *QE2* for a two-month relief period. The other great pal was the silver fox of the ocean, Executive Cruise Director, John Butt, the 'daddy' of all cruise directors and probably one of the best raconteurs afloat.

Before lunch, gathered together in John's cabin for a drink, we had been joined by a few friends, including the head of the BBC radio and television network, Bill Cotton, and film actor Jeremy Irons, who was travelling with us together with Meryl Streep for a promotion of their film, *The French Lieutenant's Woman*. We had been discussing the relative merits of British and American broadcasting, chewing the fat generally, and swapping a host of stories of our various experiences around the countries and oceans of the world.

At the end of a hard morning's work, which had been followed by a lecture on ship-board health and hygiene, and topped off with a long-winded committee meeting, the lunchtime session had been excellent therapy, and in a far more relaxed mood I headed for my cabin to put my feet up for half an hour with a book before returning to the hospital. *Beep beep beep beep beep* went the page clipped to my belt, and a crackling voice announced, 'Dr Roberts, please contact the bridge.'

I went to the nearest phone. 'PMO here. You called?'

'Yes. The captain passes his compliments Dr Roberts, and would you please join him in the radio room.'

I went back along the full length of the ship and up four decks to the radio room at the forward end of the boat deck.

'Hello, Nigel.' I was greeted by Captain Bob Arnott who was sitting with the two radio officers amidst a jungle of electronic equipment – our link with the world beyond. Dials were flickering, needles twitching, digital displays counting, the telex machine buzzing, and the radio officer, headset attached, was chatting merrily with some never-to-be-seen colleague 2000 miles away, as though he were some long lost brother.

The captain continued in his comfortable, Lancashire accent, 'I've received a call from the coastguard, Nigel. A fishing boat on the Grand Banks to the North-west of our heading has sent out a Mayday signal. Apparently, one of the crew members on board has been involved in an accident. He's had a pretty nasty head injury and they're asking for assistance. They're too far out for a helicopter rescue, and anyhow they're in thick fog. The area's been scanned for shipping and, as we're the nearest vessel, the coastguard has directed us to assist them.'

'How far off is she?' I asked.

'About six hours' full steam. I've asked the navigator for a new course and we've already turned in the general direction,' he told me. 'It'll put us way off our own course, and we'll be losing a lot of time which we won't be able to make up. We'll be quite late into Boston. I've spoken with New York office to put them in the picture. That's spoiled their day, I'm afraid! There'll be a hell of a lot of rearranging to do.'

'*C'est la vie!*' I replied. 'The passengers will hardly object to a mission of mercy, and it'll certainly add a bit of excitement! What other details do we have about the man's condition?' I asked.

'None, as yet. I've asked Alan to get us a line to the coastguard medical centre, who've been monitoring the situation. He'll have them for you in a moment.'

'Press the clip to talk, Nigel, and release it to listen,' Alan reminded me as he handed me the radio microphone. 'I'll put their transmission on the speaker so that the captain can hear.'

The coastguard medical officer came over the speaker and we introduced ourselves. There followed a vague description of the injury and developments over the past two to three hours prior to our being contacted: vague, because the description had been given by the fishing boat captain, who naturally had minimal medical knowledge. The man was conscious, but 'unsteady'. He had received a heavy blow to the forehead and face, which was complicated by a severe laceration which appeared to involve the eye, and he was unable to see from that eye. He had bled profusely, but this was now controlled with a temporary dressing, and he was apparently stable and lying on the deck of the wheelhouse.

'OK, thanks,' I replied. 'We'll get an up-to-date from their skipper as we get nearer.'

'Good luck. Over and out,' came the voice.

'What do you intend to do when we get there?' I asked the captain.

'We'll make a leeway, get the boat alongside and make the transfer through mid-ship's starboard side shell door,' he replied.

'Right. Well, there's nothing more for me to do here for the moment,' I said. 'I'll go and make sure that the hospital's all prepared,' and turned to leave.

'I'll give you a shout if they come up on the radio,' called Alan.

'Thanks,' I replied, and added as a parting comment, 'Well, at least it should be an easy transfer; nice and calm outside.'

'Don't you believe it!' Said Bob ominously. 'It may be, to us!'

I walked back to my cabin via the open boat deck. It was

miserable weather with heavy clouds. A blustery wind swept the wet decks, and little pools of water swirled around in the guttering. I looked over the side, down through wispy traces of fog to the sea below. It was grey and heaving, no white caps and no apparently high waves; the swell not severe. But here, on the boat deck, I was eighty feet above sea level. From here on this enormous ship, an eight to ten-foot swell does indeed look like a calm sea . . . I would be wiser, later.

Five hours later, the afternoon's work was done, evening passenger surgery was finished, and there had even been time to hold an abbreviated version of the doctor's cocktail party, where the buzz of the conversation was naturally centred around the rescue mission, of which everyone had been informed by the captain over the public address system. All was in hand.

As we came nearer to our rendezvous point, I took a stroll to the bridge to see how we were progressing. Through the afternoon we had been in communication with the boat, being advised of progress and giving advice. The man's condition apparently hadn't deteriorated. He was resting as best he could, but he was still in a fair degree of pain. The bridge now was dark and quiet. The captain sat in his chair in the semi-light, gazing out into the darkness beyond the windows, lost in thought.

'Not much further to go now,' he told me. 'We've worked out the rendezvous point. Everything OK in the hospital?'

'Yep, all ready. What's it like outside?'

'Go and take a look,' he replied.

I slid back the door and stepped out onto the bridge wing where a blast of sleety, cold air greeted me as we raced across the seas at almost full speed. 'Blimey!' I thought, 'not even nice weather for ducks!' The ducks, indeed, would have been lost, for without the ship's navigational equipment they could never have seen where they were in the dense rolling banks of fog, so typical of the area, which had now enveloped us since my previous visit to the bridge. Looking down, I was just able to see the waves, which, from this point, were now ninety feet below me. I was already shivering. 'I see what you mean,' I said, back inside.

The captain gave an order, and the ship started to slow. After a short time the navigator, Phil Rental, called out, 'Captain, I have them on radar. Four miles, dead ahead.' Very nice bit of navigating!

We called up their skipper and talked with him: 'No change in the patient . . . he's very quiet . . . pain easier.'

'Do you have sight of us?' we asked.

'Nothing at all. The fog's very dense.'

We had slowed almost to a stop now, and were just creeping ahead. How crazy it would be to come all this distance and then run right over the helpless little craft, in the darkness and fog, and plough them into the ocean!

'Can you see us yet?' we called.

'No, not . . . Jeeesus! We certainly can!' came the awestruck voice back from the boat.

What an absolutely incredible sight we must have looked to their amazed eyes. Sitting in a tiny boat, wallowing in an eight-foot swell, miles and miles out on the vast ocean, the wind and drizzle lashing your face, totally enveloped in a blanket of fog; scared, anxious, worried to death for your shipmate's life; sending out a call for help across the waves into the darkness; waiting, waiting, waiting. And suddenly, looming, *towering*, out of the swirling mist appears a mountain of steel and light, like a volcano erupting from the seas beside you. Having seen nothing with which to compare their relative size for days on end, and then to be abruptly confronted with an overshadowing structure, the top of which is lost in the fog, must have made their hearts leap. A small cry for help, and in response: the greatest ship on the North Atlantic, and the best medical facilities that the injured man could dream of out here on the vast empty seas.

Our searchlights pierced the dark swirling fog to pinpoint this dot on the ocean and hold it, draw it to us, in the dazzling beam. The captain commenced his manoeuvres, and instructions whistled across the two way communications systems. Before going below I looked down at the little boat ninety feet below, apparently bobbing up and down gently in the swell.

When I arrived at the shell doorway down below, two minutes later, it was a very different picture. From here the boat wasn't so little, and the bobbing wasn't so gentle. Standing four hundred yards off, she wallowed and bounced, up and down, up and down. From ninety feet up who could possibly believe that there would be that much movement? I could suddenly appreciate what an eight to ten-foot swell really meant! I looked again. What on earth was her structure? Great thick, long, booms protruded from the sides of the boat in what appeared to be every direction. She had the appearance of a spider crab, sitting on the water with huge gangling legs.

'How on earth is she going to come alongside?' I called to the chief officer, over the noise of the ocean, the wind, and engines.

'With a lot of bloody difficulty!' came the answer.

The wind, laced with rain, was whistling in through the small opening in the ship's side. The only shell door which could be used at this level, mid-ships, was perhaps seven to eight feet high by six feet wide, not the grandest of entrances, and the long awkward corridor was jammed with huge pipes, valves and other fittings.

'Why doesn't he take in his booms?' I shouted.

'Wouldn't make any odds,' was the reply. 'Even if he raised them upright, when he's alongside the ship the swell and roll would make them smack against our side. Probably break off and fall down on them!' he yelled.

'So how's he going to do it?' I asked with growing concern.

'He's going to back up and come stern-in against the ship's side.'

'In this swell?' I asked, incredulously.

'Not much choice, has he?' came the flat reply.

As predicted, the boat commenced the manoeuvre, turning in a large circle and ending up stern first towards the ship, forward of the shell door in order that the current would ease her into position, before her engines went into full reverse to hold her in against us while we transferred the injured man.

Now, as the boat neared through the swirling fog, we could see the people we'd been dealing with. I looked across in amazement. A young girl stood at the stern of the boat. A young girl! Frail, and appearing so incredibly vulnerable in this huge heaving drama. She was standing, holding tight to maintain her balance, wrapped around in oilskins, her face red and wet with the cutting drizzle, her hair knotted and dancing frantically in the wind. She rocked and lurched as the boat jumped beneath her. One other man was with her, on the deck.

'Where's the rest of the crew?' I shouted to a deck officer who was bracing himself beside me in the shell doorway.

'That's the lot!' he replied. 'Their skipper is obviously on the bridge, and the injured man would make up the full number.'

No wonder they needed help!

Alarmingly, there came a sudden and enormous THUMP! followed by a piercing, screeching, *grinding*, as the boat struck against the side of the ship and the swell shoved her up against the metal plates. She was well forward of the shell door and lost to our sight. There was another tremendous THUD! and more screeching, as metal tore against metal.

'She easing this way,' called a seaman at the top of his voice, leaning out precariously from the opening, and yelling above the noise.

'Get those ropes ready!' shouted the chief officer.

Suddenly, like a monster leaping from the bushes in the dark, the stern of the boat appeared at the opening. CRASH! . . . pause . . . CRASH! went the stern against our hull. The seaman leaped for safety, out of the way of the huge black mass which seemed as though it would burst through our side. For the briefest period, we saw the image of the girl's face at the stern rail; now white, frightened, wide-eyed, hanging on for dear life. Then the swell passed the opening, and the boat, falling away like a stone, dropped the ten foot from the crest of the swell down into the trough. The whole event had taken a fraction of time.

Suddenly, with another nerve-racking SCREECH! they were back . . . THUUUD! '*Cast the line!*' the chief officer suddenly yelled; but they were gone. Like watching the clothes appear and disappear through the window of a tumble drier, the stern of the boat came and went. THUUD! . . . SCREEECH! All the time, the wind was lashing the opening and ourselves as we stood securely on our steady, giant platform. Then, at last, she was there again, and held.

'*Get those lines across!*'

Ropes snaked out to the waiting figures on the boat. The young girl dived and scrabbled for one of the loose ends.

'*Get them secured!*' roared the chief officer.

Frantic hands lashed and tied the ropes before the boat started moving again, as wildly as before. As she dropped away, the ropes came under enormous strain. They tightened, tightened, tightened . . . and then eased as the boat rose again on the swell. The boat lurched sideways with more screaming of steel, and dropped again. The ropes tightened, tightened, tightened, hauling against the metal, their twanging notes becoming higher and higher. We held our breath. Stretching, *stretching* . . .

'WATCH OUT!' An urgent call rent the air.

CRAAAACK! went a rope, and like a scythe its end whistled through the confined space at a speed much faster than the eye could ever register, cutting the air. At these speeds the rope would take off a leg, cut a man in half, even remove his head in less than the flash of a gun, and he would never have known. The ends clattered against a bulk head, missed!

'*Let go that other rope!*' came the urgent order. Knives flashed desperately, and the rope was gone, the boat free once more.

'Jeeeez!' came an exclamation and huge sigh of relief. This was the lee-side of the ship. What would it be like on the weather side?

'Now what do we do?'

The boat eased away from the ship to stand off again and give everyone a chance to breathe and reconsider. It was decided that their skipper would take the boat around once more and try to manoeuvre again.

'What about the patient? How is he?' I asked via the bridge radio.

'No change,' came the answer.

'Can he stand unsupported? Will we need the stretchers and lashing?'

'We'll see what he can do,' replied their skipper.

From the distance we could see figures moving around in the wheelhouse, shadowy images through the fog. Then out onto the deck was led a groping figure, his head swathed in bandages, both eyes covered. Led as a blind man, he stumbled across the deck to a stern structure, which he clutched to his chest, knuckles white, desperate.

'Can you get him to the stern rail where we can grab him from you if you can lock alongside for a moment?' we asked via the radio.

'We'll see.'

Again the boat approached. THUMP! . . . SCREEEECH! it smacked into our side. The young girl fell to her knees, sprawling. She scrambled up and collided with the injured man who, in the terrifying darkness of his blindfolded world, disorientated and surely scared stiff by the thought of his injury, was still clutching with desperate strength to the deck fitting. He crashed around, the wind and rain lashing him.

She prised his fingers open as the stern approached our shell door yet again and reached out, as desperately as he, for the stern rail. The mesmerized group in the shell door – myself included – the captain and his party high above on the bridge wing, and hundreds of anxious passengers and crew leaning out over the ship's rails, held their breath, reaching out mentally across this short span of water to grasp, to help, to hold these two figures clasped together in their desperation. The boat lurched, thudded against the ship, and the injured man fell to the deck. 'I can't see! I can't see! *I can't see!*' he screamed, his cries torn away by the wind. He sprawled on the deck, arms reaching out, grasping, finding a secure point, holding on, holding!

We were all now well aware of the obvious: there was no possible way that he could make that leap, not even with a hundred hands to help. A very fit man with full sight would stand a strong chance of being crushed, or even cut in half, as the boat's stern rose at the speed of a rapid elevator past the shell door opening.

He lay there on his deck, rolling with the surge, a thin wailing on the air, the young girl holding him tight. So near, and yet so very far away.

I made my way up to the bridge. What could be done? We reappraised the situation. Obviously, if the man was fully conscious and able to stand nine to ten hours after the injury, then the chances of severe head or brain damage were less likely. Very probably, we weren't dealing now with a life saving situation; we were talking about an apparently severe facial injury and laceration, and possibly a severe eye injury. In the circumstances, the captain refused the suggestion that I, or a team, should go to the boat rather than bring the patient aboard. The chances of injury, and even death, during the transfer would be far too high. The captain categorically rejected any suggestion of heroics and considered the possible trade of a life for an eye to be out of the question. The safety of the ship and all aboard are his explicit responsibility. There would be no leaping from the shell door. Could we lower a life boat with a team already aboard? Yes, but how could we get the boat and the team back onto the ship? It couldn't be done!

There was a last desperate suggestion. The fishing boat had an inflatable dinghy aboard; perhaps we could attach a line to this, place the man aboard and draw him across to the ship's side. The practicalities were considered: the short journey across the swell would be far too dangerous. The dinghy would undoubtedly flip with its sightless passenger, and again, the transfer at this end would be dreadfully risky. The ideas were considered and explored. Other than heroic solutions which were out of the question, there were no sensible, workable answers. As ridiculously unthinkable as the situation had become, we gradually had to accept what appeared to be inevitable: despite being so enormous, and despite having every modern sea-going facility on hand, we had absolutely no choice. We had to abandon the rescue!

During the final period of our deliberations, I contacted my associate on this voyage, Dr Andrew Eardley, who organized the making up of a medical kit together with a fully detailed sheet of instructions on how to use the contents. The package was sealed in a waterproof wrapping and transferred to the boat via a line.

With heavy hearts and deep, deep frustration, we made preparations to leave. We raised our revs, engaged the propellers, and slowly slipped away. The little group of weary, frightened souls receded into the distance, and, bobbing and rocking on the North Atlantic, slowly disappeared into the enveloping, damp, eerie, penetrating fog, a memory which still makes me sad. All the effort, the distance travelled, the lost hours, the unimaginable activity in the New York offices – reorganizing, rebooking, rerouting passengers, contacting the 1800 new passengers who would be expecting to embark on time – all these complications, which would have been well worth the sacrifice had we succeeded, now appeared as fruitless effort, wasted energy.

This was an occasion which illustrated that, even with all our great resources and the expenditure of huge costs in money, time and effort, if the fates aren't with you, sometimes you just can't win.

What happened to the seaman? Having been left alone in the darkness of the ocean, the fishing boat set out for the nearest port at full speed. The patient's dressings were removed – not a pleasant sight or task for his untrained shipmates – and the wounds were treated and redressed with supplies from our emergency pack, under direction of the accompanying instructions. As dawn rose the fog banks, like the lace of the Northern lights, dissolved. Perhaps a higher authority had watched and rewarded the frustrated events of the night. To the relief and joy of all, the change in the weather conditions and visibility meant that a helicopter was able to reach and find the boat. The injured man was hoisted up and taken quickly to a shore-side establishment. There, they were able to save his damaged eye. His head injury had fortunately not caused any internal damage, and his facial injury was repaired successfully. I'm sure that, for many years to come, the scars will serve as a reminder to the injured fisherman of one of the most dramatic days of his life.

In contrast to the extremely frustrating episode above, another North Atlantic incident, which occurred prior to my joining the *QE2*, illustrates the more rewarding aspects usually resulting from these dramas at sea.

The incident occurred a number of years ago, when the *QE2* was undertaking a transatlantic voyage from New York to Southampton. As I've explained, the North Atlantic doesn't have the reputation of being one of the world's more tranquil areas of ocean, but on this particular occasion the barometer was favourable. Even so, what appears to be a relatively calm sea from the upper decks of the world's greatest liner may be a different kettle of fish, when viewed from sea level. A swell which looks pretty flat from ninety feet up can represent a significant incline in a small boat.

Early in the day, the radio room had picked up a call from a small cargo vessel, out of Russia. There had apparently been an engine room accident on board, and one of the Russian crew-members had been seriously injured. Alone in the middle of a vast ocean, the little vessel was many days from land, and consequently from professional medical attention. It is not easy to imagine the isolation of this minute speck on the ocean with the dark clouds overhead, the long swell of the sea, the chug, chug, chugging from the depths of the engine room, the endless pitching and rolling and the thud of the water on the hull as the little ship ploughed steadily on, its machinery screaming at full revs.

Lying quietly below was the injured man, frightened, lonely, in pain, suffering physically and mentally, surrounded by apprehensive, helpless friends unable to act for lack of knowledge, watching their friend slowly dying. Imagine, then, the relief, the excitement, when miraculously their radio call for help was answered by the *QE2*; and sometime later, when she appeared over the horizon like the fabled rescuing knight in shining armour!

My predecessor, Dr John Paling, was the Principal Medical Officer on this particular occasion, and he was called to the radio room to speak with the Russians. At the onset of the incident, he listened to the story, took the details and requested and advised on how to obtain more information. With all his facts assembled as best as could be, he decided that the injured sailor could not be treated via radio advice alone, he must somehow be seen and treatment commenced, otherwise his life would be in grave danger. Having confirmed his conclusion with his medical colleague, the facts were subsequently presented to the master. Without hesitation, the captain made his decisions.

The *QE2* altered course, and steamed towards the Russians. A lifeboat was readied, and a crew stood at hand.

Arriving at the location of the Russian ship, it could be seen from the movement of the smaller vessel that, despite the comparative steadiness of the Queen, a small boat would have a hazardous journey from one ship to the other across the windswept swell of the sea. On top of this, the relative movements of the lifeboat and the small ship would make embarking and disembarking extremely difficult. It would be too dangerous in the circumstances to manoeuvre an injured man in a stretcher from one to the other. The risk to his life, and to those of the rescuers, would be too great with the lifeboat rapidly rising and falling, banging back and forth against the side of the ship.

It was decided that the *QE2* would make a slow turn, create a leeway of relatively calm water, and one of our lifeboats would be lowered with its crew, together with the doctor. John Paling would go across to the Russian ship with the necessary equipment, and the patient would be treated on his own territory. Some house call!

Having boarded the lifeboat with his equipment, John steadied himself. As the boat was hoisted out over the ship's side it swung and jostled, causing him to lose his footing. He reached out quickly and caught his balance. Unfortunately, in the process, he knocked his spectacles, which fell from his nose and, inevitably, disappeared over the side of the boat, down, down into the ocean. These glasses were not for decoration – he really needed them. And so the boat set off across the wide stretch of water with the doctor groping around like a lost soul. No doubt the disorientating effect of diminished vision was a contributory factor, but the movement of the little lifeboat surging up and down across the swell – which from above had looked so insignificant – rapidly took its effect on our unfortunate medical emissary. From the bridge of the *QE2*, the groping figure of the doctor, with an increasingly green face, could be seen clutching at the side of the boat, while his stomach performed a reverse peristalsis, and that morning's bacon, eggs, toast and marmalade were fed to Davy Jones. The ordeal continued.

Arriving at the Russian ship, the lifeboat bounced and bounced, up and down, while it drew closer to the rope ladder dangling from the opening in the ship's side. The equipment was slowly transferred, when the two levels were compatible. Now came the time for John to board. Between retching and groping, he focused his whole attention on the ladder. The boat rose but moved out. He waited. It sank down again, rose up and down again, but too rapidly. He waited. Up and down, backwards and forwards, greener and greener. Eventually, the ladder was there. A sudden burst of action, a quick leap forward, a grasp for the ladder, a firm hold on the rung, and then . . . Riiiiiiiiiiiiip, the backside of his trousers burst wide open, and his shirt tail and rear end waved cheerily in the wind!

It was later reported that the Russian crewmen, who were anxiously awaiting the arrival of the answer to their colleague's prayers, were suddenly confronted with a squinting, staggering, groping, heaving, green man with his backside hanging out of his trousers! They must have been in great doubt about who was going to give help to whom.

Returning to the relative calm of the Russian ship, John soon settled down, recovered his colour and composure, and took immediate command of the situation. To the immense relief of all, he was able to treat the problem of the extremely grateful patient.

As a result of his administrations, the crisis was overcome, and the patient lived and recovered.

Not all rescue dramas involving the ship's doctor necessarily occur on the high seas or even within the confines of a ship. There was an incident in which I was involved a few years ago, in Mexico, on a beach close by the ship's berth. The circumstances and setting were so dramatic that I can visualize them now, as though I were looking at a picture. When your adrenalin is running high, your senses become acutely enhanced. You are able to see, smell and 'feel' your surroundings far more definitively. You become aware of the minutiae of a scene, as though you're able to study it in slow motion.

Back in 1976 when I worked with P&O I had the pleasure of sailing in a very beautiful ship called the *Pacific Princess* which, during my time on board, was chosen to be the setting for *The Love Boats*. Medically, she was a very busy ship. We had more than our fair share of major problems – particularly cardiac emergencies and related illnesses. Despite the very heavy geriatric carry on this occasion, the total medical staff comprised myself and one nursing sister, and that was it. The crew clinics were always packed. This, combined with the high incidence of geriatric illnesses amongst the passengers, meant a busy day even at our quietest times.

We had set sail from Los Angeles and spent a couple of days at sea, and soon after our departure we had had a cardiac emergency. A relatively young man had suffered a myocardial infarction – or coronary – and had been admitted to the hospital. He had received all the appropriate treatment and was kept under observation on a cardiac monitor. He experienced one or two complications which fortunately responded to corrective treatment each time. The upshot of the matter was that he had to be observed night and day, twenty-four hours a day, for the next two days at sea. We shared the duty: Liz, the nursing sister, and myself spent alternating spells with the patient. Meanwhile, the normal stream of problems had to be dealt with: colds, chest infections, gout, lacerations, broken bones. None of these stop just because you're busy!

By the time we arrived in Mazatlan, the patient was doing well – but I wouldn't vouch for the medical staff. The majority of the morning was taken up arranging for the patient to be admitted to a shore-side hospital for further treatment before he would eventually return home. Having finally organized the transfer, we both flopped down to a well earned cup of tea before getting on with that day's work. There was no chance to enjoy the fabulous deep sea fishing for which Mazatlan is famous on this visit!

We set sail the same evening for Puerto Vallarta, looking forward to easier times over the next day and a half at sea. No such luck. In the early hours of the following morning, we were both on the run again to another emergency, this time an elderly lady who had suffered a stroke. She was transferred to the hospital and we worked on her through the remainder of the night. Her condition was unstable and, again, she would require constant supervision. With a groan, Liz and I worked out a roster system, and once more got on with the rest of the day's work. The other officers and crew were wondering if we had both deserted! Nobody had seen the medical department out and around since the start of the cruise.

The night before Puerto Vallarta was a sleepless one. Almost staggering around the ward with exhaustion, we responded to each new crisis with a burst of adrenalin. However, we were winning, a situation which always helps to produce extra drive. By the time we arrived in Puerto Vallarta the following morning, the lady was stable, but the medics were about to collapse. Our local agents were contacted, and an ambulance duly arrived to relieve us of our patient and whisk her away to the town hospital. There were still the morning's patients to be seen! By the end of that morning, I felt that I should be sitting on the *other* side of my desk . . . as a patient.

I had been looking forward particularly to our day in port in Puerto Vallarta, where I had arranged to spend some time snorkelling with Jacques Cousteau's son, Jean Michel, who, following on from his father, had also become an authority of the sea world and had been introducing me to the fascinating thrills of the underwater realm of this coastline since we had become friends during earlier cruises. Today's lesson would have to wait; fortunately, there was always another time.

Too weary to eat, I made my way to my cabin and collapsed into a heap on my bed, exhausted. Fully clothed I sank immediately into a deep sleep.

In a nightmare setting, I was rocking about, being shoved and thumped, and from the very far distance a voice was calling, 'Doc! . . . Doc!' More shoving. 'Doc! . . . Wake up!'

I suddenly sprang bolt upright! It wasn't a dream. In the darkened cabin, a blurred figure was standing over me, shouting, 'Doc . . . Come on . . . Quick! Someone's drowned!'

'What? Where? What?' Was all I could mumble as, dragged by my arm, I stumbled from my bedroom, hitting the doors, the chairs

215

and most of the furniture in the day room. Another figure stood by the hospital door.

'The emergency bag is here, doc,' he yelled, and dashed off.

'Who was that? What?' I was running and still half asleep. I grabbed the bag. Instead of going left and up the stairs towards the swimming pool, we turned right.

'Where? Where are we going?'

'This way, doc, come on! Come on!' I was urged.

We arrived at the gangway. I stopped, gasping for breath. 'Where the hell are we going?' I called.

'Down on the beach, doc. On the beach!'

'Jesus! That's half a mile away!'

I set off in pursuit, shirt wide open, tails flapping, socks around my ankles and shoe laces undone. Unshaved and hollow-eyed, I must have looked like an escapee from a local institute. I ran out across the concrete stretch of the dock area, through the wire mesh gates. The Mexican guards, slouched against the gate posts, armed to the teeth, wondered whether to stop me, and decided not. A jump, and I was down onto the beach on all fours, the bag flying, and one shoe off.

Suddenly, from overhead, there was an enormous CRACK! The ground seemed to shake, and my ears hurt. I looked up. It was the middle of the day, but the sky was so black, so heavy that it seemed to be reaching down to press on me. A great, scything, shimmer of lightning shot outwards across the ominous, heaving, rolling thunder clouds, and as it was absorbed into their folds, the heavens rumbled again. I scrambled to my feet. Leaving one shoe behind, I set out, stumbling across the deep, soft sand.

A tremendous wind now lashed the palm trees, their branches thrashing and rattling, tearing off to be blown away. The rain started abruptly and came driving down. I fell, scrambling, gasping for breath, wondering how I was here, where on earth could I get the energy to run, but I did. Running, stumbling, my bag dragged behind me. The bag flew open, and out gushed all my gear into the sand! I gasped, then threw the bag aside and pushed on. I have often heard people use the expression, 'like in a dream'. Now I knew what they meant. I felt as though I was hardly progressing, running through treacle, shouting noiselessly into the storm.

And then, there they were, just ahead, down on the hard sand, close to the roaring, surging waves, a small circle of people, soaked through and through, their hair streaked down by the rain, rivulets running over their faces; forms, absolutely motionless, their clothes dancing frantically in the gusting wind. In the centre, a figure, a woman, was lying distorted, ungainly, lifeless, on the sand. Kneeling over her was a man, bent double, his cheek against her face, calling out to the heavens, to a god, to the world, to anyone! 'Please! No!' he sobbed, distraught and convulsed with grief and pain, his plea almost a whisper on the howling wind. FLASH! . . . CRaaaaaCK!! the thunder exploded again.

With a final dash, I burst in through the circle and fell onto my knees beside her, gasping, almost choking. She lay motionless, her posture frozen by the flashing light. She was very pale, white; her lips were blue. There was no breath, no heartbeat to detect. Her hair was knotted and her eyes, her ears and nose were full of sand. Her slender lifeless fingers were still holding pebbles which she had grasped in her desperation!

Despite knowing that the inevitable couldn't be reversed, I eased her husband aside, and pounded once on her chest. Opening her mouth, I swept out the sand with my fingers, cleared her throat, held her nose, put my mouth to hers and blew. Her still chest, inside her crumpled bathing suit, expanded. I blew again. I massaged her heart and watched her face as the storm went on, with flashes, rain, and rolling thunder, like a scene from Dante's inferno. Blow . . . massage . . . blow . . . massage. Wailing, thunder, piercing rain. Blow . . . massage . . . blow. My hair and clothes were plastered down by the torrential down-pour, rivulets of water forming in the sand around me. Blow . . . massage . . . blow.

She coughed.

'CHRIST! I'm sure she . . . was that a cough!'

Again!

'She did! SHE DID!'

I wouldn't believe it. I carried on with greater vigour. She coughed again, and took a deep breath.

'She breathed! She really breathed.'

She breathed again, and her eyes flickered, opened. I couldn't believe it. Uncontrollably, I cheered at the top of my voice. There, on that beach, in the driving wind and rain, with the howl of the storm, the thunder and the roar of the ocean, almost collapsing with exhaustion, I shouted to whoever! and laughed, and shouted out loud. Streaming down my cheeks was torrential rain, washing away tears of supercharged emotion, exhaustion, and sheer exhilaration.

A group of breathless officers and crew, who had chased me down the beach and gathered up my bag and emergency equipment, whisked up the lady. Again, we were running, stumbling, so many hands, so much unquestioning help. We ran, with an energy born of frenzy.

A runner having arrived ahead of us at the ship, Sister was all prepared. In a blur of activity, the patient was warmed, cleaned, X-rayed, cardiographed, medicated. Needles, bottles and blankets were whizzed around. And then, all was done. She sat in bed, combed, clean, warm, rosy-cheeked and smiling. It was bewildering to see the transformation. The sight was a tremendous reward! Within just two hours of the incident she stepped from the bed feeling as 'fit as a fiddle'!

As the ship sailed off down the Mexican coast, I returned to my cabin, and finally collapsed into a deep, *very* contented, and fortunately undisturbed sleep.

On our next arrival in Puerto Vallarta, the tourist board, unexpectedly but thoughtfully presented me with a medal as a token of their thanks. It was presented to me personally, but it was accepted on behalf of many people, the officers and crew from the ship, the team who had made such a tremendous contribution and without whose quick reaction, alarm, and help, a life would unquestionably have been lost.

Stowaways

It is almost impossible to stowaway on a vessel without being detected – unless it should be with the co-operation of a crew member, and even then, the occupants of the adjacent cabins, the cabin stewards or the cleaners would soon work it out. Stowing away would require the co-operation of a significant number of people, all of whom would have to keep very quiet! However, it can occasionally happen, more frequently on short trips, and particularly on overnight hops.

On most cruise ships, security staff vet the oncoming crew, passengers and visitors, and will require some form of identification or pass. The *QE2* carries its own security and policing service which, because of the international problems of more recent years and the enormous amount of attention that *QE2* attracts, maintains a particularly tight and restrictive routine. On the less security-conscious ships, however, the system is by no means infallible, especially when there is such an enormous volume of traffic.

Once on board, where can the stowaway go? For the first day, if he's dressed smartly enough, he could mix with the other fresh faces around the public rooms, and perhaps eat a buffet meal. But where does he sleep? Where does he wash and shave? A settee in a public room would be too obvious, and washing in a public toilet would certainly attract attention. In effect, he is relegated to a broom locker or a lifeboat, but there are few, if any, of these that aren't either used or checked regularly; there is very little 'wasted', backwater space on a ship.

In reality there are, not surprisingly, very few people who risk the impracticalities and give it a try – especially on the North Atlantic run. If they do try, and they are caught out, there are a few alternative outcomes. At worst, they will be locked away in the ship's brig or prison, and kept on very basic rations! However, if they're carrying sufficient funds, or their parents, relatives or friends ashore should cough up the cash, they can pay their fare and enjoy their new status. For those who don't find the money, upon arrival at the next port of call the stowaway is escorted under guard to the airport, presented with a bill, and flown straight home. Alternatively, if the ship is due to return to the stowaway's home port, then the local authorities may refuse permission for him to land, and the vessel must return him to his home, again at the stowaway's – or relative's – expense.

Unless you fancy the risk of living on bread and milk, sleeping on a hard board bed, being locked away in a cell possibly in a cold damp paint locker up at the front of the ship, where you rock and bounce around for days until you're home, then don't bother trying it! I promise you, it's really not worth it!

There have indeed been some interesting stowaways. One case in particular springs to mind.

I was on a ship some years ago, based in Los Angeles, and we were about to undertake a South Pacific cruise. On the morning of the ship's departure, our local agents received a phone call from a potential passenger, enquiring if there was any space available on the ship, as she was deciding whether to take an impromptu cruise. As it happened, there was a choice of several different grades of cabin, and the caller was advised accordingly. She had then gone on to state that she had travelled on the ship before, and knew it quite well. She felt that certain cabins were better value than others, even within the same grade. In order to help her make up her mind, she enquired which specific cabins were empty. Trying to be as helpful as he could and possibly clinch a sale, the agent gave a selection of different grade cabins which the computer showed available.

'There's an A grade cabin – cabin A123, or a C grade – cabin C234, or . . .' she was told. 'Thank you,' said the caller, 'I'll think it over, and call you back shortly if I decide to go.'

As the day progressed there was no further call.

Meanwhile, back at home, the telephone caller – a young lady who we will refer to as Sally – was packing her bags for a South Pacific cruise. Sally was a small, fairly well-proportioned, by no means beautiful, but not unattractive young lady in her mid to late twenties. Unfortunately, as was eventually to become apparent, Sally suffered from schizophrenia for which she was being adequately treated and which remained very well controlled with her prescribed medication. Although she didn't have sufficient cash, Sally had decided that she would like to take a cruise, and if she couldn't pay for it, she'd stowaway. Not for her the prospects of living in a lifeboat or linen locker; Sally was going to travel in style.

As with most people with her psychiatric condition, Sally was a particularly intelligent young lady; hence, with one phone call she now knew which of the cabins would be empty during the cruise. She duly arrived at the gangway and, having somehow bluffed her way on board, asked to be shown to cabin A123, and was, in a short time, ensconced as its occupant. There were many potential pitfalls to this plan, but luck must have been with her, because for several days it paid off.

Now we come to the first hitch. Being intelligent enough to be aware of the side-effects of her medication, Sally knew that she was photosensitive – in other words, while taking the medication she could have a sensitivity reaction on any skin which was exposed to strong sunshine. Not wanting to draw attention to herself, she reasoned that it would appear strange for her not to take the sun on a sunshine cruise. It would certainly not be in her interests to be noticed, and there was the added risk of being questioned about her reasons. Consequently, in order that she could stay out in the sun, Sally decided to stop her medication.

The third day out of Los Angeles. As usual, I strolled along to the hospital for the morning clinic. Passing through the waiting room, I found it packed. 'Morning all,' I chirped. A flutter of smiles and replies came back. No-one looked desperately ill. One young lady, I noticed, didn't respond. She was sitting in the corner, her head bowed, arms folded across her chest and a full length top coat pulled tightly around her. She appeared to be alone.

'Morning, Jane,' I said to the sister inside the surgery. 'Full house outside. Any problems before we start?'

'Well, yes, in a way,' she replied. 'There's been a string of crew members down here this morning. I don't know what for, nobody would tell me what their problem was. Most peculiar! They all want to come back and talk with you. Strange, isn't it?'

'Sounds very odd,' I agreed. 'I wonder what's going on?'

'Well, I can promise you one thing,' Jane added, 'you're going to have a very busy morning, because they're all coming back later on, after passenger clinic is finished.'

'Oh, well, we'll find out soon enough,' I said. 'We'd better push on. Let's have the first patient in.'

The morning was going well, no major problems – at least, none that we couldn't sort out. I had seen six or seven patients, and the present lady, having been examined, had been taken next door to the

221

treatment room by Jane for a dressing. I was left alone to finish writing a few notes on the lady's card before the next patient was brought in. The door behind me opened, I naturally thought it was the nursing sister, and carried on writing.

'Doctor!' said a voice unknown to me.

I glanced up. The young lady from the corner of the waiting room stood before me, Sally, of A123. She stood with her arms still clasped around her, as she had while sitting outside. Her top coat was closed up to her neck, completely enveloping her.

'Oh, I'm sorry, I didn't expect the next patient yet,' I said. 'Please take a seat for a moment, while I just finish these notes.'

Sally didn't move. 'I know you're busy, doctor,' she said in a quiet, slow, and precise voice, 'but I need to know something.'

There was an urgency in her tone . . . I looked up at her. She stood absolutely still, staring directly at me, a penetrating stare. Not a word, not a movement. Suddenly she jerked open her overcoat, wide open, a classic pose. With legs apart and arms held high, she stood stark naked. Not even a G-string!

The short silence was shattered abruptly. Yelling at the top of her voice, she stood defiantly, and demanded, '*What do you think of this?*'

The room became very still, very, *very* quiet. There was a pause.

'Not a lot!' I replied, 'but do take a seat, and let's talk about it.'

That was the tip of the iceberg. The story that emerged still amazes me.

Poor Sally; one of the unfortunate traits of her psychiatric problem was nymphomania. Released from the controlling effects of her treatment when she had discontinued her medication three days earlier, Sally's libido had gone on the rampage! On the second night of the cruise, Sally – by accident or design – had found herself in the corridor of the Italians' accommodation, where two or three men shared each cabin. Dressed in her 'fun suit' of overcoat and sandals she rapped on the first door.

'Yes?' a voice called. She didn't answer. She knocked again. The door opened. A sleepy Italian figure stood in the doorway.

'What'a you want?' he mumbled at the shrouded figure.

Sally launched into her act. With coat tails flying and legs akimbo, she revealed her bounty. '*What do you think of this?!*' she cried.

There was the merest pause, while sleepy brain cells snapped into action, then . . . WHAM! Our Italian friend was galvanized! 'Mama mia!' Like a lizard's tongue snapping up a moth, an Italian hand whipped out to grasp this fantasy before the dream ended. Then ZZZZIIP!! Sally's feet left the floor, and she flew through the doorway. BANG! went the door. Inside the cabin, the bed boards rattled as each of the inmates shared an unexpected few moments of recreational joy. Michelin calenders and Penthouse magazines were cast aside like forgotten toys. Bang, bang, bang, bang, bang . . . pause . . . the door opened, and Sally was back on the corridor, smiling, but unsatisfied!

She moved along the corridor. Next door. Knock, knock, knock! 'Whad'a you want?'

'*What do you think of this?*'

Zap!! Bang, bang, bang, bang, bang!

Knock, knock, knock. '*What do you think of this?*' ZAP!!

Of course, the stories eventually travelled all around the ship, and naturally improved with the telling. It became hard to distinguish truth from fiction, but what I do know is this. Not unexpectedly, the story quickly spread that Sally had a venereal disease – which thankfully she hadn't, or my work might have been cut out for weeks to come. However, the crew weren't taking any risks, and over the course of the next few days forty-four crew members visited the hospital to be checked out. *Forty-four*! And those were just the ones who came to see me.

The outcome of this saga, of course, was that I now had the explanation to the unusual crowd of crew who had attended the hospital earlier to discuss their 'personal matters'.

The story of one crew member amused me particularly: the night steward, a little old guy, bent and shuffling, working out his last days before retirement, described to me one day, by way of an explanation for his visit, how he had received a phone call in his pantry asking for coffee and a sandwich in the early hours of the morning. It was to be delivered to A123. He hobbled along the corridor and stood puffing and panting outside the door, holding his tray and leaning unsteadily on the door post. The door opened. Sally stood before him, stitchless. Without comment or preamble, she reached out, grabbed him by the collar, and ZZZIIIIIIP! he was gone, just as Sally herself had disappeared down below. The vision of a tray of coffee and sandwiches suspended in midair as the night steward's arthritic old bones flew through the door still tickles me to this day.

Epilogue

I trust that my reminiscences of life at sea have been interesting, educational and most of all entertaining, and that you are now aware that despite the restricted boundaries of our world on board ship, all the extremes of life and medicine are still to be found: from laughter to tears, from the romantic to the ridiculous, from the humdrum world of seasickness to the high dramas of the operating theatre, from cocktail parties to coronary care. It's not surprising, however, that the world at large still regards the life of the ship's doctor as superficial and principally social rather than professional. In this respect, a short anecdote comes to mind which perhaps sums up the whole situation. Cast your mind back to my delightful little patient, Fiona, and to the days surrounding the drama of her illness . . .

During the earlier and quieter moments of Fiona's cruise, I'd had the pleasure of meeting the actor, Robert Young, who in those days was involved with the American TV medical series, *Marcus Welby M.D.* Robert Young was with us on a holiday cruise, taking a break away from his 'medical involvements'. Nonetheless, we had found it amusing and interesting to swap stories regarding our respective medical roles, and had spent time together relaxing and chatting.

A few days after Fiona's operation, the ship had arrived in Tahiti, and we had then travelled to New Zealand where Robert Young and his wife were due to disembark. When we arrived in Auckland, the press naturally descended on the ship to interview the internationally famous Mr Young. As might be expected in view of the strong association with his character, Dr Welby, the press photographers were anxious to set their photographs in an appropriate background, the ship's hospital. Robert Young approached me to see if this would be all right, and asked if I would be in the photographs.

The shots were set up in the operating theatre, around the table and the anaesthetic machine. Amidst the bustle and the joking, one photographer called out:

'Mr Young, could we have a shot with you holding the anaesthetic mask and placing it on Dr Roberts's face to look as though you're putting him to sleep, just for a comedy shot?'

Before I could make a comment, Robert Young turned to the photographer.

'This is not a studio set, gentlemen. It is the ship's hospital, and as such I'm sure that it is usually the setting for far more than "comedy shots". Although I only act the role of a doctor,' he continued in a clipped voice, 'we take it seriously. I have no intention of making a joke out of either my role or the medical profession.'

'Oh! . . . Yes . . . OK,' said the photographer. 'No offence meant. I just thought that as it's not really a *proper* hospital . . . Well, in that case, how about a shot with . . .'

I stood quietly, and let his blusterings pass without comment.

At the close of the session, a couple of reporters were chatting casually with me.

'Thanks for the loan of the operating theatre,' said the man who had called out to Robert Young earlier. 'I don't suppose you get to use this place,' he added. 'Nice quiet life on a cruise ship, eh? Just seasickness and colds? I suppose it's a bit of a lark, doctor at sea, isn't it – champagne, girls and cocktail parties? No real medicine, no dramas or major problems, no need for all this gear,' he quipped, gesturing around the room.

I looked at the table that he had propped himself against, and pictured the small figure that had been lying there just a few days earlier. I gazed around the room, at the trolley, and the equipment now neatly stacked away, at the dials and knobs which had been turned so desperately on the anaesthetic machine. I thought of the atmosphere, the electricity, the adrenalin charging this small area such a short time ago. I paused and considered for a moment. Then, turning to the reporter with a wry smile, I replied quietly:

'We have our moments!'